Yo puedo
para empezar

**Elizabeth Silvaggio-Adams
& Ma. Del Rocío Vallejo-Alegre**

Milne Open Textbooks

Geneseo, NY

ISBN: 978-1-942341-80-2

We want to acknowledge the following websites for providing free access to openly licensed images that help illustrate and give life to our books to benefit our students:

* WPClipart
* Openclipart
* Pixabay
* Pixy.org
* Pxhere.com
* The LandView 6 and MARPLOT

Milne Open Textbooks, One College Circle, Geneseo, NY

Yo puedo hablar español

Acknowledgements

We thank the following people for their participation in providing materials and converting the Yo puedo series to the Open Educational Resources and systems support:

+ Allison Brown

+ Michelle Costello

+ Marie Shero

+ Eduardo Vallejo-Resines

****

Be The Change

The royalties from the print version of this book will be donated to Cultures Learning TOGETHER, Inc.

Mission

Cultures Learning TOGETHER is a win-win organization that enables people with different backgrounds and experiences to break linguistic barriers and embrace cultural diversity. Grounded in inclusion and belonging, we are a team of learners that exchange knowledge to unite our community with a network of cross-cultural bridges.

Vision

We aspire to create a permanent safe space to grow and connect the community through teaching, learning, and cultural integration. Cultures Learning TOGETHER is a team that believes we can do more together than we ever could imagine alone.

Values

LEARNING: We are lifelong learners who are constantly growing and evolving.

INCLUSIVITY: We accept, support, and celebrate differences. Learning new linguistic and cultural information expands our capacity to embrace and understand the perspectives of others.

BRAVERY: We empower each other and advocate for the needs of those in our community. We are brave to learn, try new things, and confront challenges TOGETHER.

To learn more about Cultures Learning TOGETHER, Inc. visit www.cultureslearningtogether. org.

****

Lifelong Learners

Because everything in this life can be improved, we would appreciate it if you were to contact us if you find any errors within the text. Our email addresses are vallejo@cultureslearningtogether.org or bethadams@cultureslearningtogether.org or adamse@geneseo.edu.

Contents

Introducción

You have learned two words in a second language just by reading the title of your book. Think about that for a moment and reflect upon your prior foreign language experiences.

Often, students enter language classes with previously acquired skills, be they from secondary school or another college. Many say, "I have studied Spanish for years and don't know how to speak or write it", while others are a bit anxious about taking a second language for the first time, but all are overwhelmed by the expensive textbooks and online packages that don't seem to be practical or relevant. We sought to change these common complaints by creating materials that take a communicative approach to learning a second language based upon the skills that we deem most useful and that will enable our students to confidently express themselves in Spanish.

How will we achieve this common goal of empowering our students with the tools to communicate effectively in Spanish? Our language courses will be based on students previewing videos or pre-reading topics that will be expanded upon in home-based and in-class assignments. Instead of giving you lectures in class and then homework, you will be studying the concepts at home using this book, along with our online materials. In the classroom we will complete exercises, discussions and projects that help you use the concepts that you studied at home, using the target language the whole time that you are in class. In other words, we are making our Spanish class a lab. Imagine a typical chemistry or biology lab: the student is expected to master the scientific concepts outside of class; the labs are all about practicing and applying concepts. In the same way, your Spanish class will not be a passive experience but rather an active learning environment. Some of the sections invoking **active learning** are:

+ **Practiquemos**→Let's practice

+ **Comprendamos** or **Entendamos**→Let's understand

+ **Escuchemos**→Let's listen

+ **Charlemos**→Let's chat

+ **Añadamos** or **Agreguemos** →Let's add (add to your knowledge while practicing what you have learned)

Pre-reading the materials, filling in scaffolded notes and stepping into the practices with some background allows you to have an idea of themes to make the classroom experience richer and more rewarding. As in any skill, you take ownership of learning by practicing and, in this case, doing the required readings, learning the vocabulary and studying the online assignments before each class. If you don't come prepared to class you will not be successful. By coming to class with a base upon which to build you will be able to understand the in-class usage and practices better, ultimately making it possible to converse with other students in Spanish. As you work through the material at home, you should take detailed notes based upon the videos, readings and other assigned material. In class, you will use your notes to enable you to participate in conversations and exercises in Spanish. While the instructor will answer questions on content, the focus of the class will be to explain grammar implicitly through examples of the use of vocabulary and grammar in daily speech so that you can begin building on your proficiency in Spanish.

Our classroom structure includes:

+ Using your book as a notebook in which you will supplement the explanations with your own notes.

+ Viewing the videos and PowerPoint presentations at home. These will be indicated with the icon images as seen here to the left to highlight the fact that you must access the online platform to view them and write the information that is required in your book.

+ Processing the information you noted in exercises that are done in the book or to be handed in separately.

+ Applying the content in discussions in the target language in class in pairs, small groups or individually with the instructor. In order to participate actively in the class, you must come prepared knowing the concepts.

+ Being prepared for daily evaluations either orally or written for the application of the concepts to achieve oral and written proficiency.

Ultimately, the goal for all language learners is to develop a functional use of another language. The American Council on the Teaching of Foreign Languages (ACTFL) divides functional use into the following categories:

+ Interpersonal Communication

+ Presentational Speaking

+ Presentational Writing

+ Interpretive Listening

+ Interpretive Reading

During the semester, you will be developing skills in the above categories, along with learning how to be a global citizen. In order to assess what language students are learning—including your strengths and weaknesses—ACTFL created a series of Can-Do statements that will help you become a more reflective learner. Yo puedo ... is structured around explicit objectives introduced at the beginning of the unit. Each unit ends with a checklist of Can-Do statements that you have learned throughout the unit. The vocabulary and grammar in that section pertain to that skill. This is your time to reflect on how well you have achieved the goals noted in the Can-Do statements and how to maximize your language skills via additional practice of concepts covered or stretching your skills toward attaining the next level of proficiency of the material covered thus refining your ability.

Vocabulary is presented in small groups with a master list found on the online platform for you to use as a self-correcting study tool. Sometimes, concepts that seem to be grammar points may be presented as vocabulary.

Grammar is presented in brief explanations within the functional use of the language with a balance of implicit (again functional use) and explicit (grammar explanations) approaches.

Cultural awareness will be fostered in a variety of ways. It may be addressed through proper pronunciation (phonetics and phonology) or activities where you read about the lives of Spanish speakers. Cultural awareness goes beyond learning discrete cultural points. This text strives to give students a competitive advantage using foreign languages so that they can succeed in a global world, work with a diverse workforce, and relate to people of other cultures. Consider the following:

"A feeling of common belonging based on linguistic and cultural diversity is a powerful antidote to intolerance. Increasing mutual understanding, multilingualism can significantly contribute to the dialogue between people, be it at school, at work or during free time".[1]

We are excited to help you on your journey to learn Spanish so…

LET'S BEGIN!! ¡EMPECEMOS!

---

[1]   Leonard Orban, European Commissioner for Multilingualism.

Los sonidos del español

Objectives

1. Learn the vowels in Spanish.
2. Learn the alphabet and all the sounds in Spanish (including some regional differences).
3. Learn how to form consonant and vowel groups and how to pronounce them.
4. Learn about similarities and differences between Spanish and English sounds and cognates (words that look and mean the same as words you already know).

Contents

¡Comprendamos el idioma español!

Language consists of a series of sounds (phonemes) and a series of symbols to represent these (written language). Some languages, such as Spanish, are phonetic—you write, speak and read with the same sounds—while others, like English, are not. However, there are similarities between Spanish and English. While both languages share many of the same vowels and consonants, they are not pronounced in the same way. Learning the sounds of the Spanish alphabet will flow into our goal for all language learners, which is to develop a functional use of the new language in four key areas: writing, reading, listening and speaking.

1. ¡Aprendamos las vocales!

A E I O U A vowel, in any language, receives this name because its sound is made by the vocal cords. The vowel sound comes from the lungs, through the vocal cords and depends on the position of the lips, tongue, and mouth opening, with nothing blocking the air for clear pronunciation. Spanish is emphatic, so you need to emphasize the positions of the lips and the mouth when you make the sound of the vowels. Something important to keep in mind is that the vowels in Spanish always have the same sound; they never change as in English. In the following pictures you can see the position of the lips and the mouth when you make the sound of each vowel. The position of the mouth remains the same throughout the pronunciation of the vowel and each vowel has only one sound.

Letra A   *Letra* E   *Letra* I   *Letra* O   *Letra* U

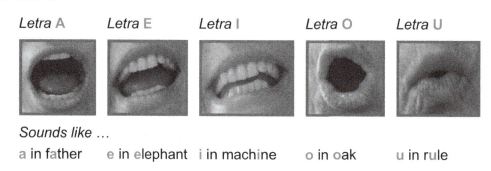

Sounds like …

a in father   e in elephant   i in machine   o in oak   u in rule

¡Practiquemos las vocales!

It is very important that you practice repeating the sounds as much as possible. In the beginning it can be a little strange and you may feel uncomfortable, which is common. With practice you will have better control of the sounds. Don't worry about your accent! Be a **"caradura"** (stubborn and persistent) as you learn. You will even sing in Spanish and can start with singing **"las vocales"**. For now, we have selected videos developed for kids. In our experience, it is the best way to approach a new language; have fun and make it simple. Later, we will have the opportunity to study the Spanish sounds with the techniques of a Spanish linguistics professor. For now, it is crucial that you listen and repeat the video until you feel comfortable with your pronunciation.

"La canción de las vocales A E I O U" is going to help you understand what we are studying. It is important that you remember to repeat the sound of each vowel until you are satisfied with your pronunciation. In the video, you will find two Spanish words for each vowel; these words are:

A   E   I   O   U

abeja, avión   enano, elefante   isla, imán   ojo, oveja   uva, uno

Observa los videos 1.1.1

on the online platform; listen and repeat what you hear. There will be times when you have to stop and repeat the section so you may take notes in this text. The videos allow you to take more ownership of learning the materials at your pace which affords you the opportunity to replay certain concepts that help you.

2. ¡Aprendamos el abecedario en español!

As previously mentioned, the vowels always have the same sound and each consonant has a specific sound depending upon the vowel that follows it. Studying each sound and the rules that each sound follows will help you avoid mispronunciations; more importantly; it gives you the opportunity to be able to hear a Spanish word and be able to spell it out because Spanish is phonetic—words are pronounced the way they are spelled. Learn the Spanish alphabet and the proper pronunciation of all letters.

¡Practiquemos el abecedario en español!

For practice. We selected a video that can help you learn the name of each letter in the Spanish alphabet and also teach you some words, pay attention to the way that the words are pronounced.

REMEMBER THAT YOU NEED TO BE A CARADURA

El alfabeto español

La letra	El nombre	El sonido	Las vocales	Los ejemplos
A, a	*a*	*Sounds like 'a' in father*		*abeja*
B,b	*be, be grande*	*Sounds like 'b' in boy*	*a,e,i,o,u*	*bebé*
C,c	*ce*	*Strong sounds like 'k' in cap*	*a, o, u*	*casa*
		Soft Sounds like 'th' in thought (North and Central Spain)	*e , i*	*cero*
		Soft Sounds like 's' in dress (America and south of Spain)	*e , i*	*cero*
D, d	*de*	*Sounds like 'd' in day*	*a,e,i,o,u*	*dedo*
E, e	*e*	*Sounds like 'e' in elephant*		*elefante*
F, f	*efe*	*Sounds like 'f' in family*	*a,e,i,o,u*	*fuente*
G, g	*ge*	*Soft sounds like 'g' in sugar*	*a, o, u*	*gato*
		Strong sounds like 'h' in home	*e , i*	*general*
		With a silent u soft sound gue/gui as in sugar	*e , i*	*guitarra*
H,h	*hache*	*Doesn't have sound, it is silent as in honor*	*a,e,i,o,u*	*hotel*
I,i	*i*	*Sounds like 'i' in machine*		*isla*
J, j	*jota*	*Strong sounds like 'h' in home*	*a,e,i,o,u*	*jabón*
K, k	*ka*	*Sounds like 'k' in karate : Occurs only in words adopted from other languages*	*a,o,u*	*kilo*
L, l	*ele*	*Sounds like 'l' in love*	*a,e,i,o,u*	*león*
M, m	*eme*	*Sounds like 'm' in mode*	*a,e,i,o,u*	*mamá*
N,n	*ene*	*Sounds like 'n' in night*	*a,e,i,o,u*	*manzana*
Ñ,ñ	*eñe*	*Sounds like 'ni' in onion or "ny" in canyon*	*a,e,i,o,u*	*araña*
O,o	*o*	*Sounds like 'o' in oak*		*ojo*
P,p	*pe*	*Sounds like 'p' in part*	*a,e,i,o,u*	*pie*
Q,q	*cu*	*Sounds like 'k' in king, only with ue/ui and u is silent*	*ue, ui*	*queso*
R,r	*ere*	*Soft sound when is not an inicial position. sound like 'd' in muddy*	*a,e,i,o,u*	*loro*
	erre	*Strong vibration when initial or after N,L, or S no equivalent in English*	*a,e,i,o,u*	*rosa*
S,s	*ese*	*Sounds like 's' in dress*	*a,e,i,o,u*	*sol*
T,t	*te*	*Sounds like 't' in telephone*	*a,e,i,o,u*	*tomate*
U,u	*u*	*Sounds like 'u' in rule*		*uva*
V,v	*uve,ve chica*	*Sounds like 'b' in Spanish*	*a,e,i,o,u*	*vaca*
W, w	*doble u, uve doble*	*Sounds like 'w' in Washington. Occurs only in words adopted from other languages*	*a,e,i,o,u*	*kiwi*
X,x	*equis*	*sounds like 'ks' in thinks*	*a,e,i,o,u*	*xilófono*
		The words of Mexican origin are written with an X, but pronounced with Spanish J	*a,e,i,o,u*	*México*
Y,y	*ye*	*Consonant: sounds like 'Y' in yes or 'J' in English 'judge'*	*a,e,i,o,u*	*inyectar*
	*Hasta 2010 conocida como i griega.	*Vowel: when it stands alone or after another vowel at the end of the word is pronounced as if you pronouncing the Spanish 'I'*	*y*	*Rosa y Juan*
				rey
Z,z	*zeta*	*Soft Sounds like 'th' in thought (North and Central Spain)*	*a,o,u*	*zapato*
		Soft Sounds like 's' in dress (America and south of Spain)	*a,o,u*	*zapato*

Observa los videos 1.1.2
on the online platform; listen and repeat what you hear.

¡Comprendamos las diferencias!

1. All the Spanish letters are treated as feminine nouns (la "a", la "b").
2. The letters are divided in vowels and consonants as in English.
3. **The vowels** are the same as in English.
4. The 'Ñ' is the only additional consonant that the Spanish alphabet has (27 letters in total).
5. The '**K**' **and** the '**W**' appear only in foreign words.
6. The '**H**' and the '**U**' are the only silent letters (in certain limited structures).
7. Each letter has only one sound except: **C, G, X** and **Y**, whose sound depends on the vowel that follows the letter.
8. The '**Y**' is a consonant when it begins a word or a syllable: "**inyectar**" (inject), but it is a vowel when it is last letter in a word; (For example: "**hoy**" or if the '**Y**' stands alone for example: Rosa y Juan).
9. Spanish is similar to English in that the two languages are affected by regional differences. There are different patterns that may be typical in one place and less common in others. For example, the different accents or vocabulary between the U.S. states (English from Texas, Minnesota or New York) or between countries (English from USA, England, New Zealand or Australia). We will explore this idea throughout the semester in the cultural sections. For now, we will briefly look at two of these differences.

¡Viva la cultura!

The grammatical aspects of Spanish are fairly uniform; the principal differences are in vocabulary and pronunciation. As we studied, some consonants have different sounds with each vowel. For example: the letter **C** has a strong sound with the vowels **a, o** and **u.** The sound is like the "c" in cap. But with the vowels **e and i,** it has a soft sound. With the "ce" and "ci" sounds is where we find the biggest linguistic differences between countries. North and Central Spain are distinct in making a sound like 'th' in **th**ought. These regions also apply a similar pronunciation when a "z" is before the vowels. This is referred to as the **ceceo or seseo** which we will practice. Other parts of southern Spain and the different countries in the Americas use the same sound as the letter "**S**" in dre**ss**.

Observa los videos 1.1.3
on the online platform; listen and repeat what you hear.

As Spain is known for the pronunciation of Z and C, Argentina is known for the pronunciation with the '**Y**' and '**LL**'. Pay attention in the next video so it will be easier for you to understand the differences.

Observa los videos 1.1.4
on the online platform; listen and repeat what you hear.

3. ¡Aprendamos agrupar consonantes y vocales para formar palabras!

Until now, we have only learned the individual vowels and the consonants in Spanish, but we also have some specific sound combinations called consonants groups. They work like one consonant and will not be separated when you divide a word in syllables. The consonant groups that we will learn here are CH, LL, and RR.

Double L or ELLE. In Spanish when we have two Ls together we have a consonant group and we never separate the **LL**, they are one consonant. In the previous video we studied the different sounds for this consonant group. The four sounds are correct but we prefer the sound for "jeans"; it is your decision what sound works for you.

RR is a double R. This consonant group will have the same sound as the consonant R when beginning a word. In this case the double R only occurs within a word, never at the beginning of the word and it is the same sound. Watch the next video and practice the sound.

Observa los videos 1.1.5
on the online platform; listen and repeat what you hear.

CH is the combination of the letter C and the letter H and is pronounced as the Ch of "Child".

CHI-na   co-CHE   cu-CHA-ra

¡Practiquemos! While watching the video, you will have the opportunity to practice the entire alphabet and the three consonants groups that we just studied; and at the same time, you will familiarize yourself with different types of accents. Remember that it's very important that you listen and repeat the words several times, until you feel comfortable with your pronunciation.

Observa los videos 1.1.6
on the online platform; listen and repeat what you hear.

¡Palabras trabadas!

"Palabras trabadas" or blended words are the words that have a consonant group with a vowel, the consonant group and the vowel form a blended syllable ("sílabas trabadas"). You never will separate the consonant group and the vowel when you divide the words in syllables. Here are some examples of "palabras trabadas." We emphasize the "sílaba trabada" in each word:

BRA - zo	→	brazo	**BLU** - sa	
CLO - ro	→	cloro	**CRE** - ma	
DRA - gón	→	dragón	consonant group with DL doesn't exist	
FRU - ta	→	fruta	**FLA** - co	
GLO - bo	→	globo	**GRA** - no	
PLA - to	→	plato	**PRI** - mo	
TRA - je	→	traje	a - **TLE** - ta	

Observa los videos 1.1.7
on the online platform; listen and repeat what you hear.

In English it is very common to find double consonants, but it is very rare in Spanish—the exceptions are the consonant groups that we just studied. Spanish has only two double consonants that are not considered **consonant groups**→ they are the double N and the double C. Because it is not a consonant group, the sound doesn't change, so we pronounce each letter. Remember that Spanish is phonetic, you write and read it like it sounds.

The double N is not a consonant group and because Spanish is phonetic we need to read each letter, for example: in**n**ovación, you pronounce **"in"** first and then the next "n" with the "**o**" → "**no**". The two "n"'s have sound.

The double C is different because, as you remember, in Spanish we have two different sounds with the C, depending on the vowel that follows the C. With the **E** and **I,** the sound is soft (with each one of the two geographic pronunciations that we studied in the **seseo or ceceo**) and a strong sound with the **A, O,** and **U.** To be phonically consistent, Spanish language uses the two sounds when you have a double C in a word. In other words, the first C, is like the strong sound of the **C** like 'k' in **c**ap. The second C will use the soft sound like 'th' in **th**ought, if you use the pronunciation of the North and Central Spain, or the soft sounds like 's' in dre**ss,** if you use the pronunciation of America and south of Spain.

As there are consonant groups, we also have vowel groups in Spanish. These vowels groups are known as **diptongos,** when the vowel group has two vowels; and **triptongos** when the vowel group has three vowels. As in the consonant groups, when we have a vowel group we have "palabras **trabadas**" or blended words. You never can separate the vowel group and the consonant or consonants when you divide the words in syllables. In Spanish we have only specific combinations of consonants that form a consonant group. The same is with the vowel groups. In this case, we have some easy rules to follow to know when we have a vowel group: **diptongo.**

The vowels A, E and O are considered strong vowels: vocales fuertes

The I and the U are soft vowels: vocales débiles

Los diptongos are the combination of one strong vowel and one soft vowel; or two soft vowels. In these two cases the two vowels stay together in the syllable.

EU - ro - pa   AU - ro - ra   CUO - ta   Se - gUIr

A diptongo can be a combination of some consonants like in Cuota, but the consonant always will start the syllable. It will never be at the end of the syllable.

Los triptongos are formed by the combination of IAI – IEI – UAI – UEI and UAU. Some words that have **triptongos** are Cuau-tla, ro-ciáis, a-ve-ri-güéis, but for now, we want you to only know that the **triptongos** exist. We will study them in the future.

Later, we will study how to divide a word in syllables and all the *different* rules, but in the mean time we would like to recommend you review the next website found on the online platform.

Observa los videos 1.1.8
on the online platform; Take notes on what you are hearing and reading.

¡Aprendamos pronunciar palabras!

The stress is the emphasis given to certain syllables. As in English, stress is occasionally used to differentiate between words. All words have a stressed syllable. in Spanish, we have only two degrees of stress: strong or weak. The stress always goes on a vowel of the syllable.

La sílaba tónica (the stressed syllable) in Spanish words is the one that is pronounced the loudest. **How do you know which syllable is pronounced the loudest?** In other words, what is the tonic syllable? Remember, el español es fonético, Spanish words are spelled just like they sound. We have these simple four rules to help show you the stressed syllable.

REGLA #1:

Words ending in vowel, n, or s are stressed on the next to the last syllable:

<u>CA</u> - ma   Li - mo - <u>NA</u> - da

<u>LI</u> - bro   <u>PLU</u> - ma

<u>COM</u> - pro   <u>ES</u> - tas

Ca - ma - <u>RO</u> - te

REGLA #2:

Words ending in any consonant except , n, or s are stressed in the last syllable:

doc - <u>TOR</u>   a - <u>MOR</u>

ciu - <u>DAD</u>   can - <u>TAR</u>

le - <u>ER</u>   ca - mi - <u>NAR</u>

pa - <u>PEL</u>   be - <u>BER</u>

REGLA #3:

When there are exceptions to the above rules, a written accent, the ORTHOGRAPHIC ACCENT = ACENTO ORTOGRÁFICO, is applied. The written accent (the tilde) is always on the vowels and looks like this: á, é, í, ó, ú.

a - <u>VIÓN</u>

be - <u>BÉ</u>

ja - <u>BÓN</u>

na - <u>CIÓN</u>

e-du-ca-<u>CIÓN</u>

(All -ción or -sión words follow regla 3.)

REGLA #4:

Written accents are also used to differentiate between words that are pronounced the same but have different meanings:

Si vs. Sí	If vs. Yes
Mi vs. Mí	My vs. Me
El vs. Él	The vs. He
Tu vs. Tú	Your vs. You

Make sure you configure your keyboard to allow for the Spanish alphabet and diacritical marks. If you need help with this, please contact CIT, the campus computing department ,for assistance.

¡Practiquemos!

Now you have the key elements for the correct pronunciation of Spanish words. Like we said before, some of the material that we are using is developed for kids, because we think that it is an easier way to learn. Now that you have a base of Spanish pronunciation, we would like you to study words that look or sound like English words but are going to add to your comprehension in Spanish.

4. ¡Aprendamos los cognados!

As we end this chapter about vowels and consonants, we have a nice surprise for you—you may already know more Spanish than you think! Many Spanish words have the same origin as English words. In fact, some words are the same word, but are pronounced differently. We have many words that are the same that in Spanish have one consonant but have two consonants in English.

Let's see some examples:

Capital	Capital	←	same word different in pronunciation.
Instructions	Instrucciones	←	same origin: From the Latin: instructǐo,-ōnis.
Impossible	Imposible	←	In Spanish, we have only NN and CC as double consonants*.
			*Notice: ch, rr, ll are consonant groups.

In linguistics a cognate (COGNADO) is a word that has the same origin or root as in another language; it can be Latin, Greek, German, etc.

How many Spanish words do you already know?

Accident	=	Accidente	List	=	Lista
Banana	=	Banana	Magic	=	Mágia
Cabin	=	Cabina	Natural	=	Natural
December	=	Diciembre	Object	=	Objeto
Elephant	=	Elefante	Paper	=	Papel
Family	=	Familia	Radio	=	Radio
Idea	=	Idea	Secret	=	Secreto
Galaxy	=	Galaxia	Telephone	=	Teléfono

The next table gives you some equivalents between English and Spanish. These are very helpful to have a better understanding of the COGNADOS and also help you to succeed in spelling Spanish. As you remember, there are some words that need to have an acento ortográfico. We didn't study the rules for the acentos ortográficos yet; but when you **memorize** these equivalents you are learning also that all Spanish words that end in ción, sión or ión use an acento ortográfico. When you learn a new Spanish word, always learn it with the correct spelling including the orthographic stress.

Inglés	Equivalencia en Español	Ejemplos:
-ade	-ada	limon**ada**
-ant	-ante	inst**ante**
-cy	-cia	infa**cia**
chl	cl	**cloro without H**
-ic	-ica/-ico	mus**ica**/publ**ico**
-ion	-ion	relig**ion**
-ist	-ista	art**ista**
mm	nm	in**m**ovil
s + consonant	es + consonante	**es**pecial
-(s)sion	-sion	pas**ion**
th	t	**t**eologia **without H**
-ty	-ad	universid**ad**
-tion	-cion	na**cion**
ph	f	**f**ilosofia
psy	psi	**psi**cologia

JUST FOR FUN!!

Although it may seem improbable, **you can** learn **100 Spanish words** in record time! We're just talking about the **cognates!** As you remember, cognates are words that are identical or nearly identical in spelling in both languages because they have the same origin or root.

Empecemos—let's get started...

Español	Inglés
accidente	accident
actor	actor
analizar	to analyze
ángel	angel
artístico	artistic
banana	banana
banco	bank
balance	balance
cabina	cabin
carro	car
canal	channel
colección	collection
combinar	to combine
concierto	concert
cultura	culture
curioso	curious
delicado	delicate
detalle	detail
distancia	distance
dividir	to divide
enorme	enormous
esencial	essential
excelente	excellent
expreso	express
extremo	extreme
familia	family
fantástico	fantastic
general	general
guía	guide
hospital	hospital
hotel	hotel
importante	important
imposible	imposible

Español	Inglés
individual	individual
infinito	infinite
interactivo	interactive
invención	invention
ilusión	illusion
isla	island
letra	letter
león	lion
máquina	machine
material	material
melodía	melody
memoria	memory
miserable	miserable
momento	momento
música	music
nación	nation
necesidad	necessity
nota	note
objetivo	objective
océano	ocean
opinión	opinión
opción	option
orden	order
original	original
papel	paper
parque	park
personal	personal
foto	photo
pino	pine
planta	plant
posibilidad	possibility
posible	possible
presidente	president

Español	Inglés
el problema	problema
proyecto	project
promover	promote
público	public
radio	radio
rancho	ranch
real	real/royal
razón	reason
recibir	to receive
reducir	to reduce
relación	relation
repetir	to repeat
reservación	reservation
restaurante	restaurant
romántico	romantic
rosa	rose
ruta	route
secreto	secret
sensación	sensation
silencio	silence
especial	special
estructura	structure
teléfono	telephone
terrible	terrible
tráfico	traffic
unido	united
urgente	urgent
usual	usual
verbo	verb
vibración	vibration
vacaciones	vacation
virgen	virgen
visitar	to visit
vocabulario	vocabulary

WE JUST LEARNED 100 WORDS IN SPANISH!!!

Please answer the following:

[ ] Yes   [ ] No   Can I understand the main differences between Spanish and English?

[ ] Yes   [ ] No   Can I say the vowels in Spanish?

[ ] Yes   [ ] No   Can I say the alphabet in Spanish?

[ ] Yes   [ ] No   Can I identify some of the geographic variances between Spanish-speakers?

[ ] Yes   [ ] No   Can I form consonant and vowel groups and pronounce them correctly?

[ ] Yes   [ ] No   Can I read and understand COGNADOS?

[ ] Yes   [ ] No   Can I apply what I learned at home to activities in the classroom?

If you answered "No" to any of these questions, review those sections again and see your professor for help.

LEARNING AT HOME AND USING SPANISH IN THE CLASSROOM

Vocabulary

Español	M/F	Inglés	Clasificación
accidente	El	accident	Sustantivo
analizar		to analyze	Verbo Regular
ángel	El	angel	Sustantivo
artístico/a		artistic	Adjetivo
así, así		so, so	Expresión
auto	El	car	Sustantivo
balance	El	balance	Sustantivo
banana	La	banana	Sustantivo
banco	El	bank	Sustantivo
bien		well	Adjetivo, Adverbio
cabina	La	cabin	Sustantivo
canal	El	channel	Sustantivo
carro	El	car	Sustantivo
chao		goodbye	Expresión
coche	El	car	Sustantivo
colección	La	collection	Sustantivo
combinar		to combine	Verbo Regular
concierto	El	concert	Sustantivo
cultura	La	culture	Sustantivo
curioso/a		curious	Adjetivo
delicado/a		delicate	Adjetivo
detalle	El	detail	Sustantivo
distancia	La	distance	Sustantivo
dividir		to divide	Verbo Regular
enorme		enormous	Adjetivo
esencial		essential	Adjetivo
especial		special	Adjetivo
estructura	La	structure	Sustantivo
excelente		excellent	Adjetivo
expreso/a		express	Adjetivo
extremo/a		extreme	Adjetivo, Sustantivo
familia	La	family	Sustantivo
fantástico/a		fantastic	Adjetivo
foto	La	photo	Sustantivo
general		general	Adjetivo, Sustantivo
guía	El, La	guide	Sustantivo
hospital	El	hospital	Sustantivo
hotel	El	hotel	Sustantivo

ilusión	La	illusion	Sustantivo
importante		important	Adjetivo
imposible		impossible	Adjetivo
individual		individual	Adjetivo
infinito/a		infinite	Adjetivo
interactivo/a		interactive	Adjetivo
invención	La	invention	Sustantivo
isla	La	island	Sustantivo
león	El	lion	Sustantivo
letra	La	letter	Sustantivo
máquina	La	machine	Sustantivo
material	El	material	Sustantivo
melodía	La	melody	Sustantivo
memoria	La	memory	Sustantivo
miserable		miserable	Adjetivo
momento	El	moment	Sustantivo
música	La	music	Sustantivo
muy bien		very well	Adjetivo, Adverbio
nación	La	nation	Sustantivo
necesidad	La	necessity	Sustantivo
nota	La	note	Sustantivo
objetivo	El	objective	Sustantivo
océano	El	ocean	Sustantivo
opción	La	option	Sustantivo
opinión	La	opinion	Sustantivo
orden	La	order	Sustantivo
original		original	Adjetivo
parque	El	park	Sustantivo
personal		personal	Adjetivo
pino	El	pine	Sustantivo
planta	La	plant	Sustantivo
posibilidad	La	possibility	Sustantivo
posible		possible	Adjetivo
presidente	El, La	president	Sustantivo
problema (Irregular in terms of gender rule—Greek origin.)	El	problem	Sustantivo
promover		to promote	Verbo Irregular
proyecto	El	project	Sustantivo
público/a		public	Adjetivo
radio	El, La	radio	Sustantivo

rancho	El	ranch	Sustantivo
razón	La	reason	Sustantivo
real		real/royal	Adjetivo
recibir		to receive	Verbo Regular
reducir (c—zc)		to reduce	Verbo Regular: Cambio Fonético
relación	La	relationship	Sustantivo
repetir (e—i)		to repeat	Verbo Irregular
reservación	La	reservation	Sustantivo
restaurante	El	restaurant	Sustantivo
romántico/a		romantic	Adjetivo
rosa	La	rose	Sustantivo
ruta	La	route	Sustantivo
secreto	El	secret	Sustantivo
secreto/a		secret	Adjetivo
sensación	La	sensation	Sustantivo
silencio	El	silence	Sustantivo
teléfono	El	telephone	Sustantivo
terrible		terrible	Adjetivo
tráfico	El	traffic	Sustantivo
unido/a		united	Adjetivo
urgente		urgent	Adjetivo
usual		usual	Adjetivo
vacaciones (pl.)	Las	vacation	Sustantivo
verbo	El	verb	Sustantivo
vibración	La	vibration	Sustantivo
virgen	La	virgin	Sustantivo
visitar		to visit	Verbo Regular
vocabulario	El	vocabulary	Sustantivo

¿Quiénes somos?

Objectives

1. Learn the beginning concepts and rules for dividing words into syllables to determine the stress of a word. Learn about enunciation and intonation to achieve authentic pronunciation.

2. Learn how to write basic sentences and ask/answer a variety of simple questions.

3. Learn how to greet others in formal and informal situations and say goodbye politely.

4. Learn to introduce yourself and others and provide basic personal information in a polite way.

5. Learn numbers for providing information.

6. Learn what subjects, pronouns, and adjectives are while recognizing if they are singular or plural, feminine, or masculine.

7. Learn what SER and TENER mean, when to use the verbs and their conjugations.

Overview

1. ¡Aprendamos a dividir palabras en sílabas!

As you know Spanish is phonetic, the consonants and the consonant groups have specific sounds with each one of the vowels, and only the vowels have a sound by themselves. In order to pronounce words correctly, you need to know how to divide the word into syllables so that you are able to identify the stress of the word. Spanish words are syllabified according to some very rigid rules.

Let analyze the next words for the number of the vowels and the number of the syllables that we have:

amigo	➜ has a, i, and o	➜ then the word amigo has three syllables.
profesora	➜ has o, e, o and a	➜ It has four syllables.
verde	➜ has two e	➜ It has two syllables
hombre	➜ has o, and e	➜ It has two syllables.
estudiar	➜ has e, u, and ia (diptongo)	➜ It has three syllables.
transporte	➜ has a, o, and e	➜ It has three syllables.
construir	➜ has o, and ui (diptongo)	➜ It has two syllables.

After you define the number of syllables that the word has, you have to follow the next 4 simple rules:

1. **A simple consonant or consonant group goes with the following vowel. You can NEVER have a consonant without a vowel in a syllable, but one vowel can be a syllable.**

amigo	→	a-mi-go	*tres sílabas.*
profesora	→	pro-fe-so-ra	*cuatro sílabas.*
tarea	→	ta-re-a	*tres sílabas ("ea" no es diptongo = dos sílabas.) Why?*

A DIPHTHONG IS COMPRISED OF A STRONG + A WEAK VOWEL OR TWO WEAK VOWELS. "E" AND "A" ARE CONSIDERED STRONG VOWELS AND HENCE CAN BE SEPARATED INTO SYLLABLES.

2. **Two consonants are usually separated; except when you have an S and a consonant, the S goes with the syllable before. Remember a consonant group never is divided.**

verde	→	ver-de	*dos sílabas.*
estudiar	→	es-tu-diar	*tres sílabas ("ia" diptongo = una sílaba).*

3. **Three consonants are usually divided after the first one, unless the second is an S:**

hombre	→	hom-bre	*dos sílabas.*

transporte → trans-por-te   *tres sílabas.*

4. **It is uncommon in Spanish to have four consonants between vowels, the rule is always divided after the second.**

construir → cons-truir   *dos sílabas ("ui" diptongo = una sílaba).*

Now you need to divide some of the words of your vocabulary in syllables. We recommend that you read aloud each one of the syllables. It is important that you control the sound of each consonant with the vowel. Like we studied before, the sound of each consonant in Spanish depends on the vowel. In Spanish, we cannot read consonants alone. We read the consonant with the vowel. If you have good control of the sound of the vowels with each consonant, you will have good Spanish pronunciation. Remember pronunciation in Spanish depends on the vowels.

You may think that this exercise is tedious but it will be crucial for your pronunciation, for your spelling and also, for you to be able to write correctly the orthographic stress. For each word, write the number of vowels, diphthongs and triphthongs that it has. This number is the number of syllables that the word has. You will write the word divided in syllables in the last column. See the example apellido: it has 4 vowels, then we divide the word in four syllables.

As you complete the exercise below and have a question, go back to review the rules above.

➔ **Remember** diphthongs or triphthongs = 1 vowel grouping.

	La palabra	El número de sílabas	Las sílabas de la palabra
1	apellido	4 vocales = 4 sílabas	a-pe-lli-do
2	mujer		
3	alcohol		
4	nueve		
5	corazón		
6	seis		
7	guante		
8	Europa		

Recordemos la acentuación en español:

As we studied in Unidad uno, the stress (acento) is the prominence given to certain syllables. The stressed syllable is the sílaba tónica. All Spanish words have a sílaba tónica; but it is important that you remember that some Spanish words need an orthographic stress (acento ortográfico) on the stressed syllable. As you remember, the orthographic stress is a little tilde that we write only on the vowel of the stressed syllable: á, é, í, ó, ú **that did not follow the stress rules learned in Unidad 1.** In Spanish not all the words need an orthographic stress and there are specific rules for the orthographic stress. To apply these rules, it is important that you know how to divide a word into syllables and identify the stressed syllable. Before we study the rules for writing the tilde or orthographic stress, do you remember **the rules that we studied to know where the stressed syllable is in the word**? Please write the **stress rules** below (you will find them in unidad 1):

Note: The **stress rules (which you write below)** *are not the same as the syllable division rules.*

Regla número uno: _____

Regla número dos: _____

Regla número tres: _____

Regla número cuatro: _____

In the next chart, you have some of your vocabulary words divided by syllables and the stressed syllable is marked with red and bold letters. Now you need to write the rule number that was applied for the specific stressed syllable. For example, in the word **a-ma-ble** la síla-ba tónica es "**ma**" porque se aplica la **regla número uno**: Words ending in vowel, n, or s are stressed on the next to the last syllable.

Palabras:	Regla
a-ma-ble	1
a-zul	
a-zu-les	
ba-jo	
bo-ni-to	
cas-ta-ño	
chis-to-so	
ge-ne-ro-sa	
gran-de	

Palabras:	Regla
es-ta-dou-ni-den-se	
pro-du-ce	
gus-tar	
ha-cer	
ser	
te-ner	
bai-lar	
le-ga-li-za-ción	
es-cu-char	

Remember bring your questions to your next class!

SUCCESS IN OUR IN CLASS PRACTICES REQUIRES THAT YOU TAKE OWNERSHIP OF LEARNING BY DOING THE REQUIRED READINGS, LEARNING THE VOCABULARY AND STUDYING THE LECTURES ONLINE AND IN YOUR BOOK BEFORE EACH CLASS!

In our vocabulary, we have the next words **bolígrafo, números, atlético, simpático y die-ciséis**. All these words have an orthográphic stress, can you tell us why? What is the rule that we apply to know that these words need el **acento ortográfico**? _____

bo - lí - gra - fo
nú - me - ros
a - tlé - ti - co

When the rules number one and number two are not followed, we use the written accent, the orthographic stress. Regla número tres.

This is the tricky part! You need to know how the word sounds!

Remember, when we write a stress, it is because the word is not following rules 1 or 2.

Analyze each example:

Palabra : bolígrafo

Número vocales: 4

Número de sílabas: 4

División silábica: bo-li-gra-fo

Sílaba tónica: La regla 1: Words ending in vowel, n, or s are stressed on the next to the last syllable. Boligrafo ends in vowel. We don't say: Bo – li – gra – fo... We say: bo – lí – gra –fo.

It is a word that doesn't follow rule 1! We need to write the stress to indicate that the pronunciation of the word is not following the rules. This applies to the next two examples as well.

Palabra : números

Número vocales: 3

Número de sílabas: 3

División silábica: nú-me-ros

Sílaba tónica: La regla 1: Words ending in a vowel, n or s are stressed on the next to the last syllable.

We don't say: nu – me – ros... We say: nú - me – ros.

Palabra : atlético

Número vocales: 4

Número de sílabas: 4

División silábica: a-tlé-ti-co

Sílaba tónica: La regla 1: Words ending in a vowel, n or s are stressed on next last syllable.

We don't say: a – tle – ti –co... We say: a – tlé – ti – co.

Notice how these examples did not follow rule 1 and as a result we wrote the stress above the appropriate vowel!

These kinds of words are exceptions. We want you to keep these in mind so you learn the correct pronunciation of the words. For now, we want you to remember this:

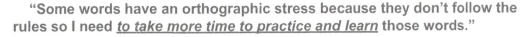

"Some words have an orthographic stress because they don't follow the rules so I need _to take more time to practice and learn_ those words."

Now let's concentrate on la regla número cuatro in which written accents are also used to differentiate between words that are pronounced the same but have different meanings. Usually these words are monosyllabic, words with only one syllable. You need to learn these words. We call this special stress el acentro diacrítico because it differentiates between the words such as tú (you) vs tu (your).

¡Practiquemos los acentos!

Here are some of your vocabulary words and some expressions in Spanish that we are studying. We want you to **write the stress of the words that need an orthographic stress and the stress of the words that need a diacritic stress.** In the next column you need to write the kind of stress that you use. Follow the examples and use your vocabulary lists to find the answers:

#	Expression in Spanish and vocabulary words	Type of stress
1	Por favor	No acento ortográfico
2	Perdón.	Acento ortográfico
3	¿Qué tal?	Acento diacrítico
4	(Muchas) gracias.	
5	Yo tambien.	
6	Buenos dias.	
7	Veintidos.	
8	Buenas noches.	
9	¿Como esta usted (Ud.)?	
10	Veintitres.	
11	¿Como se llama?	
12	Me llamo (Jose).	
13	Jugar al futbol.	
14	Escuchar musica.	
15	¿Cuantos años tienes?	

We will review answers to this exercise in class so please make sure you complete it beforehand.

¡hola!

Soy el **acento**

2. Sentence and question formation in a few easy steps:

Observa el video 1.2.1 on the online platform before beginning the next section Listen and repeat what you hear about questions and responses regarding one's origin. Watch the explanation and the conversational videos. As you watch, take notes on the word order and repeat the questions and answers that you hear. Notice the tone in the speaker's voice as he asks questions. **Does it change?** ¡Sí! **The tone changed.**

Intonation is the pattern or melody of rising or falling pitch changes in the voice when speaking. The pitch or tone pattern of a sentence distinguishes kinds of sentences as when in the video questions are asked. The pitch pattern also distinguishes the speakers of different countries in the same culture. British English has a specific pitch pattern different from the English that we speak in the States or the English that is spoken in Australia. If in the same language we have diverse patterns, imagine between languages! It's important to learn to use the Spanish tone, because like stress, **tone can change the meaning of a sentence**. Keep this in mind; we will address these changes of tone in the future.

Comprendamos la formación de oraciones:

The sentence is a set of words that is complete in itself, typically containing a subject (who is doing the action in the sentence) and a verb (the action that the subject is doing) and some extra information. Different kinds of sentences exist:

Declarative sentences: used to express any statement positive or negative.

We speak Spanish and English.

She doesn't speak French.

Exclamatory sentences: used to express great emotion such as excitement, surprise, happiness and anger, and end with an exclamation point.

What a lovely day it is!

Be careful!

We never are going to finish the book!

Interrogative sentences: used to ask questions and end with a question mark.

What's your name?

What time is it?

Let's understand sentence formation: *Subject + verb + extra information* *(Remember: keep it simple at first. This helps you focus on verb agreement but more so the aspect of communicating clearly the action.)*

1. Determine who is your **subject.**

2. Conjugate a verb that agrees with that subject in the tense you are studying.

3. **Extra information** such as an adjective, direct object or timeframe in which the action is done.

He is intelligent. → Él es inteligente.   or   She is **special.** → Ella es especial.

If you are asked to make up 10 sentences about something, keep them simple to about 5-10 words. Your thoughts in English might be more verbose, but you are learning a 2nd language so keep it simple and to things you can say (even if they are not true!). For example, if I asked "what do you study?" and you did not know your major in Spanish, then just say **Estudio medicina** o **estudio italiano en la universidad.** Your abilities will grow in time as long as you study the vocabulary and structures daily.

Exclamatory sentences: follow the same formation. The difference is the emotion that we are using and the exclamation point.

¡Subject + verb + extra information !

1. Determine who is your **subject.**

2. **Conjugate a verb** that agrees with that subject in the tense you are studying.

3. **Extra information** such as an adjective, direct object or timeframe in which the action is done.

He is intelligent! → ¡Él es inteligente!   or   She is **special!** → ¡Ella es especial!

Interrogative sentences: As in English, in Spanish the formation changes:

Questions→¿Question word +verb +subject + extra information?

That upside down question mark tells you that a question is coming so change the intonation of your voice to indicate uncertainty or a higher inflection.

1. **Know** the **question words.**

   The entire list of interrogatives or question words will be in the next unit, so for now just repeat what you hear. There are times when you won't use an interrogative but rather start with the verb.

2. **Identify who your** subject is but conjugate the **verb** for that first as the word order differs in Spanish.

3. **State who the subject is** –*note the word order is different in Spanish.*

4. **Extra information** Is he intelligent?→ ¿Es él inteligente? or Is she special? →¿Es ella especial?

Because Spanish uses the upside down question mark at the beginning of the sentence and a question mark at the end of the question Spanish has the option to not change the formation. With the change of the intonation it is enough to indicate the question. For example:

Is he intelligent? →¿Es él inteligente? In Spanish we can ask ¿Él es inteligente? ¿Es él inteligente?

Is she special? → ¿Es ella especial? → ¿Ella es especial? ¿Es ella especial?

This is the reason why in Spanish it is very important that you mark when a question starts "¿" and when a question ends "?".

A word about vocabulary before we begin... **It is important to realize that you are the one responsible for learning the vocabulary.** Your goal should be a deep processing of words. Deep processing implies that these words become part of you, almost as your native language is part of you.

While they are not required of each word that you see, we recommend you write flashcards for the words that you have difficulty recalling. Flashcards are also helpful to help you remember verbs and any patterns for verb conjugations that you will learn.

Why use flash cards.

+ Flash-card technology is still better than the most expensive educational computer gear that you can buy.

+ It is the quickest way to get just the repetition that you need on just the words that you need to repeat.

+ It is so simple: it is tried and true.

   1. Visualize and vocalize: We all know that a picture is worth a thousand words, you can facilitate the recall of vocabulary using drawings, stickers, pictures, etc. To help our memory we will use the color red for the Spanish words and blue for the English. We will use red for the Spanish words because it is a very emotionally intense color. It enhances human metabolism, increases respiration rate, and raises blood pressure. It has very high visibility; which is why stop signs, stoplights, and fire equipment are usually painted in red.

   2. Visualize by imagination and vocalize: Meditate on an image that the word represents or suggests as you say it aloud. If you see a house, say: "casa", if you see a dog say "perro", if you pass in front of the cafeteria say: "cafetería."

   3. Use the diglot weave – to understand: Insert palabras en español into English sentences, until you get their meanings quickly. For example: el perro = dog, so repeat to yourself several sentences like:

El perro is a nice pet.   She loves her perro.   Your perro is a puppy.

   4. Repeat, repeat, and repeat again: Especially for learning important parts and forms of words, sometimes only repetition will secure your deep learning for certain hard-to-retain items. Frequent vocal repetition impresses the forms on your "mental ear." We want to be able to communicate, we need to say words, but also we need to listen and understand the words when the other person talks. That is the reason why we need to work with our "mental ear."

3. ¡Comencemos con los saludos y despedidas!

Let's start with greetings and pleasantries. You should know that when one meets someone

other than a child, it is always best to be polite and use a formal way of addressing the other person. Let's familiarize ourselves with expressions to help you put your best foot forward in a Spanish speaking country.

Observa los videos 1.2.2 through 1.2.4 where you will watch videos on Greetings and Introductions.

In these videos, you will hear the pronunciation for basic greetings, introductions and questions related to **"how are you?"** and how to describe yourself. Listen to the videos and repeat the phrases or answer the questions when prompted. This will help you with the in-class practices. The videos are set up in 2 sections—one that explains the concepts and the other that is more conversational. Pay attention to the usted forms since this is the polite way to address those you do not know or who are not among your family and friends.

Make sure you select the greetings and good-byes video as well as the video on asking someone's name.

4. Preguntando y dando información básica.

After having watched the videos to familiarize yourself with the different greetings and introductions, you should begin learning the vocabulary and phrases associated with the topics that we are learning in this chapter. It is divided into 2 sections —one for questions color-coded to correspond to possible replies in the following section.

Unos saludos—Formal Greetings

Buenos días	Good day/good morning
Buenas tardes	Good afternoon
Buenas noches	Good evening/night
Hola	Hi

Unas Despedidas—Some goodbyes

Adiós	Goodbye
Con permiso	A polite way to excuse yourself
Nos vemos	See you later.
Chao	Goodbye

Conociendo a otra persona—Meeting someone

¿Cuál es su nombre?	What is your name?
¿Cómo se llama usted?	What is your name? (Literally, What do you call yourself?)

¿Quién es usted?	What is your name? (Literally, Who are you?)
¿De dónde es usted?	From where are you?
¿Cuál es su dirección?	What is your address?
¿Cuál es su número de teléfono?	What is your phone number?
¿Qué estudia usted?	What do you study?
¿Dónde estudia usted?	Where do you study?

Respuestas—replies

Soy _____	I am ____
Mi nombre es	My name is
Me llamo	My name is ____ (Literally, I call myself)
Mucho gusto	Nice to meet you
Encantado (just males say this)	Nice to meet you
Encantada (just females say this)	Nice to meet you
Igualmente	Mutually/likewise
Soy de	I am from
Mi dirección es la calle ____ número__	My address is __ number _____
Mi número de teléfono es	My phone number is
Estudio español	I study Spanish.
Estudio español en Geneseo	I study Spanish at Geneseo

Let's learn about how to ask one's origin. In the next video, you will see various photos of people and determine based on their age whether or not one would use Usted or Tú with that person. You will also see flags from the various Spanish speaking countries to help you determine the answer to ¿De dónde es usted? or ¿De dónde eres tú?

Observa los videos 1.2.5 on the online platform. You will note that this is the same video as 1.2.1 but the purpose is now for context rather than tone. Reflect on the videos. on the online platform; listen and repeat what you hear. There will be times when you have to stop and repeat the section so you may take notes in this text. The videos allow you to take more ownership of learning the materials at your pace which affords you the opportunity to replay certain concepts that help you.

1. How would you greet someone you do not know?_____
   _____

2. You hear the phrase, "**muy bien, gracias**". What do you think the question was?_____
   _____

3. Which greeting do you use with a friend?_____

4. It is 9:00 AM, which greeting do you use?_____

5. You heard "**soy de**". What do you think that means? _____
_____

6. How would you answer "**De dónde es usted**" for yourself? _____
_____

Practiquemos:

Let's practice putting these phrases together—read the dialogue with a partner or by yourself. Remember to pay attention to the vowels' sounds so you sound **auténtico** (authentic).

Alejandro Sanz:	Buenos días.
Talía Soto:	Buenos días.
Alejandro:	¿Cómo se llama usted?
Talía:	Me llamo Talía Soto Iglesias. ¿Cuál es su nombre?
Alejandro:	Encantado, Señora Soto. Soy Alejandro Sanz Laredo.
Talía:	Mucho gusto, Señor Sanz.
Alejandro:	¿De dónde es usted?
Talía:	Soy de Costa Rica. ¿Y usted?
Alejandro:	Soy de México. ¿Estudia usted?
Talía:	Sí, estudio en Geneseo. Mi clase es en cinco minutos. Adiós.
Alejandro:	Chao.

Comprendamos:

Answer the questions based on the brief reading and your knowledge of the vocabulary.

1. ¿Cuál es el apellido de Talía? _____

2. ¿Cuál es el apellido de Alejandro? _____

3. ¿De dónde es Alejandro? _____

4. ¿De dónde es Talía? _____

5. ¿Quién estudia en Geneseo? _____

6. ¿Cómo se dice "It is nice to meet you?" _____

Did you notice that Talía and Alejandro have two last names? This is common to Hispanic families. The first last name refers to the father's family and the second last name refers to the mother's last name. You will study more about this practice later in this unit.

> REMEMBER HOW IMPORTANT THAT FIRST IMPRESSION IS SO PUTTING YOUR BEST FOOT FORWARD AND BEING POLITE WILL LEAD TO BETTER RELATIONSHIPS WITH OTHERS WITH WHOM YOU MEET.

Homework= La Tarea:

Create a dialogue in which you ask and answer the questions about yourself and a partner in class. Make up both sides of the dialogue. Use the above as a guide. **Bring your written dialogue to class with you to practice and to submit as part of your homework.**

Añadamos:

Let's add to what you know. There are two ways of addressing people—formally as in the conversation above and more friendly or informally for people who may be peers in school or acquaintances/friends. These greetings come in handy when you are among friends and meet one of their friends for the first time or you are talking among people you know already.

Unos saludos Informales—Informal greetings

| Hola, ¿qué tal? | Hi, how is it going? |
| Hola ¿cómo estás? | Hi, how are you? |

Unas despedidas—Some goodbyes

| Hasta luego | Until later/see you later |
| Hasta mañana | See you tomorrow. |

Conociendo a otra persona—Meeting someone

¿Cuál es tu nombre?	What is your name?
¿Cómo te llamas tú?	What is your name? (Literally, What do you call yourself?)
¿Quién eres tú?	What is your name? (Literally, Who are you?)
Mucho gusto	Nice/pleasure to meet you
¿De dónde eres tú?	From where are you?
¿Cuál es tu dirección?	What is your address?
¿Cuál es tu número de teléfono?	What is your phone number?
¿Qué estudias tú?	What do you study?

¿Dónde estudias tú?	Where do you study?

Respuestas—replies

Soy _____	I am _____
Mi nombre es	My name is
Me llamo	My name is _____ (Literally, I call myself)
El gusto es mío	The pleasure is mine.
Es un placer.	It is a pleasure.
Soy de	I am from
Mi dirección es la calle _____ número_____	My address is number ___ _____
Mi número de teléfono es	My phone number is
Estudio español	I study Spanish.
Estudio español en Geneseo	I study Spanish at Geneseo

Otro vocabulario—other vocabulary

Por favor	Please
Gracias	Thank you
Yo también	Me too.
Este es mi amigo.	This is my friend. (male friend)
Esta es mi amiga.	This is my friend. (female friend.
Bien	Well
Muy bien	Very well
Así, así	So so

Practiquemos:

Let's practice putting these phrases together assuming now that Alejando and Talía are peers in school and Talía has another friend with her. Read the dialogue with a partner or by yourself at home.

Alejandro:	Hola, ¿Qué tal?
Talía:	Hola, ¿Cómo estás?
Alejando:	Bien gracias, ¿y tú?
Talía:	Muy bien gracias. Alejandro, este es mi amigo José.
Alejandro:	Es un placer, José.
José:	El placer es mío, Alejandro. ¿Estudias en Geneseo también?
Alejandro:	Sí, estudio matemáticas.

José:	¡Yo también estudio matemáticas!
Talía:	Alejandro es de México.
Alejandro:	José, ¿eres tú de Costa Rica como Talía?
José:	No, yo soy de Panamá.
Talia:	Alejandro, ¿nosotros estudiamos luego? ¿Cuál es tu número de teléfono?
Alejandro:	Sí, amiga, mi número de teléfono es cinco, uno, cinco, dos, dos tres, tres.
Talia:	Gracias, amigo. Hasta luego.
José:	Nos vemos.

Comprendamos:

Answer the questions based on the brief reading and your knowledge of the vocabulary.

1. ¿Quién es el amigo de Talía? _____

2. ¿Qué estudian Alejandro y José?_____

3. ¿De dónde es José?_____

4. ¿Cuál es el número de teléfono de Alejandro? _____

5. ¿Ellos estudian italiano? _____

Comparemos:

Let's compare--think about the similarities in your culture with those of the Spanish speaker's culture.

1. What do you do when you see an acquaintance, a friend, a co-worker? Do you stop to chat or do you greet them in passing without stopping?

2. How do you greet a professional person, a person of title or someone with whom you may have an interview?

3. How do you feel about people speaking to you in close proximity to you? If in a Spanish speaking country, you would need to become more comfortable with it.

Leamos:

Read for pronunciation. You will then read the translation to yourself to learn about physical cues that occur when one greets someone else; think about what you do in terms of your gestures and non-verbal communication.

Dos amigos

Cuando dos amigos pasan uno al otro, se saludan con "Hola", ¿Cómo estás?", Ellos esperan la respuesta de su amigo y paran para charlar.

Si ellos son de España, generalmente se dan dos besitos en cada mejilla o cerca a la mejilla de su amigo.

Si ellos son de Latinoamérica, generalmente se dan un besito o un abrazo al verse.

Los chicos se dan la mano o se abrazan.

Dos profesionales solamente se dan la mano. No se dan besitos ni se abrazan.

La práctica de hablar muy cerca el uno al otro es normal.

Traduzcamos: Let's translate.

Two friends: When two friends see each other, they greet each other with "Hi, How are you?". They wait for the friend to reply and stop to chat.

If they are from Spain, generally they kiss upon seeing each other with one kiss on each cheek or near their friend's cheek.

If they are from Latin America, generally they give one kiss or a hug upon seeing each other.

If they are two male friends, they shake hands or hug.

Two professionals only shake hands. They do not kiss or hug. Speaking close to each other is normal.

Repasemos:

A. In the previous unit, you learned the alphabet and the fact that Spanish is phonetic. That is to say that the majority of the words are spelled exactly the way they sound. To practice speaking ask various classmates words from the list of vocabulary and phrases to spell. Spelling the words may be especially helpful to you if you are trying to provide demographic information to a Spanish speaker of words that are not of Spanish origin, for example, perhaps your last name or street name.

B. Practicing greetings, introductions and polite phrases by yourself daily and/or with a partner will increase your confidence and skills.

If practicing by yourself: **You will find the list below on the online platform.** Print and fold the list in half and quiz yourself by writing and speaking the answers to the expressions. Unfold the list, to check your answers. Place a checkmark next to the ones you have mastered well and practice again those that you did not recall easily.

With a partner, you can ask the expressions and place a checkmark by the ones your partner has mastered. The master list below may be found on the online platform for you to print to bring to class for practice with other classmates.

#	En español	1	2	3	4	En inglés
1	Por favor.					Please.
2	De nada.					You're welcome.
3	Con permiso.					Excuse me, when you need to physically move
4	Perdón.					Excuse me. When you cough or sneeze
5	¿Qué tal?					How is it going? (informal.)
6	(Muchas) gracias.					Thank you (very much).
7	Yo también.					Me, too. (I also)
8	Buenos días.					Good morning.
9	Buenas tardes.					Good afternoon.
10	Buenas noches					Good evening.
11	¿Cómo está usted (Ud)?					How are you? (formal)
12	¿Cómo estás tú?					How are you? (informal)
13	(Muy) bien, gracias.					(Very) well thank you.
14	¿Cómo se llama Ud?					What is your name?
15	¿Cómo te llamas tú?					What is your name?
16	Me llamo …(José)					My name is… (José.)
17	Mi apellido es … (Ramos)					My last name is …(Ramos.)
18	Hasta luego.					See you later.
19	Hasta mañana.					See you tomorrow.
20	Adiós.					Good bye.
21	Este es mi amigo, Juan. Esta es mi amiga, Ana.					This is my friend, Juan. This is my friend, Ana.
22	Mucho gusto.					Pleased to meet you.
23	Encantado (m)/ Encantada (f).					Pleased to meet you.
24	Igualmente.					Likewise. It's mutual.
25	El gusto es mío.					The pleasure is mine.

5. ¡Aprendamos los números!

In this section you will learn numbers. To study the vocabulary for the numbers from 0-100+ below, we recommend you make flashcards for numbers 0-20 then the tens up through 100. Remember Spanish in Red, English in Blue (and use the numbers, not the English words to help you learn easily). Say them aloud and pay attention to spelling. Notice that you may spell numbers from 16-29 in two ways. After 30, you will spell them using the **tens place and (y) (the word for "and") ones place. Keep this summary of number related vocabulary with you as you listen and watch the videos. Seeing the spelling as you listen to the words helps reinforce the pronunciation and recall of the words.**

Unos números	Some numbers		Más números	More numbers
cero	0		quince	15
uno	1		diez y seis / dieciséis	16
dos	2		diez y siete /diecisiete	17
tres	3		diez y ocho / dieciocho	18
cuatro	4		diez y nueve / diecinueve	19
cinco	5		veinte	20
seis	6		veinte y uno / veintiuno	21
siete	7		veinte y dos / veintidós	22
ocho	8		veinte y tres / veintitrés	23
nueve	9		veinte y cuatro / veinticuatro	24
diez	10		veinte y cinco /veinticinco	25
once	11		veinte y seis / veintiséis	26
doce	12		veinte y siete / veintisiete	27
trece	13		veinte y ocho / veintiocho	28
catorce	14		veinte y nueve / veintinueve	29
Notice now that there is 1 way to spell the numbers				
treinta	30			
treinta y uno	31		cuarenta	40
treinta y dos	32		cincuenta	50
treinta y tres	33		sesenta	60
treinta y cuatro	34		setenta	70
treinta y cinco	35		ochenta	80
treinta y seis	36		noventa	90
treinta y siete	37		cien (100) / ciento (101-199)	100
treinta y ocho	38		doscientos	200
treinta y nueve	39		trescientos	300

Observa los videos 1.2.6, 1.2.7, 1.2.8. As mentioned in the previous unit, some of the videos are geared toward the elementary grades; but as a first time learner of a second or third language, it may be a confidence builder to start with simple videos and songs to help you remember..

Práctica: Write the answers in words rather than numbers. (ie: cero instead of 0)

1. ¿Cuál es tu número de teléfono? _____

2. ¿Qué es cuarenta más veinte? _____

3. ¿Cómo se dice 15 en español? _____

4. ¿Hay (are there) cien estudiantes en la clase? No, hay _____
(#) en la clase.

5. ¿Cuánto es sesenta menos dieciocho? _____

You will practice more numbers later in this chapter as related to expressing one's age.

6. ¡Aprendamos los pronombres!

Now it's time to learn a bit more about others and perhaps people that they know. In order to know about whom you are speaking, you need to know **subjects**. Subjects tell us **who or what** in a sentence. It can be a person, place or thing—a noun. In our earlier conversation practices, Alejando, Talía and José were our subjects for the most part. The sentences in the conversation were **declarative, interrogative** and only **one exclamatory**: ¡Yo también estudio matemáticas! José expresses his excitement, because Alejandro and he study the same thing.

Let's analyze the subjects of the conversation:

+ Names such as Alejandro o Talía are called **proper nouns**. They are specific and clearly identifiable.

+ General names such as students, people, books, pets are called **common nouns**. One knows what these refer to but it is not very specific.

+ When one does not want to repeat the proper nouns or common nouns, one may use what is called a **pronoun**. A pronoun takes the place of a proper or common noun.

Once you have identified the proper or common noun, often you may refer to that as **he, she, you or they**. These are pronouns and are often used in daily language.

Observa el videos 1.2.9 as an introduction to the pronouns in Spanish. Take notes on the pronouns—you will define them in the section below.

As you watch, try to determine what it means to be a singular or plural subject or object? Can you classify the pronouns as singular or plural?

The only thing to re-think about this video is that since the Spanish language is derived from Spain, it is important to know the "Vosotros/ Vosotras" forms. We would like to emphasize that the pronoun "tú" in plural is "vosotros/vosotras".

In Latin America, the **"vosotros/as"** form is not used. Instead, they use the plural formal form of **"usted → ustedes"** for both formal and informal ways of addressing several people at the same time. In the Spanish grammatical context, you must use the appropriate subject for the situation as it has consequences in the way that we conjugate the verbs. It is very important that you know that the plural pronoun of tú is **vosotros/vosotras**. In Latin America, they use the plural pronoun **"ustedes"** to address a group of friends or family members. Gain familiarity with the singular subjects and their plural counterparts (tú has a plural form in Spain. In Latin America it does not.) Usted has a plural form→Ustedes which is used for formally addressing a group of people in Spain. In Latin America, "ustedes" can be used to address formally or informally a group of people.

Subject Pronouns

> NOTE: IN SPANISH, THE SUBJECT PRONOUN WHEN USED WITHIN THE SENTENCE, MEANING IT DOES NOT START THE SENTENCE, WOULD BE SPELLED IN LOWERCASE. THE DIFFERENCE IS THAT IN ENGLISH THE SUBJECT PRONOUN "I" IS ALWAYS CAPITALIZED.

Below you will find vocabulary and phrases that you should learn. As you replay the video (1.2.9) or look at your notes, define the words in English and to whom these pronouns pertain (male(s) vs female(s).)

Español	Inglés	To whom does the pronoun refer in terms of gender? (Males only; Females only; Both Males and Females)
yo		
tú		
él		
ella		
usted (ud.)		
nosotros		
nosotros		
nosotras		
vosotros		
vosotros		
vosotras		
ellos		
ellos		
ellas		
ustedes (uds.)		

Practiquemos:

Let's practice. Reflecting back on Alejandro, Talía and José:

1. What word would you select to replace José? _____

2. What word would you select to replace Talía? _____

3. What about Alejandro y Talía? _____

4. What about Alejandro y José? _____

5. Why are 3 and 4 similar? _____

6. What word would you select if Talía brings her friend María and you are referring to the both of them? _____

7. What word would you select if María comes with her Grandmother and you are referring only to her? _____

8. What word would you select if María's Grandmother brings her sister and you are referring to the both of them (Maria's Grandmother and Maria's aunt)? _____

Aprendamos:

Just like in English, we have subject pronouns in Spanish. The subject pronoun takes the place of a specific name. For example instead of saying Joe eats, Joe plays, Joe sleeps, you could say "He" eats, he plays, etc. The subject pronouns in Spanish should be learned. Pay attention to the number preceding the English meaning. Awareness of the terms first, second and third person will be helpful as you learn how these subjects correspond to the action words or verbs. The subject pronouns are:

English	Spanish (note: may be in upper or lowercase.)
1. I (singular)	yo
2. you (informal-singular)	tú
3. he (singular)	él
3. she (singular)	ella
3. you (formal-singular)	usted (ud.)
1. we (all male-plural)	nosotros
1. we (male and female-plural)	nosotros
1. we (females only-plural)	nosotras
2. all of you (informal, plural and male only in spain)	vosotros
2. all of you (informal, plural and male and females in spain)	vosotros
2. all of you (informal, plural and females only in spain)	vosotras
3. they (all male-plural)	ellos
3. they (male and female-plural)	ellos
3. they (females only-plural)	ellas
3. all of you (formal, plural and male and females)	ustedes (uds.)
3. all of you (informal, plural and male and females in latin-american)	ustedes (uds.)

In this version, you will see that some of the pronouns are combined on one line. **This does not mean that the words have the same definition.** You will find this organization useful as you work with verbs with these pronouns. NOTE: The pronoun it doesn't exist in Spanish—all words are feminine, masculine or neuter. Do not rely on biological gender to indicate the word's gender: The word "person" (persona) is always feminine yet we can be speaking about a person: man or a woman.

The subject pronouns are divided into three groups: **first, second and third person pronouns**. The word **person** in this case does not necessary mean a human being. It is a grammatical term that can refer to any noun. In the following chart are the subject pronouns in English and in Spanish grouped by persons. Notice the "person" has number: singular and plural.

Person singular	Subject pronoun	Pronombre personal	Person plural	Subject pronoun	Pronombre personal
1st	I	yo	1st	we	nosotros/as
2nd	you	tú	2nd	you	vosotros/as
3rd	he, she, it	él, ella, usted	3rd	they / you	ellos/ellas/ustedes

7. ¡Aprendamos! Los verbos SER (to be) y TENER (to have)

You have now mastered the subject pronouns but let's add meaning to them by pairing them with an action word—**a verb**. Verbs are broken down or conjugated according to the subject just as in English. A verb conjugation is a list of the six possible forms of the verb of each of the six persons used as the subject of the verb. For each tense: present, past or future, there is one verb form for each of the six persons.

Let's conjugate the verb to be in the present tense in English.

Person singular	Subject pronoun	Verb: to be	Person plural	Subject pronoun	Verb: to be
1st	I	am	1st	we	are
2nd	you	are	2nd	you	are
3rd	he,she,it	is	3rd	they	are

The verb "to be" is the English verb that changes the most. Other English verbs only have two forms such as in "to have":

Person singular	Subject pronoun	Verb: to have	Person plural	Subject pronoun	Verb: to have
1st	I	have	1st	we	have
2nd	you	have	2nd	you	have
3rd	he,she,it	has	3rd	they	have

In Spanish, verb forms change from one person to another so that when you learn a new verb, you must also learn how to conjugate it. Let's learn to conjugate the verb "to be" = **SER**.

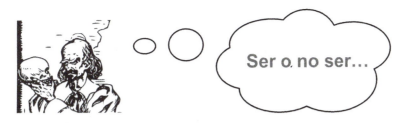

Person	Inglés	Verb To be	español	Verbo ser	Put these words together in Spanish	If you put these words together in Spanish they mean
1st singular	I	am	yo	soy	yo* soy	I* am
2nd singular	you (informal-singular)	are	tú	eres	tú eres	you are
3rd singular	He, she, you (formal, singular)	Is or are	Él, ella, Ud	es	Él es Ella es Usted es	He is She is You are
1st plural	We	Are	Nosotros (as)	somos	Nosotros somos Nosotras somos	We are
2nd plural	All of you (informal, plural)	Are	Vosotros (as)	sois	Vosotros sois Vosotras sois	All of you are
3rd plural	They and all of you (formal, plural)	Are	Ellos, ellas, Uds	son	Ellos son Ellas son Ustedes son	They are They are All of you are

*Notice: In English the subject pronoun "I" is always capitalized, in Spanish "Yo" is capitalized only if it is starting the sentence.

Practiquemos:

Using the list of adjectives or describing words from the previous unit's cognates and the structures above of the pronoun and the verb **ser**, let's form questions and sentences. Notice how the questions and replies were formed.

1. ¿Es usted artístico? or ¿Usted es artístico?   **Sí**, yo soy artístico(a).

2. ¿Es usted inteligente? or ¿Usted es inteligente?   **Sí**, yo soy inteligente.

3. ¿Es usted presidente? or ¿Usted es presidente?   **No***, yo **no*** soy presidente.

*note the placement of the **"no"**.

 Let's try describing others!

1. ¿Es romántico Alejandro? or ¿Alejandro es romántico?

Sí, él es romántico. *(Note the replacement of Alejandro with the subject pronoun "él".)*

2. ¿Es especial Talía? or ¿Talía es especial?

Sí, ella es especial. *(Note the replacement of Talía with "ella".)*

3. ¿Es interesante José? or ¿José es interesante?

No, él no es interesante; él es aburrido (boring). *(Note the replacement of José with "él".)*

Añadamos más vocabulario—Let's add more vocabulary

REMEMBER YOUR WORD LISTS FOR CLASS! FOR NOW, LEARN THE VOCABULARY. AFTER THE NEXT SECTION, YOU WILL USE THIS VOCABULARY WITH THE VERB TO BE "SER" TO FORM THE THREE TYPES OF SENTENCES: DECLARATIVE, EXCLAMATORY AND INTERROGATORY.

Español	Inglés
de	of / from
dónde	where?
cómo	how/what?
los Estados Unidos	The United States
México	Mexico
¡Qué chévere!	How great!
cumpleaños	birthday
Unos adjetivos	**Some adjectives**
bueno (buena)	good
malo (mala)	bad
famoso (famosa)	famous
simpático (simpática)	nice
bello (bella)	beautiful
bonito (bonita)	pretty
guapo (guapa)	handsome
moreno (morena)	brunette
rubio (rubia)	blonde

Unas nacionalidades : Never use capital letters	Some nationalities
estadounidense	**United States citizen** (*some refer to this as American—however American refers to someone from North through South America.*)
mexicano (mexicana)	Mexican
alemán (alemana)	German
francés (francesa)	French
inglés (inglesa)	English
africano (africana)	African
chino (china)	Chinese
Unas profesiones	**Some professions**
estudiante	student
doctor (doctora)	doctor
actor (actriz)	actor/actress
colega (used for male or female)	colleague
recepcionista (used for male or female)	receptionist
ingeniero (ingeniera)	engineer
abogado (abogada)	lawyer
dentista (used for male or female)	dentist
contador (contadora)	accountant
profesor (profesora)	teacher/professor
Unos títulos de respeto use capital letters as in English	**Some courtesy titles**
Don/Doña	Title of respect (usually with elders)
Señor (Sr.)	Sir, Mr.
Señora (Sra.)	Mrs. Madam, lady
Señorita (Srta.)	Ms. Miss, young lady
Los posesivos (note: they agree with the item possessed not the possessor. This is part of another unit.)	**The possessives**
mi/mis	my
tu/tus	your
su/sus	his, her , your
nuestro, nuestros nuestra nuestras	our
vuestro, vuestros, vuestra, vuestras	your (belonging to all of you & used in Spain)
su/sus	their/your

Comprendamos:

In Spanish, there are two verbs that can be translated as "to be". One of these verbs is SER that we just learned about; one of the most important Spanish verbs. To make it simple for you to remember when to use, read the following memory aid or mnemonic where the first letter of each situation or reason spells a word when you look at them vertically.

Dr EE

D—date

O—occupation

C—characteristics (permanent characteristics, personality traits, origin)

T—time

O—ownership/possession

R—reaction/opinion (cognates—es fabuloso, es importante, es posible...)

E—events taking place

E—essence—what something is made of

TAREA=HOMEWORK

.**Observa el ppt 1.2.10 on the online platform** and follow the prompts after the explanation to create the questions and sentences required. Remember to bring them to class to hand in as well as to help you prepare for the in-class dialogues.

Practiquemos:

Fill in the correct form of SER for the following sentences. Pay attention to who your subject is. Also observe how the adjectives agree in number and in gender with your subject.

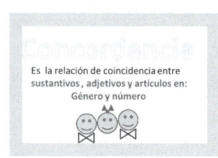

Concordancia

Es la relación de coincidencia entre sustantivos, adjetivos y artículos en: Género y número

1. What does the verb **ser** mean?

a) to dance   b) to be   c) to sing

2. Yo _____ **estadounidense.** *(singular, neuter)*

3. Ella _____ **simpática.** *(singular, feminine)*

4. Nosotros_____ **abogados.** *(plural, masculine)*

5. Ellos _____ **inteligentes.** *(plural, masculine)*

6. La maestra _____ **creativa.** *(singular, feminine)*

7. Ashley y yo_____ **estudiantes.** (plural, neuter)

8. Nosotras _____ **americanas.** *(plural, feminine)*

9. El chico _____ **guapo.** *(singular, masculine)*

10. Beth _____ mi **amiga.** *(singular, feminine)*

11. Los doctores _____ **inteligentes.** *(plural, masculine)*

12. Vosotras _____ **bonitas.** *(plural, feminine)*

13. Ustedes _____ **españoles.** *(plural, masculine)*

14. La universidad _____ **grande.** *(singular, feminine)*

15. Tú _____ **creativo.** *(singular, masculine)*

Number and Gender:

+ In Spanish, all adjectives must agree in number and gender with the nouns they describe:

-Gender: nouns are **masculine, feminine** or **neuter**.

-Number: nouns are either singular or plural.

+ Masculine personal pronouns can apply as neuter:

A group of females: ellas, vosotras, nosotras

A group of males: ellos, vosotros, nosotros.

A group of females and males: ellos, vosotros, nosotros.
←NEUTER:

MASCULINE = NEUTER

+ Personal pronouns "usted, ustedes" apply to all, masculine, feminine or both.

+ Adjectives ending in"e/es" are neutral and apply for a masculine or feminine noun:

Nosotras (all females) somos estudiantes.

Ellos (all females) son estudiantes.

El niño	La niña
pequeño	pequeña
castaño	rubia
simpático	simpática
él	ella

Ella es **inteligente**
Él es **inteligente**
inteligente = neutro

TENER—**to have** and, believe it or not, in some expressions TENER **means to be.**

Remember for every subject there is a specific conjugation for a verb (an action word.) When a verb is not conjugated, like TENER, we say that it is the infinitive. It means you know the name of the action, but just like the word "infinity" implies an unknown end, the infinitive means one does not know who is doing the action since it is not broken down to correspond to a specific noun. When the verb is conjugated it means that the action is happening and that a specific subject is doing the action.

Study the following chart to learn the conjugations of the verb TENER. You will see that we have noted the meaning as to have but later in your studies, you will see that TENER is used to indicate hunger, thirst, success, age and other expressions.

TENER:

Person	Subject/Subject Pronoun	Conjugation of Tener	Meaning
1st singular	yo	tengo	I have Do I have? (for a question)
2nd singular	tú	tienes	You have Do you have? (for a question)
3rd singular	él , ella, ud	tiene	He has She has You have (*Note:* these also can be flipped into a question, Does he have...)
1st plural	nosotros (as)	tenemos	We have
2nd plural	vosotros (as)	tenéis	You all have Do you all have?
3rd plural	ellos, ellas, uds	tienen	They have You all have Do they have? Do you all have?

 ## Practiquemos:

Let's practice. Write the answer to the question according to your knowledge of subjects and conjugated verbs.

1.Which form of the verb tener corresponds with Marco?

¿Cuál forma del verbo tener corresponde a…?

Marco _____ → Marco has.

2. ¿Cuál forma del verbo tener corresponde a mi amiga Rocío?

   Rocío _____ → Rocío has.

3. ¿Cuál forma del verbo tener corresponde a los estudiantes?

   Los estudiantes _____

4. ¿Cuál forma del verbo tener corresponde con mi amiga y yo?_____

5. ¿Cuál forma del verbo tener corresponde a mí misma (yo)? _____

6. ¿Cuál forma del verbo tener corresponde cuando deseas determinar algo de tu amigo y

   preguntas (you ask) a tu amigo? _____

Apliquemos:

Let's apply los números and tener with age (edad) when one wishes to express one's age, tener is conjugated for the subject and the number is provided. It literally means we have a certain number of years instead of we are a certain number of years old. When you look at it philosophically, it makes sense. We are not a number but we have or own our years of experience.

In Spanish, we have years but in English you are old.

In Spanish, we never consider ourselves old but rather we have years of experience.

Yo tengo veinte años. I am 20 years old.

Tú tienes veinte y dos años. You are 22 years old.

(Remember you can also express numbers from 16-29 in 2 ways: the way noted above with 3 words or in one word **veintidós**.)

¿Cuántos años tienes tú? **Vs**. ¿Cuántos años tiene Ud.?

Note: *that this question is only asked in situations where one needs to provide demographic information such as at a hospital or filling out forms.*

Él tiene treinta años.Celia Cruz tiene setenta y siete años. Usted (Ud.) tiene ochenta y cinco años. Nosotros tenemos diecinueve años. Vosotros tenéis quince años. Ellos tienen noventa años. Mis amigos tienen treinta y cuatro años. Ustedes (Uds.) tienen sesenta y siete años.

Did you recognize another aspect of Spanish that you studied in the previous chapter? The "o" in veintidós tiene un acento. That's because it does not follow one of the rules you learned—about words ending in a vowel, n or s typically have the accent on the second to the last syllable. This word broke that rule so the written accent is noted to show you where to put more stress in your pronunciation.

Review the statements again above and indicate the age of the individuals noted in terms of a number next to the sentences above starting with "Él tiene treinta años."*

Leamos:

Let's read. Read the passage aloud about Celia Cruz and highlight all the words you recognize or are able to understand. Pay attention to a cultural difference in the Spanish culture related to names. In English we use our first name, middle name and last name. In Spanish, the first and the middle name are call **"nombre de pila"** and it can be one or several names. The last name is called **"apellido"**. The proper translation to English is surname. The Spanish speaking culture uses two surnames, one by the father (first) and one by the mother (second).

Celia Cruz es la reina de la salsa. La salsa es un baile (dance) pero también es un estilo de música. Ella es de Cuba. Su padre es Símon Cruz. Su madre es Catalina Alfonso. Su esposo es Pedro Knight. Ella estudia para ser profesora en la Universidad Nacional de Maestras y en el Conservatorio Nacional de Música de la Havana, Cuba. Su nombre completo es Úrsula Hilaria Celia de la Caridad Cruz Alfonso. Por su música, tiene veintitrés álbumes de oro y muchos premios de Grammy Latin. Es honrada por su música y su historia de perseverancia.

Más información está disponible a http://www.biografiasyvidas.com/biografia/c/cruz.htm

Our final application for now of this concept brings us back to the comment in the short reading about **Celia Cruz. Ella tiene veintitrés álbumes de oro.** She has 23 gold albums. WOW! Listen to her music and learn more about her life. She was amazing!

--Ella tiene veintitrés álbumes de oro. **¿Cuántos álbumes tienes tú?**

--Yo no tengo un álbum de oro pero tengo una pluma morada para indicar todas las metas que tú tienes como experto en español.

Apliquemos:

Let's apply your understanding of the passage above to the questions

1. ¿Es famosa Celia Cruz? _____

2. ¿Cuál es el nombre de pila completo de Celia Cruz?_____

3. ¿Qué es salsa? (aparte de ser comida→besides being food)_____

4. ¿Cuántos apellidos **tiene** Celia Cruz?_____

5. ¿Cuál es el apellido de su madre? _____

6. ¿Cuál es el apellido de su padre? _____

7. ¿Cómo se llama su esposo?_____

8. ¿De dónde es Celia Cruz?_____

9. ¿Dónde estudia ella? _____

10. ¿Qué **tiene** ella? (What does she have?) _____

11. ¿Qué diferencia cultural observas en la lectura?_____

Tarea:

Think again about the short reading on Celia Cruz. Identify what was familiar to you. Now using the vocabulary and the verbs **ser and tener,** create 10 sentences about yourself. **Bring this assignment with you to class to submit as homework and to use as part of our discussions.**

8. Aprendamos el verbo GUSTAR.

.**Observa el el ppt 1.2.11 on the online platform** on Gustar **(PPT 1.2.11).** For **HOMEWORK** fill in the notes document that is also on the online platform titled "Gustar Notes" and submit the assignment in the next class.

Leamos:

Let's read. Read the dialogue with a partner. Pay attention to the pronunciation of the vowels and consonants. After reading for pronunciation you will re-read for comprehension.

Dos amigos see each other in the **plaza** (the main square in town). They stop to chat. **(charlar)**

Emma:	Hola Carlos, ¿Cómo estás? *(as she leans in to give him dos besitos—2 little kisses)*
Carlos:	Hola amiga, muy bien; ¿y tú?
Emma:	Muy bien gracias. ¿Cómo son tus clases en la universidad?
Carlos:	¡Ay Emma!, son buenas; me gustan mis clases. ¿Y tú, no eres una estudiante de medicina?
Emma:	Sí, amigo. Mis clases son difíciles pero buenas también. Me gusta estudiar medicina. Mis profesores son inteligentes y simpáticos. Uno es de Argentina. Él es fantástico e interesante. Es famoso en Argentina por curar problemas cardiacos.
Carlos:	¡Qué chévere! Mi profesora es abogada y maestra. ¡Es increíble! Estudio mucho en su clase porque a ella le gustan los exámenes.
Emma:	¡Ah! Veo a mi profesor. Te presento a mi profesor. Doctor Vargas, buenos días.
Dr. Vargas:	Muy buenos días, Emma. ¿Cómo estás?
Emma:	Bien gracias Doctor, ¿Y usted?
Dr. Vargas:	Muy bien, Emma.
Emma:	Doctor Vargas, este (this) es mi amigo Carlos.

Carlos:	Mucho gusto, Doctor Vargas.
Dr. Vargas:	Es un placer. ¿Eres tú un estudiante en la universidad también?
Carlos:	Sí, estudio para ser abogado
Dr. Vargas:	¡Qué bueno! Es una buena e importante profesión. Gusto en saludarles, yo voy al hospital. Hasta luego.
Emma y Carlos:	Adiós, Doctor.
Carlos:	Es el cumpleaños de mi mamá. Es un día especial. Ella tiene sesenta años.
Emma:	Tu mamá es muy inteligente y es una bella persona. Además (besides), ella es famosa por sus enchiladas.
Carlos:	Gracias, Emma. Es muy especial a mí. A ella le gusta la torta de chocolate. Es por eso que estoy aquí. Yo compro una torta para mi madre.
Emma:	Te acompaño a casa para cantar.

> Feliz cumpleaños a ti,
>
> Feliz cumpleaños a ti,
>
> Feliz cumpleaños querida mamá,
>
> Feliz cumpleaños a ti.

Carlos:	¡Tú cantas como Shakira!
Emma::	Carlos, tú eres muy cómico.
Carlos:	¡Compremos la torta!

Añadamos:

Let's add a little more vocabulary to help you understand what you re-read above.

mi	my
tu	your
su	his/hers/ your
cumpleaños	birthday
tener	to have
gustar	to like or to be pleasing
ahora	now
compro	I buy or am buying
cantas	You sing

As you may have noticed above there were a few new elements. They dealt with the verb **gustar** (to like). In this next section, you will learn how to use it.

In our last dialogue above, Carlos and Emma were chatting when Carlos says

¡A ella, le gusta la tarta de chocolate!

This literally means: to her (referencing his mother) chocolate cake is pleasing to her.

So, you are thinking that the above is a typo because there are two occurrences of the phrase "to her". The first part of "a ella," just refers to the mother—to her→it gives more emphasis. One could say, a mi mamá→to my mother directly but you would still need what is called an **indirect object pronoun** in Spanish to communicate correctly; this is to say to be grammatically correct. In order to communicate the concept of "to *someone*" in Spanish, we use an **Indirect Object Pronoun,** which in this case was "le".

The pronouns that tell **TO WHOM or FOR WHOM** something happens are the Indirect Object Pronouns (IOP) = Pronombres de Objeto Indirecto. ***Note:*** These pronouns go BEFORE **gustar** or any other verb, *when needed*, when it is conjugated.

Singular		
ME:	To me, for me.	
TE:	To you, for you.	
LE:	To her/him/you, for her/him/you.	

Plural		
NOS:	To us, for us.	
OS:	To y'all, for y'all.	
	(corresponding to the vosotros/vosotras subject used in Spain only.)	
LES:	To you all, for you all, to them, for them.	

The Indirect Object Pronouns (IOP) are always used with the verb **gustar.** Do you remember "**mucho gusto**" from the beginning of this unit? It is an expression meaning it is nice to meet you or it is a pleasure to meet you. As you know from the PowerPoint you viewed, **GUSTAR** means to be pleasing. Although in English, we say, "I like, you like, he likes…", in Spanish the concept is reversed in a way to indicate something or someone is pleasing to a person. That is exactly what the purpose of the **Indirect Object Pronoun is within the context of gustar**→**to indicate to whom something is pleasing.**

Repasemos:

Let's review by filling in what you know already from studying this concept at home.

Gustar means _____.

If one thing pleases you use:	
If one or more activity (VERBS) pleases you, use:	

If more than one thing pleases you, use:	

How to form sentences (declarative, exclamatory or interrogative) using the structure **gustar:**

+ Generally, the placement is :

+ Indirect object pronoun **+** gusta **+** the one thing that is pleasing.

+ Declarative sentences:

Me gusta **el español.**   Spanish pleases me. → I like Spanish.

Me gusta **mucho la clase.**   The class pleases me a lot. → I like the class a lot.

+ Exclamatory sentences:

¡Nos gusta **el español!**   Spanish pleases us! → We like Spanish!

¡Nos gusta **mucho la clase!**   The class pleases us a lot! → We like the class a lot!

+ Interrogative sentences:

¿Te gusta **el español?.**   Does Spanish please you? → Do you like Spanish?

¿Te gusta **mucho la clase?** Does the class please you a lot? → Do you like the class a lot?

Also the grammatical structure **gustar** as we studied before, has an option in case we would like to **emphasize** who is pleased. The emphasis is not a required element in the structures that work like **gustar but rather serve as a clarification for the third persons or simply emphasis for the first and second persons.** The elements that are required however, are the Indirect Object Pronoun and the correct verb form of **gustar.** Let's analize this concept in the following sentences:

(A mí,) me **gusta** la clase.	The "a mí" can be included for more emphasis or clarification but is not required. *Notice the diacritic stress: Mi The diacritic stress distinguishes between mi (my) and mi (me).*
(A ti,) te **gusta** la clase	a ti→to you.
(A él,) le **gusta** la clase.	a él→to him; a ella→to her; a usted→to you (formal).In this case we are not only emphasizing, we are clarifying who is the person that is pleased: él, ella or usted.
(A ella,) le **gusta** la clase.	
(A usted,) le **gusta** la clase	
(A nosotros/as,) nos **gusta** la clase	a nosotros/as → to us.
(A vosotros/as,) os **gusta** la clase	a vosotros/as → to you all.
(A ellos,) les **gusta** la clase.	a ellos→to them; a ellas→to them; a ustedes→ to you all. Again, we are not only emphasizing, we are clarifying who are the people that are pleased: ellos, ellas or ustedes.
(A ellas,) les **gusta** la clase.	
(A ustedes,) les **gusta** la clase.	

What happens when we like not only one class (la clase), but we like several classes (las clases)?

If more than one thing is pleasing, use GUSTAN.

> Me **gustan** las clases.

> The classes are pleasing to me→I like the classes.

It is very important that you keep in mind that the verbs are conjugated to agree with the **subject** of the sentence. In this case, "**las clases**", the subject, is at the end of the sentence yet it still is the subject with which the verb needs to agree. "Clases" would correspond with "ellas" so you would use the 3rd person plural form of gustar to agree with "clases".

Me gustan las clases. gustan corresponds with the third person plural.

NOTE: If you do not like something, simply write "No" before me gusta(n) and the object(s).

> No me gusta el color de la casa.

> No me gustan las personas antipáticas *(unkind)*.

As you know Spanish is a phonetic language, but also it is an emphatic language. When we answer a question in the negative form, in general the "no" is repeated:

> ¿Te gusta el color de la casa? No, no me gusta el color de la casa.

> ¿Te gustan las personas antipáticas? No, no me gustan las personas antipáticas.

Let's try the next exercise: We are giving you a tip that the word "taco" is masculine. How do you say, "you like the taco?"

> The taco is pleasing to me→I like the taco _____ vs

> Tacos are pleasing to me→I like tacos _____

Practiquemos:

Let's practice with some likes. Read for pronunciation and take note of the definition.

1. **Me** gusta el perro → The dog is pleasing to me.→I like the dog.
2. **Me** gustan las pizzas → The pizzas are pleasing to me.→I like the pizzas.
3. **No me** gustan los libros → The books are not pleasing to me.→I don't like books.
4. ¡**Me** gustan los gatitos! → The kittens are pleasing to me! → I like the kittens.
5. ¿**Me** gusta la lasaña? → Is lasagna pleasing to me? → Do I like lasagna?

Let's see the next example: (A nosotros,) nos **gusta** bailar y cantar.

> *We like to dance and sing = Singing and dancing are pleasing to us.*

In the sentence, we are talking about two activities that we like to do. In this case we are not talking about things. Bailar y cantar are actions. The actions remain in the infinitive form, in other words they are unconjugated verbs. No one is doing the action, we are only making a reference to the action. When we are talking about likes or dislikes related to actions, we use "**gusta**", never "**gustan**". We can talk about one action or several actions, but we always are going to use "**gusta**". The reason is because we are talking about actions (actions as an entity—singular)

We like the action of singing = nos **gusta** la acción de cantar..

We like the action of singing and the action of dancing = nos **gusta** la acción de cantar y la acción de bailar.

We are talking about different actions, but each one of the actions are singular = **La acción = GUSTA**.

All verbs in infinitive in English or in Spanish, are actions. To avoid redundancy we refer directly to the name of the action that we like: Nos **gusta** cantar, nos **gusta** cantar y bailar, nos **gusta** cantar, bailar y reír.

Practiquemos:

Let's practice with some actions that we like. Again, read aloud for pronunciation and take note of the definition.

(A mí,) **Me** gusta hablar en español. →Speaking in Spanish is pleasing to me.

→I like speaking in Spanish.

(A ti,) **te** gusta nadar. →Swimming is pleasing to you.

→You like swimming.

(A ella,) **le** gusta nadar y hablar en español. →Swimming and speaking in Spanish are pleasing to her.

→She likes swimming and speaking in Spanish.

It might be a little difficult to do these two activities together but now you can see how to form statements using gustar and actions/verbs ☺.

(A nosotros,) **nos** gustan las plantas. →The plants are pleasing to us.

→We like the plants.

(A vosotros,) **os** gusta el gato. →The cat is pleasing to you.

→You like the cat.

(A ellos,) **les** gusta caminar y tomar el sol. →Walking and taking in the sun (sunbathing) are pleasing to them.

→They like walking and taking in the sun (sunbathing.)

(A ustedes,) **les** gustan las empanadas. →The empanadas (a delicious food similar to a turnover) are pleasing to you.

→You like the empanadas.

At this stage, you should be able to ask the question to a friend, ¿**Que te gusta?** (What is pleasing to you?). How do you think you would ask this same question of your teacher? Remember to use the polite forms. Check the chart above for the indirect object pronoun that corresponds to the **"usted"** form.

There are more verbs that follow the structure **gustar** in terms of agreement with the item or items that one finds interesting, boring, fascinating, lacking or displeasing. In the future we will study them.

TAREA:

Write 5 questions about likes and dislikes that you will ask your teacher and 5 questions for your friend. Remember to use the polite forms with your teacher and the informal forms with your friend. Bring this assignment with you to class to submit as homework and to use as part of our discussions.

¡Nos gusta la clase de español!

Yo puedo
hablar español

Do you realize how much you have learned in a short period of time? You can read, understand, write and speak in Spanish. Indicate what you believe you have mastered on the checklist below.

Please answer the next questions:

[ ] Yes   [ ] No   Can I explain the rules to divide Spanish words in syllables?

[ ] Yes   [ ] No   Can I explain which is the stressed syllable in a Spanish word?

[ ] Yes   [ ] No   Can I explain the rules to divide Spanish words in syllables?

[ ] Yes   [ ] No   Can I explain which is the stressed syllable in a Spanish word?

[ ] Yes   [ ] No   Can I ask and answer a variety of simple questions?

[ ] Yes   [ ] No   Can I greet others in formal and informal situations and say good-bye politely?

[ ] Yes   [ ] No   Can I introduce myself and provide personal information politely?

[ ] Yes   [ ] No   Can I use numbers correctly to indicate my phone number, age and address?

[ ] Yes   [ ] No   Can I present information about myself and others including de-mographic information and descriptions?

[ ] Yes   [ ] No   Can I identify people and objects?

[ ] Yes   [ ] No   Can I talk about what someone has and does not have?

[ ] Yes   [ ] No   Can I understand short readings in Spanish?

[ ] Yes   [ ] No   Can I discuss what I like and that which I do not like?

[ ] Yes   [ ] No   Can I read aloud based on the phonetic background knowledge I have that words in Spanish are pronounced exactly as they are written with each vowel having a particular authentic sound?

If you answered "No" to any of these questions, review those sections again and see your professor for help.

Vocabulary

Español	M/F	Inglés	Clasificación
(muchas) gracias		thank you (very much)	Expresión
(muy) bien, gracias.		(very) well thank you	Expresión
¡Qué chévere!		How great!	Expresión
¿adónde?		where?	Adverbio
¿Cómo está Usted (Ud.)?		How are you? (formal)	Expresión
¿Cómo estás tú?		How are you? (informal)	Expresión
¿Cómo se llama Ud.?		What is your name?	Expresión
¿Cómo te llamas tú?		What is your name?	Expresión
¿cómo? ¡cómo!		how? How!	Adverbio
¿cómo? ¡cómo!		what? What!	Adverbio
¿cuál?		which?	Pronombre
¿cuáles?		which ones?	Pronombre
¿cuándo?		when?	Pronombre
¿cuánto?		how much?	Pronombre
¿cuántos?		how many?	Pronombre
¿de dónde?		from where?	Preposición
¿dónde?		where?	Adverbio
¿por qué?		why?	Pronombre
¿Qué tal?		How is it going? (informal)	Expresión
¿qué?		what?	Pronombre
¿quién?		who?	Pronombre
¿quiénes?		who? (pl.)	Pronombre
actor	El	actor	Sustantivo
actriz	La	actress	Sustantivo
adiós		good bye	Expresión
africana		African	Adjetivo
africana	La	African woman	Sustantivo
africano		African	Adjetivo
africano	El	African man	Sustantivo
alemán		German	Adjetivo
alemán	El	German language	Sustantivo
alemán	El	German man	Sustantivo
alemana		German	Adjetivo
alemana	La	German woman	Sustantivo
bello/a		beautiful	Adjetivo
bonito/a		pretty	Adjetivo
buenas noches		good evening	Expresión
buenas tardes		good afternoon	Expresión

bueno/a		good	Adjetivo
buenos días		good morning	Expresión
catorce		14	Adjetivo
cero		0	Adjetivo
china	La	Chinese woman	Sustantivo
chino	El	Chinese language	Sustantivo
chino	El	Chinese man	Sustantivo
chino/a		Chinese	Adjetivo
cien		100	Adjetivo
ciento >101…199		100 > 101…199	Adjetivo
cinco		5	Adjetivo
cincuenta		50	Adjetivo
colega (used for male or female)	El, La	colleague	Sustantivo
como		like, as	Preposición
con permiso		excuse me, when you need to physically move	Expresión
cuarenta		40	Adjetivo
cuatro		4	Adjetivo
cumpleaños	El, Los	birthday	Sustantivo
de		of / from	Preposición
de nada		you're welcome	Expresión
dentista (used for male or female)	El, La	dentist	Sustantivo
diez		10	Adjetivo
diez y nueve / diecinueve		19	Adjetivo
diez y ocho / dieciocho		18	Adjetivo
diez y seis / dieciséis		16	Adjetivo
diez y siete /diecisiete		17	Adjetivo
doce		12	Adjetivo
doctor/a	El, La	doctor	Sustantivo
Don/Doña		title of respect (usually with elders)	Sustantivo
dos		2	Adjetivo
doscientos		200	Adjetivo
Él or él		he	Pronombre
El gusto es mío.		The pleasure is mine.	Expresión
ella		she	Pronombre
ellas		they (all women)	Pronombre
ellos		they (all men or neuter)	Pronombre
encantado/a		pleased to meet you	Adjetivo
Esta es mi amiga, Ana.		This is my friend, Ana.	Expresión

Estados Unidos	Los	United States	Sustantivo
estadounidense	El, La	United States citizen	Adjetivo, Sustantivo
famoso/a		famous	Adjetivo
francés		French	Adjetivo
francés	El	French language	Sustantivo
francés	El	French man	Sustantivo
francesa		French	Adjetivo
francesa	La	French woman	Sustantivo
guapo/a		handsome	Adjetivo
gustar		to be pleasing (like)	Verbo Regular (Requires IOP)
hasta luego		see you later	Expresión
hasta mañana		see you tomorrow	Expresión
igualmente		likewise, it's mutual	Adverbio
inglés		English	Adjetivo
inglés	El	English language	Sustantivo
inglés	El	English man	Sustantivo
inglesa		English	Adjetivo
inglesa	La	English woman	Sustantivo
malo/a		bad	Adjetivo
me llamo …(José)		my name is… (José)	Expresión
mexicana	La	Mexican woman	Sustantivo
mexicano	El	Mexican man	Sustantivo
mexicano/a		Mexican	Adjetivo
México		Mexico	Sustantivo
mi (mis)		my	Adjetivo
mi apellido es … (Ramos)		my last name is …(Ramos)	Expresión
moreno/a		brunette	Adjetivo
mucho gusto		pleased to meet you	Expresión
nosotros/as		we	Pronombre
noventa		90	Adjetivo
nuestro/a		our	Adjetivo
nueve		9	Adjetivo
números	Los	numbers	Sustantivo
ochenta		80	Adjetivo
ocho		8	Adjetivo
once		11	Adjetivo
perdón		excuse me; when you cough or sneeze	Expresión

por favor		please	Expresión
quince		15	Adjetivo
recepcionista	El, La	receptionist	Sustantivo
rubio/a		blonde	Adjetivo
seis		6	Adjetivo
Señor (Sr.)	El	Sir, Mr.	Sustantivo
Señora (Sra.)	La	Mrs. Madam, lady	Sustantivo
Señorita (Srta.)	La	Ms. Miss, young lady	Sustantivo
ser (muy irregular)		to be	Verbo Irregular
sesenta		60	Adjetivo
setenta		70	Adjetivo
siete		7	Adjetivo
simpático/a		nice	Adjetivo
su		his, her, your	Adjetivo
su		their/your	Adjetivo
tener (go + e—ie)		to have	Verbo Irregular
trece		13	Adjetivo
treinta		30	Adjetivo
treinta y cinco		35	Adjetivo
treinta y cuatro		34	Adjetivo
treinta y dos		32	Adjetivo
treinta y nueve		39	Adjetivo
treinta y ocho		38	Adjetivo
treinta y seis		36	Adjetivo
treinta y siete		37	Adjetivo
treinta y tres		33	Adjetivo
treinta y uno		31	Adjetivo
tres		3	Adjetivo
trescientos		300	Adjetivo
tu		your	Adjetivo
tú		you (friendly, familiar)	Pronombre
uno		1	Adjetivo
Usted (Ud.)		you (formal)	Pronombre
Ustedes (Uds.)		you all (formal & both formal and informal in latin america)	Pronombre
veinte		20	Adjetivo
veinte y cinco /veinticinco		25	Adjetivo
veinte y cuatro / veinticuatro		24	Adjetivo
veinte y dos / veintidós		22	Adjetivo

veinte y nueve / veintinueve		29	Adjetivo
veinte y ocho / veintiocho		28	Adjetivo
veinte y seis / veintiséis		26	Adjetivo
veinte y siete / veintisiete		27	Adjetivo
veinte y tres / veintitrés		23	Adjetivo
veinte y uno / veintiuno		21	Adjetivo
vosotros/as		you all (Spain only)	Pronombre
vuestro/a		your	Adjetivo
yo		I	Pronombre
yo también		me, too (I also)	Expresión

Mis planes

Objectives

1. Learn how to identify the gender and number of Spanish words to achieve agreement.
2. Learn about definite articles and their usage rules.
3. Review how to divide words into syllables and the rules associated with each word's stressed syllable to achieve authentic pronunciation.
4. Gain the ability to read, write, listen and speak about vocabulary related to school and professions while indicating your preferences about your studies.
5. Understand the structures associated with telling time and the date.
6. Recognition of some irregular verbs and how to conjugate them.
7. Learn the question words (interrogatives) in Spanish.
8. Learn to express how you are and where you are.
9. Understand some grammatical structures in Spanish to form sentences andquestions correctly.

Contents

1. Aprendamos los conceptos del género y número

As you recall, all Spanish words are feminine, masculine or neuter and do not rely a person's biological gender to indicate the word's gender. Another important characteristic of Spanish is that the articles work hand-in-hand with the noun to which it belongs--matching the noun's gender and number. Spanish has some rules to know the gender of the nouns, but to make it simple for you, each time that you study a new Spanish word, learn the word with the article.

Singular-Maculino   Plural-Masculine   Singular-Femeninio   Plural-Femenino

When we have the definite article of a Spanish word, we know the gender of the word and the number of the word.

El Libro

Book

In this case the word "El libro"is masculine and singular.

To express a noun in plural is very simple; if the word ends in a vowel we only attach an **S** like in English:

El libro (singular) = Los libros→(plural).

El día (singular) = Los días→(plural).

When the Spanish word ends in a consonant, we attach an **ES**:

La televisión = Las televisiones→(plural).

Did you notice the accent is not necessary in the plural? The stress naturally falls on the "o" in the second to the last syllable. This follows stress rule #1 for words ending in vowels, n or s, the natural stress is on the penultimate syllable and thus no longer requires the orthographic stress.

Los artículos definidos:

	Singular		Plural
Masculine	El	→	los
Feminine	La	→	las

Los Nombres-Nouns:

Singular	Plural
If a noun ends in "o" →El perro	Add "s"→Los perros
If a noun ends in "a"→La pluma	Add "s"→Las plumas
If a noun ends in a consonant→la nación	Add "es"→Las naciones

2. Aprendamos los artículos definidos

As you remember, we studied the nouns in Unidad Dos ¿Quiénes somos? We defined a noun as a word that can be the name of a person, animal, place, thing, event or idea. We can have **common nouns** and **proper nouns**. All **nouns have a gender**: masculine or feminine. All nouns can be identified as singular or plural, known as **the number of** the noun. **The articles** are the word placed before a noun. We use articles more in Spanish than in English.

For example:

I sing **the song** that you love →it is a specific song.

Yo canto **la canción** que tú amas.

I like cats (in general) and dogs (in general).

Me gustan **los gatos** y **los perros**.

Keep in mind that a proper noun doesn't use a definite article.

Felix is my cat→Félix es mi gato.   **Or**   Rachael is my mom→Raquel es mi mamá

I like Spain→Me gusta España.

I like **the** capital of Mexico→Me gusta la capital de México.

I like cats→Me gustan los gatos.

I like Felix→Me gusta Félix.

Common nouns don't begin with a capital letter, unless it is the first word in the sentence. A noun that is the name of a specific person, place, thing, etc. is called a proper noun and always begins with a capital letter.

As an aside, **a beginning student of the Spanish language should focus on the above rules** *but in some regions of the south of Spain, it is the opposite! They use the definite article with a proper name of a person to show a close relation.*

Notice: These are exceptions as used in Southern Spain.

El Noé es mi sobrino→Noah **is my nephew.**

La Marimar es mi hija→**Marimar is my daughter**

You've learned how to say "**the**" (**the definite articles**) before a noun, however, there is another type of article, **the indefinite article**, which translates as "**a**" in the singular and "**some**" in the plural.

Indefinite articles work in the same way as definite articles in terms of agreement in gender (masculine or feminine) and number (singular and plural).

Singular-Masculine   **Plural-Masculino**   **Singular-Femenino**   **Plural-Femenino**

Practiquemos

In Spanish we use the definite and indefinite articles the same as English. The only difference is that in Spanish we have number and gender. Translate the following sentences to English:

Tengo un libro._____   Tengo el libro_____

Tengo una novela._____   Tengo la novela._____

Tengo unos libros._____   Tengo los libros._____

Tengo unas novelas. _____   Tengo las novelas. _____

Complete the sentences in Spanish with the correct article. You will use both definite and indefinite articles as you need it:

1. Yo tengo _____ gato. _____ gato es negro.

*I have **a** cat. **The** cat is black.*

2. Hay _____ libro en mi mochila. _____ libro es muy grande.

*There is **a** book in my backpack. **The** book is very big.*

3. Me gustaría _____ galleta de chocolate. Yo solo tengo _____ galletas de vainilla.

*I'd like **a** chocolate cookie. I have only **some** vanilla cookies.*

4. María tíene _____ perro. _____perro se llama "lucky".

*Mary has **a** dog. **The** dog is called "lucky".*

Translate the following examples:

un libro→_____las novelas→_____

unasplumas:→_____unosprofesores→_____

el doctor:→_____la dentista→_____

3. Recordemos cómo dividir palabras en sílabas

Do you remember how to figure out the number of syllables that a Spanish word has?

_____

Keep in mind that Spanish phonetics are controlled by vowels unlike in English. In Spanish, a consonant doesn't have sound, and we cannot read it if it is not with a vowel. But a vowel has its own sound and doesn't need a consonant. A vowel can be a syllable by itself. The more you control the sounds of the Spanish vowels, the better your pronunciation will be. Remember the correct position of the lips, tongue and mouth when you produce the sound in Spanish.

Do you remember la sílaba tónica (the stressed syllable)?

¿En español cuál es la sílaba tónica? _____

Remember the rules about the stressed syllable:

Regla número UNO:

Words ending in vowel, n or s are stressed _____

CA-ma   Li-mo-**NA**-da   **LI**-bro   **PLU**-ma

Regla número DOS:

Words ending in any consonant except n or s are stressed _____

—

Le-ER   **ca-mi-NAR**   **be-BER**   **di-bu-JAR**

Regla número TRES:

When rules number one and number two above are not followed that is when we use the written accent. The name of this written accent is the _____

Regla número CUATRO:

Written accents are also used to differentiate between words that are pronounced the same but have different meanings. This orthographic stress is known as _____

If you did not recall what to fill above, go back to Unit 2 to check your notes.

We studied these words in Unidad 1, please complete the next table by filling in their English translation.

¿qué?	vs	
que		
tú	vs	
tu		
¿cuándo?	vs	
cuando		
más	vs	
mas		
sí	vs	
si		
¿cuánto?	vs	
cuanto		
él	vs	
el		

Your flashcards will help you remember when to use the **acento diacrítico.**

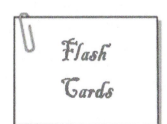

Practiquemos cambiar palabras del singular al plural:

Typically one would make a word plural by adding' "**s**" if a word ends in a vowel or "**es**" if the word ends in a consonant. We have only **one exception,** when a Spanish word ends with the letter Z like el lápiz, the letter Z changes to C, los lápices. Remember the letter Z only goes with the vowels a, o, u for the sound th/s. With the vowels e and i, Spanish has the letter C for the soft sound. Examples:

cruz--cruces   actriz--actrices   arroz--arroces   lápiz--lápices

When we change the number of the word (singular vs plural), **the stressed syllable changes,** because the number of the *syllables* changes. In the next exercise, we want you to change the number of the words (singular, plural). If the word is in the singular, write the plural and vice versa. In case you have a doubt about the syllable division or the stressed syllable review our last unit and use the website *BUSCAPALABRAS.*

In the next chart, you will find several examples. Analyze each one and then finish the exercise.

palabras	Género	número	Sí-la-bas		Plural/ singular	Sí-la-bas
La mesa	femenino	singular	**Me**-sa		Las mesas	**Me**-sas
El sillón	masculino	singular	Si-**llón**		Los sillones	Si-**llo**-nes
Las ventanas	femenino	plural	Ven-**ta**-nas		La ventana	Ven-**ta**-na
Los coches	masculino	plural	**Co**-ches		El coche	**Co**-che
El radio						
La silla						
Las lámparas						
Los bolígrafos						
La flor						

os árboles					
el avión					
la voz					
las narices					
las casas					
el zapato					
os gatos					

Apliquemos los conceptos a la fecha (date):

We will start with the days of the week. Observe the words in the following table. We will use all the concepts that we have been studying: syllables, definite articles, orthographic stress, etc. Our objective is that you not only learn words, we want you to learn the words with the correct phonetics **so you can write, read, speak and listen in Spanish.**

What gender are they?

What number are they? (singular/plural)

Los **días** de la **semana**:

el/los lunes

el/los martes

el/los miércoles

el/los jueves

el/los viernes

el/los sábado (s)

el/los domingo (s)

el **fin de semana** / los **fines de semana**

Now answer the next questions:

1. How do you say "days" in Spanish?_____

2. El número de la palabra "días" es singular o plural:_____

3. ¿Qué género tiene **la** palabra "días"? _____

4. ¿Qué significa en inglés "**la** semana"? _____

5. ¿Qué número tiene la palabra "**la** semana"?_____

6. ¿Qué género es **la** palabra "semana"?_____

El lunes significa on Monday, el martes significa on Tuesday, el miércoles significa on Wednesday. The word "el" and "los" in this case means "on". This only occurs for the days of the week where one uses the definite article "el" or "los" to indicate "on" which day.

7. ¿Qué significa **el** jueves?_____

8. ¿Qué significa **el** viernes?_____

9. ¿Qué significan **los** sábados?_____

10. ¿Qué significan **los** domingos?_____

El fin de semana means the weekend.

11. ¿Qué significan **los** fines de semana?_____

12. ¿Qué género es la palabra "el jueves"?_____

13. ¿Qué género son todos" **los** días de **la** semana"?_____

14. ¿Qué género son "todas **las** semanas en **el** mes" (month)?_____

15. ¿Qué género es la palabra "**el** mes"?_____

16. ¿Cómo se escribe (write) el mes en plural?_____

Did you notice that in Spanish the words for the days of the week are the same for singular and for plural? The definite article is the word that lets us know if it is singular or plural:

El lunes vs los **lunes**, el **martes** vs los **martes**, el **miércoles** vs los **miércoles**, etc...

*NOTE: IN SPANISH WE DON'T USE CAPITAL LETTERS EN LOS DÍAS DE LA SEMANA OR THE MONTHS AND SEASONS.

Los días de la semana: divide the days of the week in syllables and identify the stressed syllable.

Artículo definido	Sustantivo/nombre	Sí – la - bas	Sílaba tónica
El / los	lunes	**lu - nes**	**Lu**
El / los	martes		
El / los	miércoles		
El / los	jueves		

El / los	viernes		
El / los	sábado/s		
El / los	domingo/s		
El / los	fin/es		
La/las	semana/s		

Observa el video 1.3.1 on the online platform. Listen and repeat the days of the week out loud. Pay attention to the pronunciation. You can listen to it several times until you feel comfortable with your Spanish. If some day of the week is giving you problems review the chart above. Pay attention to the syllables for the day and identify the stressed syllable. Remember the vowels are a key part of the Spanish phonetic.

Las estaciones del año = Divide the seasons of the years in syllables. Identify the stressed syllable, the gender and the number.

Artículo	Estación del año	sí – la – bas	número	género	
La	primavera				
El	verano				
El	otoño				
El	invierno				

Los meses del año: divide the months of the year in syllables and identify the stressed syllable. Remember a difference with English; the months in Spanish don't begin with a capital letter within a sentence. Remember there are three kinds of sentences: interrogative (questions), declarative or exclamatory.

Sin artículo	**enero**	e-**ne**-ro	Sin artículo	**julio**	
Sin artículo	**febrero**		Sin artículo	**agosto**	
Sin artículo	**marzo**		Sin artículo	**septiembre**	

Sin artículo	abril		Sin artículo	**octubre**	
Sin artículo	mayo		Sin artículo	**noviembre**	
Sin artículo	junio		Sin artículo	**diciembre**	

In Spanish, as in English, the months of the year don't use the definite article. In English, the months are written with a capital letter. They are considered proper names. In Spanish, on the other hand, we don't write the months of the year with a capital letter and also we don't use a definite article before the names of the months. Only capitalize a month if it begins the sentence.

Observa el video 1.3.2 on the online platform. Watch the
vocabulary tutorial for seasons and months. It's very important that you listen to the video and observe the syllables of the word. Pay attention to the stressed syllable. Repeat until the Spanish sounds and the Spanish words become natural to you.

Aprendemos a pronunciar correctamente los lugares:

Let's practice the correct pronunciation of the next words. At the same time, you will practice making the words plural.

Pay attention to **ca-fe-te-rí-a** and **li-bre-rí-a**

In both, we have a diphthong **ia**   → soft vowel **i** + strong vowel **a**.

In both words the diphthong is broken→ **rí – a**.

When we have an orthographic stress on the soft vowel the diphthong is broken: **ca-fe-te-rí-a / li-bre-rí-a**

We just learned rule number five: If the soft vowel in the diphthong or in the tripthong is stressed, the diphthong or tripthong is destroyed:

ca-fe-te-rí-a → rí –a   the soft vowel i has an orthographic stress = it breaks the diphthong.

li-bre-rí-a   → rí –a   the soft vowel i has an orthographic stress = it breaks the diphthong

Now we will learn rule number six: We have some words in Spanish that have an "h" between vowels. If the vowels are the combination of a soft and strong vowel, the diphthong exists even with the "h" in the middle (*Remember the " h" is silent producing a diphthong*).

Ahi – ja – do → Godson

Prohi – bir → To ban

Los lugares: places

Artículo	Singular	Sílaba tónica	Significado	Artículo	Plural
el	apartamento	a-par-ta-**men**-to			
la	Biblioteca	bi-blio-**te**-ca			
la	cafetería	Ca-fe-te-**rí**-a			
el	edificio	e-di-**fi**-cio			
el	estadio	es-**ta**-dio			
el	laboratorio	la-bo-ra-**to**-rio			
la	libreria	li-bre-**rí**-a			
la	residencia estudiantil	Re-si-**den**-cia es-tu-dian-**til**			
la	tienda	**tien**-da			

4. Aprendamos a hablar, escribir y escuchar temas de la escuela.

You are studying Spanish because you want to be a responsible citizen with skills and values important to the pursuit of an enriched life and success in the world. You want to have a competitive advantage using Spanish to succeed in a global world, and be able to work with a diverse workforce, that can understand people of other cultures. **To be successful in any language or career, you need to have good listening skills along with the ability to express yourself via spoken and written communication so that you can understand others and they can understand you.**

We have studied how to pronounce words and we understand some of the meanings. Now we will start using the words to communicate! Let's start with days of the week. When you want to talk about your class schedule, you can say that you have certain classes on certain days of the week. You will also be able to talk about what you do on different days during the week, as well as on the weekend. Remember in Spanish the first day of the week is Monday and the days of the week don't begin with a capital letter. To proceed there are some grammar elements that we studied in Unit 2 that need to be fresh in our mind to progress with our Spanish communication about classes and times.

El verbo SER: as you remember SER is to be, SER is the name of the verb (infinitive). We studied each form of the verb SER with each one of the personal pronouns. Complete the next table.

To be – Ser

Personal pronouns	Verb: To be	Pronombres personales	Verbo ser	Put these words together in Spanish	If you put these words together in Spanish they mean in English
I	am	yo*	soy*	yo soy	I am
you (informal-singular)	are	tú	eres		
he,	is	él	es		
she,	is	ella			
you (formal, singular)	are	Ud.*			
we	are	nosotros (as)	somos		
all of you (informal, plural)	are	vosotros (as)	sois		
they	are	ellos	son		
they		ellas			
all of you (formal, plural)		Uds.*			

*__Note:__ *Personal pronouns in Spanish are only capitalized when a sentence starts. With "usted and ustedes", note these are capitalized when we use the abbreviation "Ud. or Uds."*

What is the subject pronoun that we have in English, but not in Spanish?_____

Spanish doesn't have the subject pronoun "it." Sometimes we will use the personal pronouns él or ella, when we are talking about things or animals. Often the pronoun is not used simply because the "it" is understood. For example:

It is **my dog.**　　　→　　Él es mi perro.　　　→　　Es mi perro.

It is **my book.**　　　→　　Él es mi libro.　　　→　　Es mi libro.

They are **my books.** →　　Ellos son mis libros.　　→　　Son mis libros.

Since Spanish is very detail oriented and all words have gender and number, you need to ensure that **articles, nouns and adjectives** agree in number (singular, plural) **and gender** (feminine, masculine.) With this in mind, write the Spanish subject pronoun (él or ella) for the following nouns:

El día_____　　　La semana _____

El mes_____　　　La estación_____

　　　　　　El año_____

5. Expresando la fecha y la hora (date and time):

Do you remember the mnemonic that we studied: **Doctor EE** to memorize situations associated with SER? If not, refer back to Unidad 2. Write for each letter the situation or reason.

DR EE

D—_____

O—_____

C—_____

T—_____

O—_____

R—_____

E—_____

E—_____

When you want to talk about your class schedule, you want to say that you have certain classes on certain days of the week. This is a situation for **SER**, dates are the D of **Doctor EE**.

¿**Qué día es hoy?**→What day is it?

Hoy es domingo→Today is Sunday or It's Sunday.

¿**Qué fecha es hoy?**→What is the date?

Hoy es jueves, el tres de marzo→Today is Thursday, March 3th.

Complete the next sentences with los días de la semana:

El primer día de la semana es:_____

The first day of the week is? In Spanish the week starts on Monday and not on Sunday as in English.

El último día de la semana es:_____

El segundo (*2th*) día de la semana es:_____

El tercer (*3th*) día de la semana es:_____

El cuarto (*4th*) día de la semana es:_____

El quinto (*5th*) día de la semana es:_____

El sexto (*6th*) día de la semana es:_____

For each of the months listed, say the season in which it falls, and then write the month that comes before (**antes**) and after (**después**). Write and say aloud your answers.

Antes de junio es_____ después de junio es_____

Antes de octubre es_____ después de octubre es_____

Antes de diciembre es _____después de diciembre es_____

Antes de febrero es _____ después de febrero es_____

Antes de septiembre es _____ después de septiembre es_____

Other differences between Spanish and English dates:

+ In Spanish the days of the week or the months don't begin with capital letters. → **lunes /enero**

+ On the first of any month, you will need to use the word **primero** (*first*). → **el primero de enero**

+ For all days of the month after the 1st, you will just use the actual cardinal number. → **el 31 de diciembre**

+ Remember the days of the week start **on Monday,** not on Sunday.

Antes de julio es _____ después de julio es_____

Antes de enero es _____ después de enero es_____

Write the dates (las fechas) following the example. Pay attention as in Spanish the day of the month and the name of the month are reversed from the order we normally use in **English.**

"Today is December **10th,"** → 12/10. In Spanish "hoy es el 10 de diciembre" → **10/12**

Note the presence of the definite article "el" and the use of cardinal numbers 10th → 10. In Spanish, only for the first day of the month do we use ordinal numbers el primer de mayo (the first of May).

22/1 → **el veintidós de enero** → January 22th 17/10 → _____ → October 17th

05/04 → _____ → April 5th   17/11 → _____ → November 17th

Juan, 20/05, lunes   Juan, ¿qué fecha es hoy?   Hoy es lunes, el 20 de mayo

Dolores, 15/12,viernes   _____   _____

Carmen, 31/01,domingo   _____   _____

Sergio, 27/9, miércoles   _____   _____

Ismael, 5/10, viernes   _____   _____

We can also talk about estaciones y meses del año. As you know, the seasons of the year change between the Northern and the Southern Hemispheres. Not all Spanish speaking countries have the same seasons of the year at the same time. When México is in summer, Argentina is in Winter. In the next chart you will find the differences between the Hemispheres.

Meses	Hemisferio Norte	Hemisferio Sur
enero, febrero, marzo	invierno	verano
abril, mayo, junio	primavera	otoño
julio, agosto, septiembre	verano	invierno
octubre, noviembre, diciembre	otoño	primavera

¿En qué mes empieza (start) el verano en el hemisferio norte?_____

¿En qué mes termina (ends) el invierno en el hemisferio sur?_____

¿En qué meses es primavera en el hemisferio norte?_____

¿En qué meses es otoño en el hemisferio sur?_____

¿En qué mes es el día de Acción de Gracias (Thanksgiving)?_____

¿En qué mes es el día de Navidad (Christmas day)?_____

¿En qué mes Cristóbal Colón descubrió América?_____

¿En qué mes empieza el semestre en el otoño?_____

We can also use the following phrases to talk about the weather in any given month.

¿Qué tiempo hace en…?   *What is the weather like in…?*

Observa el video 1.3.3 on the online platform. Watch the video on weather. **PRACTICE THE PRONUNCIATION OF THE WEATHER EXPRESSIONS, AND FILL IN THE CHART WITH THE ENGLISH EQUIVALENTS.**

Expresiones para el clima:	Weather expressions
Hace mal tiempo.	
Hace viento.	
Hace buen tiempo.	
Hace sol.	
Hace calor.	
Hace frío.	

 **Recordemos:**

As you know articles are the words placed before a noun. In Spanish, we use the definite articles (la, las, el, los) when we are speaking in general terms and also when referring to a specific person, place, animal, thing. We also studied some exceptions: In Spanish we **don't use definite articles** with the **months and with proper names.** But what happens with the definite article and the days of the week in Spanish?

¿Qué día es hoy? → What day is it?

Hoy es domingo. → today is Sunday or It's Sunday.

¿Qué fecha es hoy? → What date is today?

Hoy es jueves, el tres de marzo. → Today is Thursday, March 3th.

Agreguemos:

La fiesta es en martes. → The party is on Tuesday.

¿Tienes clase en jueves? →Do you have classes on Thursdays?

Mi mamá viene en domingo. → My mom is coming on Sunday.

In Spanish the single definite article is used with the days of the week, but it is omitted in expressions that answer the question ¿Qué día es hoy? Analyze the next sentences and you will see how we use the definite article with the days of the week to express an event or a given day:

La fiesta es el martes.   → The party is on Tuesday.

¿Tienes clase el jueves?   → Do you have classes on Thursdays?

Mi mamá viene el domingo. → My mom is coming on Sunday.

Juan se equivoca, hoy es sábado.→ Juan is wrong, today is Saturday.

¿Qué día es hoy? Hoy es lunes. →What day is it? It is Monday.

The Spanish definite article + day of the week are expressed in English by on + day of the week.   Under NO circumstances in Spanish do we use "en" with the days of the week.

When the event or circumstance takes place every week, we use the plural form of the definite article in Spanish. The adjective **todos** (all) + **los** + **día de la semana** also indicates a regular occurrence each week on the day mentioned.

Me gustan las fiestas todos los viernes. → I like parties every Friday.

Tengo clases de español los jueves. → I have Spanish classes on Thursdays.

As we studied, the definite article is always used before dates when the day occurs in a complete sentence. **Hoy es el 7 de marzo de 1963** → Today is March 7th, 1963. The exception is when we use the date in a letter or in a practice exercise; no article normally proceeds the day of the month:

5 de mayo de 1970 → 5 de mayo, 1970 → May 5th, 1970.

The day of the month is followed by the preposition "de" before the month. The year may or may not be separated from the month by "de". The name of the month is **always used without the definite article.**

The definite article is normally used with seasons, with a couple of exceptions. For practical reasons we will use the definite article always. We want you to be aware of these exceptions: after the preposition "en" use of the article is optional and when the season is followed by the **impersonal use of SER.**

En **invierno** → En **el invierno** → In winter.

Cuando es verano en E.U.A. → When it is summer in the USA.

Practiquemos:

Write the definite article as needed, or an X in cases where you don't need it. Keep in mind which article you use if you do something every Monday for example.

Todos _____ lunes tengo laboratorio de biología. Todos _____ martes como mi almuerzo

(lunch) con mi amigo Pedro. Esta (this) semana _____ miércoles voy a hacer la lavandería

(laundry) antes de _____ clase de español y _____ jueves voy a hacer gimnasia después

de _____ clase de español. _____ viernes voy a _____ fiesta de mi amiga Teresa. _____

domingo es _____ 20 de _____ noviembre, voy a dormir (to sleep) todo _____ día. _____

20 de _____ noviembre es mi cumpleaños.

Demos la hora (time):

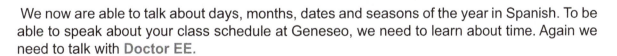

Las 9 en punto	Las 9 y cuarto	Las nueve y media	Las 10 menos cuarto	Las 10 en punto
9:00	9:15	9:30	9:45	10:00

We now are able to talk about days, months, dates and seasons of the year in Spanish. To be able to speak about your class schedule at Geneseo, we need to learn about time. Again we need to talk with **Doctor EE.**

D—date → **fecha : días, meses, estaciones**

O—occupation

C—characteristics

(permanent characteristics/physical or personality traits/origin)

T—time → the hour → **La hora**

O—ownership/possession

R—reaction/opinion

(cognates—es fabuloso, es importante, es posible, es interesante…)

E—events taking place

E—essence—what something is made of

Aprendamos: ¿Qué hora es? What time is it?

Observa el video 1.3.4 on the online platform and watch
¿Qué hora es?..

We use the verb **ser** to tell time in Spanish. You will use either the singular form "es" or the plural form "son", depending on the number that follows.

Es la una en punto   **It is** 1:00 o'clock.   → *Es* will always be used if the time includes number is one.

Son las tres en punto   **It is** 3:00 o'clock   → *Son* will be used to tell time for any number that is plural, or more than one.

In other words, the only time we will use "**es**" is in reference to "**one = la una**". The rest of the hours always will be plural. We will use "**son with las dos, las tres, las cuatro, las cinco, las seis, las siete, las ocho, las nueve, las diez, las once y las doce.**"

When we are telling a time between: 01 and: 29, we use the word y (and) to say the minutes after the hour.

Son las ocho y cinco.   It is 8:05.

Es la una y veinte.   It is 1:20.

Son las tres y quince.   It is 3:15.

Son las tres y cuarto*

Son las ocho y treinta.   It is 8:30.

Son las ocho y media*

*Notice *that we have two options: the number 15 (quarter of an hour) can be replaced by* cuarto, *30 (half an hour) is replaced by* media.

Es mediodía.   It is 12:00 pm/ It is noon.

Es medianoche.   Is is 12:00 am/ It is midnight.

*Notice how "medio" is masculine for "el día" (day) and "media" is feminine for "la noche" (night).

In Spain, when we are telling a time between: 31 and 59, we subtract the minutes from the next hour, and use the word menos to tell the minutes until the next hour.

This means that if you want to say it is 6:50, you will:

+ Take the hour, 6, and add an hour → 7

+ Take the minutes, 50, and subtract them from 60 (since there are 60 minutes in an hour, the answer would be 10.)

+ The result is 6:50 and would be expressed as Son las siete menos diez.

In Latin America, it is more common to express the time as in English in the U.S.A.

Son las ocho menos veinte.   It is 7:40.   Son las siete y cuarenta.

Son las once menos diez.   It is 10:50.   Son las diez y cincuenta.

Pay attention to the following example:

Es la una menos cuarto.   It is 12:45.   Son las doce cuarenta y cinco.

Remember "es" is used because "one" is singular. Notice that "la hora" is a feminine word then we use "una" instead of "uno".

You can also add the following information to add more details about the time of day.

De la madrugada   in the early morning, between 12:01 and 4:00 AM.

De la mañana   in the morning, between 5:00 AM and 11:59 AM.

De la tarde   in the afternoon, between 12:00 PM and 6:00 PM.

De la noche   in the evening, between 6:00 and 11:59 PM.

As you remember, Spanish is very detail oriented. If someone asked the hour it is common to give more specific references as in "in the morning or in the afternoon" for example.

Nos vemos a las tres y diez de la tarde.   See you at 3:10 PM.

Tengo clase a las diez y media de la mañana.   I have class at 10:30 AM.

La cena es a las ocho y cuarto de la noche.   Dinner is at 8:15 PM.

Estudio hasta las 3 de la madrugada.   I study until 3 AM.

In Spanish, when you write the time you need to be very specific, to avoid confusion. It is common to use military time: 24 hours or use the abbreviations AM or PM.

La boda es a las 21 hrs. *

La boda es a las 9:00 p.m.*   The wedding is at 9:00 PM

Notice that we abbreviate hour → hr. and we write AM or PM → a.m. or p.m. In Spanish, we don't use capital letters, and because they are abbreviations, we use points or periods a.m. or p.m.

Escriba la pregunta y respuesta. The video that you just watched (¿Qué hora es?) is from Spain. As we studied in Europe and in America, we say the hour in different forms and write it using different expressions.

TAREA:

For the next exercise, write the question and **all the possible** answers that are correct in Spanish for **the following times: 5:40 PM, 7:15 AM, 2:45 PM, 1:00 PM, and 3:30 AM**. This exercise is a **homework** assignment; you need to write the information on a sheet of paper that you will submit at the beginning of your next class.

6:15 PM	¿Qué hora es?	**Son las seis y quince de la tarde.**
		Son las seis y cuarto de la tarde.
		Son las seis y cuarto p.m.
		Son las dieciocho y cuarto.

Más preguntas: More questions: Answer in Spanish.

If I don't have a watch and you ask me for the time, how will I answer you?_____

In the video we saw clocks from different places that we already studied at the beginning of this unit. Write the places that we visited in the video in Spanish :_____

_____

¿Cómo son los relojes en el video?_____

Notice in Spanish we use the word Reloj for Watch and for Clock. If we want to point out the difference we say:

Reloj de pulsera
Wristwatch

Reloj de pared
Wall Clock

¿A qué hora?   To tell or ask "at" what time something is, starts, ends, etc., we use the preposition "a" and a verb such as *ser, empezar, comenzar, terminar or any verb conjugated according to what you have learned about agreement.*

¿A qué hora es la clase de español?   Mi clase de español es a las dos y media de la tarde.

My Spanish class is at 2:30 PM.

¿A qué hora estudiáis vosotros?   Estudiamos a las cuatro de la tarde.

We study at 4:00.

¿A qué hora empieza la película? La película empieza a las ocho en punto de la noche.

La película empieza a las veinte horas.

La película empieza a las ocho en punto p.m.

The movie starts at 8 o'clock at night / at 20 hours / 8 o'clock PM.

Notice: *we use the preposition "a" in the question and in the answer → to tell or ask "at" what time.*

Comuniquémonos:

We still need to learn the vocabulary about our classes and our majors, but right now we can explain our schedule for our Spanish classes. Complete the next dialogue

Carla: Hola, ¿Cómo estás?

You: _____.

Carla: Bien también, ¿Tienes clase de lenguas extranjeras?

Tú: _____

Carla: ¿Cuántas clases de español tienes en la semana?

Tú: Yo tengo tres clases de español cada_____.

Carla: ¡Me gustaría estudiar español! ¿A qué hora empiezan tus clases?

Tú: Todas mis clases de español empiezan a las _____

Carla: ¿A qué hora terminan tus clases?

Tú: Terminan a las _____. Cada clase dura(lasts) **_____ minutos.**

Carla: ¿Qué estación del año es este semestre?

Tú: Es_____.

Carla: Me gustaría tomar clases en la primavera ¿En qué mes empieza el semestre de la primavera?

Tú: _____. Yo voy a estudiar español en la primavera también.

Carla: Pero… ¿cuándo termina el semestre? En el verano quiero ir a visitar a mis padres.

Tú: ¡El semestre termina en _____ antes del verano!

Carla: ¿Qué hora es?

Tú: Son_____.

Carla: ¡Tengo clase!

Tú: ¿A qué hora empieza tu clase?

Carla: ¡Mi clase empieza a las 10:15!

Tú: Tienes _____ minutos para que tu clase empiece.

Carla:¡Tengo un examen! ¡Adiós!

Tú: ¡Mucha suerte en tu examen! _____

Apliquemos

Apliquemos los conceptos al vocabulario sobre las clases y las especializaciones.

Before we study the new vocabulary, it is important that we understand when we use or we omit the articles with the nouns that are related to special fields of knowledge as our classes, majors, etc.

+ When we are talking in general about a noun related to a field of study, in Spanish we use the definite article: La biología me interesa → Biology interests me

+ When we ask or give a definition for a field of knowledge, the definite article may or may not be used.

> ¿Qué es la biología? **Or** ¿qué es biología? → What is biology?

+ When verbs such as estudiar (to study), examinar (to examine), tomar (to take) and tener (to have) are used in the sense of study no definite article is needed.

> Estudio biología → I study biology.

> Los martes y jueves tomo español → Tuesdays and Thursdays I take Spanish.

> El miércoles tenemos examen de química → On Wednesday we have a chemistry exam.

> Mañana tengo matemáticas → Tomorrow I have math.

With this in mind we can start studying our new vocabulary about fields of knowledge, in other words we will study the names of subjects (materias/asignaturas) and majors (especializaciones). We need to pay attention to some abnormalities that we will find in the number and the gender of the words that express each field of knowledge that we are going to study.

Almost all the areas of knowledge are singular with some exceptions:

Las ciencias/ la ciencia = **sciences/science** → can be plural or singular if we are talking about several or one. In Spanish "Las ciencias políticas" is plural, in English **"political science"** is singular.

For languages, we have three synonyms frequently used in Spanish: La lengua/las lenguas, el idioma/ los idiomas or el lenguaje/ los lenguajes. In all cases you can have singular or plural, as we have in English.

Las matemáticas = **mathematics** → which will always be plural because mathematics is a group of related sciences, including algebra, geometry, and calculus, concerned with the study of number, quantity, shape, and space and their interrelationships by using a specialized notation.

El arte = **art** → singular when you are talking about a category of art: Dance is an art.

Las artes = **arts** → plural when you are talking about all branches of study in a college or university, including history, languages, music, philosophy, or literature, as opposed to scientific subjects. Pay attention as the word **arte** has one more particularity. In singular it is "**el arte**" and in plural it is "**las artes**". Later we will study this particularity that other words have such "**el agua – las aguas** (water), **el águila – las águilas** (eagle)".

Learn the new vocabulary; the words in red are the ones that have the abnormality that we just studied. **It is important that you work on your pronunciation, read each word aloud by syllables and underline the stressed syllable.** Use the web site **BUSCAPALBRAS** to check the syllabic division and review the rules to find the stressed syllable.]

Las materias, las asignaturas y las especializaciones

la administración de empresas	Business administration	
el arte/ las artes	Art	
el cálculo	Calculus	
el español	Spanish	
el inglés	English	
el/los idioma/s la/las lengua/s el/los lenguaje/s	Languages	
la antropología	Anthropology	
la biología	Biology	
la educación	Education	
la geografía	Geography	
la historia	History	
la informática	Computing/IT	
la literatura	Literatures	
la medicina	Medicine	
la música	Music	
la pedagogía	Pedagogy	
la psicología	Psychology	
la sociología	Sociology	
la/las ciencia/s	Science	
las ciencias política	Political science	
las matemáticas	Mathematics	

Flashcards can be useful!

Is yours missing? If so look it up on Wordreference.com and write it here so you can use it in class.

Mi especialización es _____

Charlemos→

contesta las preguntas en español:

1.   ¿Qué clases tienes este semestre?_____

2.   ¿Qué clases tienes los lunes?_____

3.   ¿A qué hora empieza tu primera clase?_____

4.   ¿Tienes clases los fines de semana?_____

5.   ¿Qué día es tu cumpleaños (birthday)?_____

6.   ¿En qué estación estamos?_____

7.   ¿Cuál es la fecha de hoy?_____

6. Los verbos irregulares en el modo indicativo en el tiempo presente:

 You know the verb is the heart of the sentence. It tells you the action that the subject is doing. Understanding some basic grammar elements will make forming verbs easier.

We have several verb tenses that are used within a **mood in languages**. The following chart summarizes them and what "**mood**" means. In English as in Spanish we have **three moods: indicative, imperative and subjunctive**. Each one of the moods has specific **tenses**. For now, we will focus on what is actually happening in the **present tense** in the **indicative mood** → the **Present Indicative**. The rest of the chart gives you an idea of how, in several Spanish courses, you will communicate about actions depending on **the time period** referenced and the mood (the reality vs the opinion based).

Indicative	Imperative	Subjunctive
Is defined as an action that is actual, factual and certain. • **Several tenses** that you will learn throughout your courses are: • Present • Preterit • Imperfect • Future • Conditional • Present perfect • Past perfect • Preterit perfect • Future perfect • Conditional perfect	Is based on commands and giving orders. • There is one tense • The timeframe is the present • One commands someone to do something at this moment (the present.) *** The imperative mood only has one tense or time—present**—which makes sense when you think about if you give someone a command you want them to do the action now (in the present.)	Is defined as something that is uncertain, doubtful, hypothetical, based on the emotions, wishes, wants, hopes, needs of one subject toward the actions of another subject. • **Several tenses** that you will learn throughout your courses are: • Present • Imperfect • Present perfect • Past perfect (pluperfect)

We already know that **subject pronouns** are divided into 3 groups: first, second and third person. In English or Spanish grammar the word person doesn't mean a human being; it is grammar term that can refer to any noun. Also you will remember that we have **singular and plural** for each **person**.

Número	Singular	Singular	Plural	Plural
Personas	Pronombre personal	**Personal Pronoun**	Pronombre personal	**Personal Pronoun**
Primera/first	yo	I	nosotros/as	we
Segunda/second	tú	you	vosotros/as	you (you all)
Tercera/third	él, ella, usted	He, She, You (it*-understood)	ellos, ellas, ustedes**	they, You (all of you)

* "It": doesn't exist in Spanish as a subject pronoun *

* Usted / Ustedes: for the Spanish formal "you."

As we studied in Unit One, a **verb** is a word that indicates the **action** of the sentence. The **in-finitive** form of the verb is the **name of the verb**, for example **tomar = to take**. In English, the infinitive is composed of two words: **to + the dictionary** form of the verb: **to speak, to eat, to live**. Spanish doesn't have the word **"to"** to identify the infinitive; Spanish has only **one word for the infinitive**; but **all the infinitive verbs in Spanish end** in ar, er or ir.

See the following example:

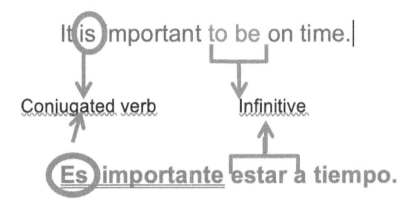

For each tense (present, past, future...) one verb form exists for each one of the six persons that we studied before. Each one of the six persons is the subject of the verb. The person or thing that **does the action of the verb** is called the subject. The verb form for each one of the persons is the **conjugated verb**.

The grammar importance is that each person **has a specific form of the verb**. In other words, the subjects that correspond to each one of the persons have the **same form of the verb or conjugated verb**. Let's see the next example:

 She is intelligent →She → subject of the verb.

She → third person singular

Is → verb form for the 3th person singular

Infinitive: to be

 He is intelligent → He → subject of the verb.

He → third person singular

Is → verb form for the 3th person singular

We are intelligent → We→ subject of the verb.

Infinitive: to be

We → first person plural

Are → verb form for the 1st person plural

Infinitive: to be

For English speakers it is very difficult to understand the **conjugation of the verbs**. The reason is because our verbs change so little that we don't need to study "how to conjugate a verb". For example, the verb to be is the English verb that changes the most in the present tense:

Persona	singular	To be	plural	To be
first	I	am	we	are
second	you	are	you	are
third	she, he, it	is	they	are

The other English verbs only have two forms:

Persona	singular	To eat	plural	To eat
first	I	eat	we	eat
second	you	eat	you	eat
third	she, he, it	eats	they	eat

In Spanish the verb form **changes for each one of the persons, for each one of the tenses!** Each time that we study a new verb in Spanish, we need to study how to conjugate it. We have two types of verbs: **regular and irregular.**

Spanish regular verbs follow a pattern. The Spanish irregular verbs are the ones that don't follow it. So far, we studied two irregular verbs in Spanish: **SER and TENER; we refer to these as unique verbs.**

Keep in mind that the infinitive form of the verb in Spanish is a verb that is **NOT CONJUGATED** and always ends in **AR, ER** or **IR**. It is so important because these three endings tell us the pattern that we will follow for the conjugation of regular verbs. In other words, all the regular verbs that end in **AR** follow one pattern, all the regular verbs that end in **ER** another pattern and those that end in **IR** another pattern.

Learning the conjugation of one sample verb for each ending: ar, er, and ir, will enable you to conjugate all the regular verbs for each group.

 Observa el video 1.3.5 on the online platform to study the forms of the regular endings for the present tense in Spanish (ar verbs).

Write the endings for the conjugation of the AR verbs:

First person singular		First person plural	
yo		nosotros/as	
Second person singular tú		Second person plural	
		vosotros/as	
Third person singular		Third person plural	
él, ella, usted		ellos, ellas, ustedes	

Write the conjugation for the **regular verb toma**r:

yo		nosotros/as	
tú		vosotros/as	
él, ella, usted		ellos, ellas, ustedes	

Observa el video 1.3.6 on the online platform to study the forms of the regular endings for the present tense in Spanish (er/ir verbs).

Write the endings for the conjugation of the **ER verbs**:

First person singular		First person plural	
yo		nosotros/as	
Second person singular tú		Second person plural	
		vosotros/as	
Third person singular		Third person plural	
él, ella, usted		ellos, ellas, ustedes	

Write the conjugation for the **regular verb come**r:

yo		nosotros/as	
tú		vosotros/as	
él, ella, usted		ellos, ellas, ustedes	

Write the endings for the conjugation of the **IR verbs**:

First person singular		First person plural	
yo		nosotros/as	
Second person singular tú		Second person plural	
		vosotros/as	
Third person singular		Third person plural	
él, ella, usted		ellos, ellas, ustedes	

Write the conjugation for the **regular verb vivir**:

yo		nosotros/as	
tú		vosotros/as	
él, ella, usted		ellos, ellas, ustedes	

The endings for the regular er and ir verbs are the same with the exception of two persons. What are these persons?_____ What are the subject pronouns that belong to these persons? _____

We form verbs in the **present tense** of the **indicative mood** to talk about daily or ongoing activities, as well as events that will take place in the near future. In the following chart, you can see the endings studied.

**Notice: *the endings for "ER" and "IR" verbs are the same with exception of the 1st and 2nd persona plural.*

Pronombres personales	Verbo AR Estudiar To study	Verbo ER Comer To eat	Verbo IR Escribir To write
yo	estudio	como	escribo
tú	estudias	comes	escribes
él, ella, usted	estudia	come	escribe
nosotros/as	estudiamos	comemos**	escribimos**
vosotros/as	estudiáis	coméis **	escribís**
ellos, ellas, ustedes	estudian	comen	escriben

Let's describe what you do on a daily basis as a student in Geneseo:

Yo estudio arquitectura*.   **I study** architecture.

Ella estudia matemáticas*.   **She studies** mathematics.

Notice we don't use the definite article with areas of knowledge.

Ellos comen en la cafetería*.   **They eat** in the cafeteria.

Tú comes en la casa*.   **You eat** at home.

Notice we use the definite article with common nouns (places, things).

Nosotros escribimos los apuntes. **We write** the notes.

Mario escribe la tarea.   **Mario writes** the homework.

Notice we use the definite article with common nouns (places, things).

Los verbos importantes: Let's look at some of the verbs that we'll be using to talk about our lives as students in this unit. We will use the most common mood: Indicative in the present tense. With the vocabulary that we know and the cognates look how much you can say in Spanish!

Write the simple sentence in Spanish in the last column.

Infinitivo	Infinitive	English sentence	Oración en español
abrir	to open	I open the book.	
aprender	to learn	We learn the regular verbs.	
asistir a	to attend	They attend the class	
bailar	To dance	We dance every weekend.	
beber	to drink	He drinks a lot of water.	
comer	to eat	You eat the hamburger.	
comprar	to buy	The students buy books.	
comprender	to under-stand	She understands Spanish.	
contestar	to answer	You (formal) answer the question.	
correr	to run	You all (masculine) run in the stadium.	
creer	to believe	I believe that I can.	
enseñar	to teach	They teach biology.	
escribir	to write	We write the report	
esperar	to wait for	He waits for the bus.	
estudiar	to study	You all (feminine) study.	
faltar	to miss	They miss the class.	
fracasar	to fail	I don't fail.	
hablar	to talk/speak	We (masculine) speak Spanish!	
leer	to read	She reads a book.	
llegar	to arrive	I arrive at 3:00 PM.	
necesitar	to need	You (informal) need to study.	
preguntar	to ask	He asks a question.	
regresar	to return	You all (informal) return to the library.	

sacar (bue-nas/malas) notas	to get (good/bad) grades	We study and we get good grades.	
terminar	to finish	I finish the flashcards.	
tomar apunt-es	to take notes	They take notes each class.	
trabajar	to work	We work every Saturday.	
usar	to use	She uses the lab.	
vivir	to live	He lives in Geneseo.	

Remember there are several tools to help you study the verbs, their meaning and conjugations. Make sure you review them in the back of your text.

TAREA:

Write 20 original questions for your peers in class on a paper that you will hand in at the beginning of class. The more original the questions, the more interesting the class will be.

To study the conjugations of the verbs we recommend using flashcards. You don't need to write all the conjugations, you need only to write the infinitives in Spanish and in English, as we did before. In this case you should write (reg or regular) to help you to remember that the verb is regular.

Correr	To run

You can make the flashcard for SER that we studied in our first unit and that we know is irregular. Did you know that the pattern that this verb follows is unique? No other verb follows this pattern.

SER		(irregular-único)	
yo	soy	nosotros/as	somos
tú	eres	vosotros/as	sois
él, ella, usted	es	ellos,ellas, ustedes	son

For each new verb that we study, you need to identify if the **verb is regular or irregular.** You will be surprised when you see that the **irregular verbs** will have some type of pattern too! **For that reason, it is so important** that you identify in your flashcards what "pattern = model" of conjugation each verb follows. Below are the patterns:

a)   When it is a **regular verb** as **HABLAR, COMER** and **VIVIR.**

b)   When it is an **irregular verb** with a unique conjugation as SER.

c)   When it is an **irregular verb** with a **similar conjugation to other irregular verbs.**

Let's learn some irregular verbs that have **similar conjugations to these in the present tense.** Don't forget, we are studying the Indicative Mood in the present tense.

HACER→ When one wants to say "I do" or "I make", use the verb hago. This verb does not follow the regular pattern for "er" conjugated verbs in the yo form in the indicative mood of the present tense.

GO verbs: have the same formation in the "yo" form, that is to say, the "yo" form ends in "go", or there is a "medial g" placed before the regular yo "o" ending after "l or n". If that helps you recall this particular group, note that in your flashcards.

Some of the verbs that can be classified in the "GO verb" group, are:

Hacer (to do/to make) → hago, haces, hace, hacemos, hacéis, hacen

Salir (to go out/leave) → salgo, sales, sale, salimos, salís, salen

Poner (to put/place) → pongo, pones, pone, ponemos, ponéis, ponen

Valer (to be worth) → valgo, vales, vale, valemos, valéis, valen

---

SALIR
(irregular–GO verb

Another rule add "ig" when the root ends in a vowel, or substitute "g" for "c". Many of these verbs are also irregular in other ways.

Caer—to fall: yo caigo, tú caes...

Traer—to bring: yo traigo, tú traes...

Oír—to hear: yo oigo, tú oyes...

For now, learn the patterns of the verbs that have the "go" changes to them as in the chart below.

If the infinitive ends in er/ir and	then	examples
*the root ends in L or N	add G before the yo ending "o"	Poner→pongo → Go verbs
* the root ends in a vowel	Add IG before the yo ending "o"	Traer—traigo → IGo verbs

There are exceptions to this pattern such as the difference between hacer and decir that you will learn with practice.

Decir—to say or tell; **(ojo—this has multiple changes)**

	Singular		Plural
yo	digo	nosotros	decimos
tú	dices	vosotros	decís
él, ella, Ud	dice	ellos, ellas, Uds	dicen

Practiquemos

Complete the sentences with the correct forms of the verbs-some are regular and a few are those that change in the yo form.

1. Yo siempre me_____ (caer) cuando esquío.

2. Nosotros _____ (esperar) a la profesora.

3. Mis compañeros de clase _____ (contestar) en español.

4. Mi amiga _____ (asistir) a la Universidad de Salamanca este semestre.

5. ¿Dónde _____ (vivir) tú?

6. Yo nunca _____ (traer) comida a clase.

7. El profesor _____ (enseñar) cuatro clases.

8. ¿Qué _____ (leer) tú?

9. Yo _____(salir) con mis amigos.

10. Mi hermano me_____(preguntar) por el profesor.

11. Hoy yo _____ (regresar) a mi casa con mis padres.

12. Juan y María _____(decir) todas las preguntas del examen?

13. ¿Vosotros_____ (llegar) a tiempo a la clase?

Comprendamos

Read the following conversation out loud.

Ana: Paco, ¿Comprendes la tarea de la clase de matemáticas?

La profesora habla muy rápido y no tomo apuntes.

Paco: ¡Sí, claro!, es mi clase favorita. Siempre saco buenas notas.

Ana: ¡Qué suerte! Necesito tu ayuda, por favor

Paco: Tengo tiempo a las dos de la tarde. ¿Trabajamos en la biblioteca?

Ana: ¡Sí, perfecto!. Terminamos la tarea, y después estudiamos un poco.

Paco: Buena idea. Nos vemos a las dos.

Ana: Hasta pronto, Paco.

Paco: Chao.

Now, go back through the conversation again, but change all of the words in bold to something else, to create your own conversation.

Ana: Paco, ¿Comprendes la tarea de la clase de _____?

La profesora habla muy rápido y no _____.

Paco: ¡Sí, claro!, es mi clase favorita. Siempre _____.

Ana: ¡Qué suerte! Necesito tu ayuda, por favor

Paco: Tengo tiempo a las dos de la tarde. ¿Trabajamos en la _____?

Ana: ¡Sí, perfecto!. Terminamos la tarea, y después _____.

Paco: Buena idea. Nos vemos a _____.

Ana: _____, Paco.

Paco: _____.

Agreguemos nuevo vocabulario... Artículos escolares

Let's study new vocabulary. Analyze what words are new for you? What words are very similar in English and Spanish? Read aloud each word and underline the stressed syllable. Now write a sentence using a verb that you identify with each one of the school supplies = "artículos escolares", as in the following examples. The subjects for the sentences are provided for you in the following exercise. Finish the sentence with a verb and school supply.

el bolígrafo	pen	Yo escribo con la pluma
la calculadora	calculator	Ella estudia matemáticas con la calculadora
el cuaderno	notebook	Nosotras
el lápiz	pencil	Usted
el libro	book	Juan y Carmen
el mapa	map	El Doctor Gómez
el papel	paper	Susana
el diccionario	dictionary	El profesor
la mesa	table	Mi mamá
el escritorio	desk	El director
la silla	chair	Los chicos
la novela	novel	Federico
la mochila	backpack	Ellas
la lámpara	lamp	Yo

Charlemos →

Contesta las siguientes preguntas en español.

1. ¿Qué necesitas para la clase de español?_____

2. ¿Tomas apuntes en tus clases? _____

3. ¿Siempre terminas la tarea?_____

4. ¿Estudias mucho?_____

5. ¿Comprendes a la profesora (o al profesor) cuando habla español?_____

6. ¿Comes en casa o en la cafetería?_____

7. ¿Lees muchas novelas?_____

8. ¿Te gusta leer novelas románticas? _____

9. ¿Vives en una residencia estudiantil o en un apartamento? _____

10. ¿Asistes a tus clases todos los días?_____

11. ¿Necesitas una calculadora para la clase?_____

12. ¿Compras un diccionario inglés-español?_____

13. ¿Haces la tarea en la mesa o en el escritorio?_____

14. ¿Escribes tus notas con lápiz?_____

15. ¿Estudias el mapa de los países de Hispanoamérica?_____

16. ¿Necesitas una lámpara nueva?_____

17. ¿José Luis tiene una mochila nueva?_____

18. ¿Te gusta leer novelas?_____

19. ¿Escribes la composición con bolígrafo o con lápiz?_____

20. ¿Te gustan las prácticas de español? _____

Completa el cuestionario 1.3.7 and 1.3.8 on the online platform We will practice some more grammar exercises using the regular verbs in the next two videos. Make a note of your scores: _____

What are the two irregular verbs that were used in the exercises? _____..

7. Los Interrogativos

Los Interrogativos or interrogative pronouns are a word that introduces a question. We already studied that all the interrogative pronouns in Spanish use the orthographic stress. Questions in Spanish will start with an opened question mark and will end with a question mark. Read the examples in the chart below:

Pronombres interrogativos:

¿Adónde?	To where?	¿Adónde vas?	(To) Where are you going?
¿Cómo?	How?	¿Cómo está Ud.?	How are you?
¿Cuál?	Which/What? (singular)	¿Cuál es tu clase favorita?	What is your favorite class?
¿Cuáles?	Which/What? (plural)	¿Cuáles son sus clases favoritas?	What are his favorite classes?
¿Cuándo?	When?	¿Cuándo es tu clase de español?	When is your Spanish class?
¿Cuánto?	How much?	¿Cuánto cuesta el libro?	How much does the book cost?
¿De dónde?	From where?	¿De dónde es él?	From where is he?
¿Dónde?	Where?	¿Dónde viven ellos?	Where do they live?

¿Por qué?	Why?	¿Por qué no estudias?	Why don't you study?
¿Qué?	What?	¿Qué estudia Rosa?	What does Rosa study?
¿Quién?	Who?	¿Quién enseña la clase de historia?	Who teaches the history class?
¿Quiénes?	Who(pl)?	¿Quiénes viven en esta casa?	Who lives in this house?

Observa el video 1.3.9 on the online platform to help you learn the question words or interrogatives. Learn the interrogative pronouns with the song. It will be fun and it is a melody that all of us know by heart!!! ..

Practiquemos→

Write which question word would be used to ask about the information in bold.

1. Yo vivo **en una casa en la calle Main.**_____

2. **Mi compañero de cuarto** estudia las matemáticas._____

3. Mi compañero de cuarto estudia **las matemáticas.**_____

4. Ellos son **de México.**_____

5. Mi clase de matemáticas es **los martes y jueves a la una y media.**_____

Completa con la palabra interrogativa correcta

1. ¿ _____ es tu clase de español?

   -Los lunes, miércoles, y viernes por la tarde.

2. ¿_____ idiomas hablas?

   -Hablo dos; el inglés y el español.

3. ¿_____ vives?

   -Vivo en Rochester, Nueva York.

4. ¿_____ estudias español?

   - Yo estudio español porque necesito hablar otro idioma.

5. ¿_____ es tu mejor (best) amigo?

   - Mi mejor amigo se llama ____.

6. ¿_____ haces después de clases?

   -Después de clases yo como en la cafetería.

7. ¿_____ usas para la clase de español?

   - Uso un cuaderno y un bolígrafo

¿Qué o cuál? can be confusing to people learning Spanish, because they both are often translated as the same words into English → what? With time you will master the different uses of these question pronouns and you will learn that sometimes you can use one or the other without changing the meaning. The following chart can help you to identify some differences.

WHAT	WHICH
When asking for definitions: ¿**Qué** es una ciudad? → **What** is a city?	**Used to suggest a selection or choice from among a group:** ¿**Cuál** prefieres? → **What** do you prefer?
Most often used before nouns: ¿**Qué** color es el coche? → **What** color is the car?	**Usually is used before es and demographic data:** ¿**Cuál** es tu teléfono? → **What** is your phone number?

A trick: To keep it simple and easy translate "qué as what" and "cuál as which."

Memorize some common idiomatic uses for "WHAT":

¿Qué hora es?	**What time is it?**	*¿Cuánto?*	**How much?**
¡Qué lástima!	**What a shame!**	*¡Qué susto!*	**What a fright!**
¡Qué hermoso!	**How beautiful!**	*¡Qué día más horrible!*	**What a horrible day!**
¡Qué bonito!	**How pretty!**	*¿Y qué? ¿Y a mí qué?*	**So what?**

8. Learning to express how you are and where you are.

So far we can say what we are doing and when we are doing it, but it is also helpful to talk about where we are, and even where we are going. You have already learned one verb for "being"—to be→ser.

Do you remember Doctor EE? Sí, sí

We use "SER" for the following reasons:

D—date → fecha : días, meses, estaciones

O—occupation

C—characteristics

    (permanent characteristics/physical or personality traits/origin)

T—time → the hour → La hora

O—ownership/possession

R—reaction/opinion

(cognates—es fabuloso, es importante, es posible, es interesante…)

E—events taking place

E—essence—what something is made of

El **verbo estar** is another word for to be. We use the verb **estar** to describe where we are, or where something or someone is located. When we want to talk about **how we are feeling and where we are, always use the verb estar. (It rhymes!)** The forms of estar are:

yo	**estoy**	nosotros/as	**estamos**
tú	**estás**	vosotros/as	**estáis**
Ud./él/ella	**está**	Uds./ellos/ellas	**están**

¿Ser o estar?

Looking at **ESTAR**, you see it is an "AR" verb so the tendency is to think it will conjugate like an AR verb. It is very close. Note that **ESTAR** is irregular in the yo form "**Estoy**", but that some of the other forms have the written accent mark. Recalling the accent or stress rules, you know that words ending in a vowel, n or s have the stress on the second to the last syllable. In the case of estar, this rule is broken for several of the verb conjugations and hence the written accent mark. Practice and, of course, writing the exception on your flashcards will help you remember the conjugations.

Below are just a few of the reasons when we choose **ESTAR** instead of **SER**. The reasons when you will use ESTAR in a sentence may be easily recalled by remembering this mnemonic device or memory tool:

Health	Estoy bien. Estoy enfermo. Estoy mal.
Emotion	Estoy feliz. Estoy contenta.
Attitude	Estoy segura (I am certain.)
Location	Estoy en Geneseo.
Temporary Condition	La sopa está fría (no me gusta). (Something contrary to what you expected.)
Happening now	Estamos aprendiendo español. (This is the present progressive which combines the use of the present tense conjugation of estar with a gerund → "ing" form.)

Mastering the different reasons for **SER** vs **ESTAR** early in your studies will help you tremendously. You can see these reasons above are very much different than those used for SER and go beyond how you are feeling and where you are.

Agreguemos unos lugares (some places) to practice the verb **ESTAR.**

> **Observa el website 1.3.10 on the online platform** and find the English equivalents of the following places on campus. Where possible, also listen to the pronunciation of the words and practice saying them aloud. In the extra spaces in the table, add any other important places on campus that you might go to spend time.

Más lugares =more places

el apartamento	
la biblioteca	
la cafetería	
el edificio	
el estadio	
el gimnasio	
el laboratorio	
la librería	
la residencia estudiantil	
la tienda	
el centro para lenguas y culturas	

Ejemplos:

Nosotros estamos en la biblioteca.	We are in/at the library.
Yo estoy en la cafetería.	I am in the cafeteria.
El cuaderno está en la mesa.	The notebook is on the table.
Nos vemos en la iglesia.	See you at church.

*Notice the use of "en" with estar, to say that someone or something is located **in**, **on** or **at** (inside of) a place.

Añadamos→

You have also learned to use the verb estar to ask and answer the question, ¿Cómo estás? As you may notice, we also use the verb estar to talk about our emotions or feelings.

Observa el video 1.3.11 on the online platform about estar.
As you are watching, write down the meaning of the following common emotions or feelings that we can use with estar.

Adjetivos para expresar emociones o sentimientos con estar:

aburrido(a,os,as)	
cansado (a,os,as)	
emocionado (a,os,as)	
enfermo (a,os,as)	
feliz (felices)	
preocupado (a,os,as)	
ocupado (a,os,as)	
triste (es)	

Remember that when we use adjectives to describe the way that someone is feeling, we must make the adjectives agree with the person that we are describing. This is referred to in Spanish as "concordancia" or agreement. You have been creating sentences where the verbs agree with the subject (person/number). Prior to that you learned how the definite article agrees with the noun in the sense of is the noun masculine or feminine while also considering singular or plural. These very same concepts apply to making adjectives agree with the noun.

Hablemos de la concordancia y los adjetivos:

+ If you are describing un libro (a book), notice the word for book is masculine and it is singular. Therefore all words describing the book will also be masculine and singular.

+ Es un libro largo y rojo. It is a long red book.

+ Es un libro interesante. It is an interesting book.

+ If you are describing una casa (an house), think about the word "casa". It is feminine and singular.

+ Es una casa amarilla. It is a yellow house.

+ Es una casa grande. It is a big house.

+ How do I make these plural? Consider that the verb will change but for the adjectives simply add "s".

+ Son unos libros largos y rojos.

+ Son unos libros interesantes.

+ Son unas casas amarillas y grandes.

Practiquemos

Answer in complete (Spanish) sentences, using the information in parenthesis.

1. ¿Cómo está Ana? (sick)_____

2. ¿Cómo están ellos? (busy)_____

3. ¿Cómo estás? (bored)_____

4. ¿Dónde estamos? (the gym)_____

5. ¿Dónde están los estudiantes? (the library)_____

6. ¿Dónde está Miguel? (the stadium)_____

TAREA

Write 10 questions and answers using "ser" and 10 questions and answers using "estar" on a sheet of paper that you will submit at the beginning of your next class.

You have been creating sentences where the verbs agree with the subject!

One of the last uses for "**estar**" is noted with "H" for happening now. This refers to an action in progress at this moment. The term for this is a progressive form and if the action is happening at this moment, it is referred to as the present progressive. It makes sense, right? It is happening now in the present and is an action in progress→present progressive (presente progresivo—it is another cognate too).

El presente progresivo:

We form this grammatical structure with the present tense indicative of the verb estar plus a gerund. What is a gerund? It is the "ing" form of the verb. In English, we don't say running or talking as actions by themselves, correct? We say someone is running or someone is talking. This requires two parts:

The present tense of **estar**   plus   the gerund.

yo	nosotros/as
estoy	**estamos**
tú	vosotros/as
estás	**estáis**
Ud./él/ella	Uds./ellos/ellas
está	**están**

AR verb root + ando→hablando

ER verb root + iendo→bebiendo

IR verb root + iendo→viviendo

(Notice the er/ir verbs have the same gerund ending.)

The examples above outline a few regular gerunds; those that do not have any spelling changes in the pattern. However, there are a few common actions that have unique spellings in the gerund.

Many of them come from IR verbs that have stem or root changes. We will study extensively the stem change verbs in the next unit however, below please learn the verbs that have a unique spelling in the gerund form to say some of the actions you are doing.

IR—to go   The gerund is **yendo.**   Estoy yendo a la tienda. *I am going to the store.*

Leer—to read The gerund is **leyendo.** Rocío e Isa están leyendo un libro. *Rocío and Isa are reading a book.*

Dormir—to sleep. The gerund is **durmiendo.** Maxie está durmiendo. *Maxie is sleeping.*

For now, learn these common gerunds with their unique spelling as part of vocabulary.   With practice you will incorporate them into your daily speech.

Use the prompts below to answer ¿Qué estás haciendo?

Decir	Diciendo	Telling	
Preferir	Prefiriendo	Preferring	
Servir	Sirviendo	Serving	
Pedir	Pidiendo	Asking for	
Venir	Viniendo	Coming	

There are more gerunds with unique spellings but for now, become familiar with the idea of the use of **ESTAR** with the **GERUND** to form a thought about what one is doing at this moment.

 Remember the gerund is not a verb as it is **not conjugated**. It belongs to a grammatical group called **a verboide** in Spanish or **verbals** in English. Within this group, you will find the terms **infinitive, gerund** and **participle**. We have studied the first two and in another course you will study the participles.

9. Estructuras verbales

Grammatical structures are formulas that help us express a thought. You already studied **the first structure: GUSTAR** to indicate something or someone is pleasing to a person.

¡Me gusta comer tacos!

The formula for the sentence (declarative, exclamatory or interrogatory) is:

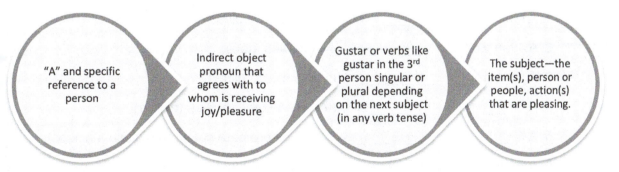

"A" and specific reference to a person

Indirect object pronoun that agrees with to whom is receiving joy/pleasure

Gustar or verbs like gustar in the 3rd person singular or plural depending on the next subject (in any verb tense)

The subject—the item(s), person or people, action(s) that are pleasing.

The correct understanding of the Indirect Object Pronouns (IOP) is fundamental to properly use this structure. Feel comfortable reviewing these concepts in Unit 2. We noted other verbs that follow this structure; hence the reason for the name: **Gustar and similar verbs**. Here are examples of some of the verbs that follow this structure:

+ Gustar: to like: ¡A mí me gusta el chocolate!

+ Encantar: to like a lot, to love (not romantic):

¿A ti te encanta cantar?, *¿ Te gusta mucho cantar?*

+ Fascinar: to like a lot, to find fascinating: **A ella le fascinan los chocolates.**

+ Molestar: to be bothered by, to find annoying: **A nosotros nos molesta estudiar.**

+ Faltar: to lack, to be missing, to need: **¡A vosotros, os faltan las tareas de español!**

Remember the use of the preposition "a" and the reference to a specific person is optional; we use it when we would like to emphasize or clarify (3rd person).

For this extra practice, you will use the correct Indirect Object Pronouns (me, te, le, nos, os, les) and then the correct form of gustar to get warmed up to the constructions.

1. A mí _____ _____las playas de Florida.

2. A nosotros no _____ _____ bailar en la tarde.

3. Mary piensa comprar una computadora nueva. _____ _____ las computadoras que venden en Best Buy.

4. ¿A ti _____ salir con tus amigos los viernes?

5. A Juan y a Sara siempre se acuestan a las diez. _____ dormir mucho.

6. Yo no hago ejercicios. No _____ correr ni caminar.

7. ¿A ellos _____ las clases que toman este semestre?

8. Tú nunca limpias la casa. _____ descansar y mirar la tele. ¡Qué perezoso eres!

9. A mis amigos y a mí _____jugar y nadar todo el día.

10. A mis amigos y a mí _____ las fiestas de Sara.

For this extra practice, you will use the correct Indirect Object Pronouns (me, te, le, nos, os, les) and then the correct form of the various verbs that work like gustar such as doler, importer, aburrir, fascinar etc.

1. A Maria ___ _____ ir de compras. (like/pleases)

2. A Juan y a mí ___ _____ los trajes. (love)

3. A nosotros ___ _____ mirar la moda. (like)

4. A mí _____ _____la ropa con agujeros (holes). (dislike)

5. A ti _____ _____el dinero para comprar la blusa. (lacking)

6. A Pedro y a Miguel _____ _____ los pantalones cortos. (love)

7. A las chicas, _____ _____ la lana mucho. (bothers)

8. A vosotros _____ _____ la moda de Oscar de la Renta. (fascinate)

9. A Ud _____ _____ ir de compras y gastar mucho dinero en las prendas. (matters/to be important)

10. A mí no _____ _____ lo que llevan las celebridades. (interest)

Check your answers for the free form practices below.

1. A mí _____me ___gustan_____las playas de Florida.

2. A nosotros no _____nos_ _gusta_____ bailar en la tarde.

3. Mary piensa comprar una computadora nueva. _____le__ _gustan_____ las computadoras que venden en Best Buy.

4. ¿A ti __te gusta_____ salir con tus amigos los viernes?

5. A Juan y a Sara siempre se acuestan a las diez. ____les gusta_____ dormir mucho.

6. Yo no hago ejercicios. No ____me gusta_____ correr ni caminar.

7. ¿A ellos ____les gustan_____ las clases que toman este semestre?

8. Tú nunca limpias la casa. ___te gusta_____ descansar y mirar la tele. ¡Qué perezoso eres!

9. A mis amigos y a mí _____nos gusta_____jugar y nadar todo el día.

10. A mis amigos y a mí _____nos gustan_____ las fiestas de Sara.

* * *

1. A Maria _le__ ____gusta_____ ir de compras. (like/pleases)

2. A Juan y a mí _nos__ __encantan_____ los trajes. (love)

3. A nosotros _nos__ ____gusta_____ mirar la moda. (like)

4. A mí ___me____ __disgusta_____la ropa con agujeros (holes). (dislike)

5. A ti _te_____ ___hace falta_____del dinero para comprar la blusa. (lacking)

6. A Pedro y a Miguel _les_____ _encantan_____ los pantalones cortos. (love)

7. A las chicas, _les_ __molesta_ la lana mucho. (bothers)

8. A vosotros _os_ _fascina_____ la moda de Oscar de la Renta. (fascinate)

9. A Ud _le_ __importa_ ir de compras y gastar mucho dinero en las prendas. (matters/to be important)

10. A mí no __me__ _interesa_ lo que llevan las celebridades. (interest)

- **Study the new verbs**, review their conjugations in the conjugation feature of Word Reference and answer:

Are they regular or irregular verbs?_____

Other useful expressions are formed by combining two verbs. Because a sentence cannot be a sentence without a conjugated verb, these structures always have first a conjugated verb and then second an infinitive. As you recall the infinitive is the name of the action.

Ejemplo:	Yo puedo hablar español = I can speak Spanish.
Pronombre personal:	Yo
Verbo conjugado:	poder → yo puedo
Acción:	hablar→ **infinitive**

 We cannot have two conjugated verbs back to back in a sentence for the same thought or action.

I cannot have: Yo puedo habio español. ←**wrong!**

The second verb needs to be an infinitive: **Yo puedo** hablar español.

Keep in mind a sentence typically contains a subject, a conjugated verb and extra information. For example:

Yo puedo hablar español. In this example the thought is I am able to do something. What is it that I am able to do? Speak. I am able= puedo. To speak = hablar. Put them together→Yo puedo hablar.

Pay attention to the following example: Yo hablo, leo, escribo y canto en español.

It seems that we have 4 conjugated verbs together in a sentence! This is fine as these are four separate actions that the subject does.

Yo hablo, leo, escribo y canto en español.

In Spanish, it is not necessary to repeat the subject pronoun with each conjugated verb, because the conjugation of the verb indicates the subject of the action.

We already studied a couple verbs that often have an infinitive follow them, and these verbs are **PREFERIR or QUERER:**

Tú **quieres estudiar** español, yo **prefiero estudiar** francés.

(You want to study Spanish, I prefer to study French.)

The third kind of grammatical structure that we are going to study is when the conjugated verb is followed **by a preposition** and then an infinitive. It is important to understand that the meaning of these verbs is completely different without the preposition. An example is the verb "have" that we already studied: TENER:

Yo **tengo** 20 años.

Mi hermano **tiene** una casa.

Nuestros hijos **tienen** muchos juguetes (toys).

If we use the verb "TENER" plus the preposition "que" plus the infinitive, the meaning is different:

TENER QUE = HAVE TO

As in English, we are expressing obligation or necessity. This expression can be translated as "someone has to do something." **Tener** is conjugated according to the subject of the sentence, while **que + infinitive** is used to express the idea of it is necessary to do something. **It is a responsibility.**

Tengo que estudiar los verbos en español.   → I **have to** study Spanish verbs.

Mi hermana **tiene que** leer un libro en francés. → My sister **has to** read a book in French.

No **tenéis que** correr todas las mañanas.   → You do not **have to** run every morning.

In Spanish, there is another structure to express obligation, but in this case it is a **DUTY**. We use the verb **Deber+ infinitive. Deber also means to owe.** In that sense, one would not use an infinitive after the conjugated form of deber.

Observe how deber is used in the sentences below to indicate duty.

Él **debe** ir al hospital.   → He **must** go to the hospital.

Paco **debe** tomar su medicina. → Paco **must** take his medicine.

Ellos **deben** apagar el fuego.   → They **must** put out the fire.

Deber is a regular verb:

yo	debo	nosotros/as	debemos
tú	debes	vosotros/as	debéis
él, ella, usted	debe	ellos,ellas, ustedes	deben

As a college student and a member of a family you have responsibilities and duties. Complete the next sentences practicing the structures "tener que" and "deber" with "yo" as the subject.

1. _____ llegar a todas las clases a tiempo.

2. _____ ayudar a mis padres en la casa.

3. _____ hacer mi tarea para cada clase.

4. _____ hablar con mi mamá "todos los días".

5. _____ pagar por mi almuerzo (lunch).

IR is another irregular verb that may be considered "**unique**" as **SER** was considered "**unique**" in its conjugation. Notice they have 2 things in common, the "**oy**" sound in the "**yo**" form and that there are no accents on the verbs. Single syllable verbs in the present tense indicative do not have written accents; this is a pattern you can recall.

You noticed on the video the conjugations for el verbo **ir**: to go.

yo	voy	nosotros/as	vamos
tú	vas	vosotros/as	vais
Ud.él/ella	va	Uds./ellos/ellas	van

Ejemplos:

Ellos van a la librería.	They are going to the bookstore.
¿Vas al* gimnasio hoy?	Are you going to the gym today?
Ella va a la biblioteca mucho.	She goes to the library a lot.

***Notice** that the preposition "a" comes after ir when you want to say that someone is going to a place.

a la librería	to the bookstore (feminine noun)
al* gimnasio	to the gym (masculine noun)

*In the second example, a + el *(definite article) combine to form one word,* al.

When we are on campus, we can talk about where we are right now, but we should also be able to discuss where we are going. To talk about movement to a place, we will use the verb "IR", or to go.

Observa el video 1.3.12 on the online platform and take notes on the concept "IR.".

Write the examples of what you see and hear below from the part after **"We are going to the mall,"** from the video 1.3.12 you just watched.

They go to the movies. _____

Yo _____

Tú _____

Nosotros _____

Juan y Salvador _____

Ud _____

Señor Ortiz _____

Los estudiantes _____

Maxie, mi perro, _____

Comprendamos→

Let's understand what is happening by reading the following conversation.

Jorge:	Hola, amigo. ¿Cómo estás?
Armando:	Bien, ¿y tú?
Jorge:	Así así. Tengo mucha tarea y necesito estudiar para un examen de matemáticas.
Armando:	¿Adónde vas?

Jorge:	Voy a la biblioteca. Nunca termino mi tarea en la residencia porque mis amigos están allí (there) y hablan mucho. Y tú, ¿adónde vas?
Armando:	Voy al laboratorio. Mis libros y los apuntes para la próxima clase están allí. Nunca voy a las clases sin mis apuntes.
Jorge:	¡Qué buen estudiante! ¿Dónde está Ana?
Armando:	Está enferma. Va a ver al médico. No va a clases hoy.
Jorge:	Ay, qué pena. Bueno, amigo, me voy. No quiero fracasar el examen mañana.
Armando:	Buena suerte, Jorge. Adiós.
Jorge:	Chao.

Contesta en español

1.   ¿Adónde va Ana? ¿Por qué?_____

2.   ¿Adónde va Armando? ¿Por qué?_____

3.   ¿Adónde va Jorge? ¿Por qué?_____

Practiquemos

Write the correct form of the verb estar or ir depending on the context.

1. Nosotros _____ en casa.

2. Ellos _____ a la clase.

3. Yo no _____ al gimnasio hoy. No tengo tiempo.

4. ¿Dónde _____ (tú)?

5. Mi familia y yo _____ al estadio esta noche para ver el partido de fútbol.

Looking back at the conversation between Jorge and Armando, we read: Ana va a ver al médico. We can use this structure, ir + a + infinitive, to talk about what we are going to do. As students, we not only want to talk about what we are studying and why, but how our choices relate to our plans for the future. Let's look at how we can also use the verb ir to talk about what we are going to do in the future.

TAREA

With the objective to use all the structures that you know, you need to write three sentences for each of the types of verbs we have studied to hand in at the beginning of class.

•   Write one declarative, one interrogative and one exclamatory sentence for each of the following:

• Gustar and similar verbs

• Conjugated verbs followed by an infinitive

• Conjugated verbs followed by a preposition and infinitive

Remember these last two requirements refer to the verbs we just studied (ir + a + infinitive, tener que and deber.)

Repasando el verbo ser:

We studied the verb SER before with Doctor EE.

Now we will learn **"O" of DOCTOR EE**, O = OCCUPATION

When we are referring to what someone "is," as when talking about his or her profession.

Some examples are:

Yo **soy** profesora.	*I am a professor.*
Mi madre **es** abogada.	*My mom is a lawyer.*
Mis hermanos **van a ser** médicos.	*My brothers are going to be doctors.*

Let's also look at some common professions in Spanish.

Observa el link 1.3.10 again on the online platform and
look up the meanings of the following professions. Listen to the pronunciation of the Spanish words and say them aloud. In the extra space, add either your future profession if it isn't included, or the profession of a friend or family member that you would like to know how to say.

Las profesiones:

el/la abogado/a		el/la farmacéutico/a	
el/la arquitecto/a		el/la ingeniero/a	
el/la contador(a)		el/la maestro/a	
el/la enfermero/a		el/la médico/a	
el/la estudiante		el/la profesor(a)	

Charlemos:

Answer these questions in complete Spanish sentences. Be prepared to discuss your answers in your next class.

1. ¿Qué vas a ser en el futuro? _____

2. ¿Cuándo tienes que pagar la universidad?_____

3. ¿Qué tienes que hacer en la tarde?_____

4.   ¿Qué puedes decir en español?_____

5.   ¿Dónde vas a trabajar?_____

6.   ¿Qué prefieres comer pizza o hamburguesas?_____

7.   ¿Qué debe hacer tu mejor amigo hoy?_____

8.   ¿Qué vas a hacer en la mañana? (morning)_____

9.   ¿Tienes que ir a tus clases mañana? (tomorrow)_____

10.   ¿Qué vas a hacer después de clases hoy?_____

11.   ¿Qué deseas hacer el fin de semana?_____

12.   ¿Tienes que sacar buenas notas este semestre?_____

13.   ¿Vas a estudiar este fin de semana?_____

14.   ¿Tienes que terminar esta unidad?_____

15.   ¿Qué debes hacer durante las vacaciones? _____

16.   ¿Qué deporte te gusta practicar?_____

17.   ¿Dónde prefieres estudiar?_____

18.   ¿Qué te gusta comer en Navidad?_____

19.   ¿Dónde quieres vivir a los 30 años?_____

20.   ¿Cuál es tu coche favorito?_____

**Why did I need to answer so many questions? Wow!!!!!
All of them were in Spanish!**

Indicate what you believe you have mastered on the checklist below.

[ ] Yes   [ ] No   **Can I identify the gender and number of Spanish words?**

[ ] Yes   [ ] No   **Can I use definite articles in agreement with the noun that follows?**

[ ] Yes   [ ] No   **Can I divide words into syllables to aid in pronunciation?**

[ ] Yes   [ ] No   **Can I apply the rules associated with the stressed syllable to achieve an authentic pronunciation of a word?**

[ ] Yes   [ ] No   **Can I write what I hear in Spanish when Spanish is spoken slowly and clearly?**

[ ] Yes   [ ] No   **Can I read, write, listen and speak about my school and profession?**

[ ] Yes   [ ] No   **Can I tell time, the date and at what time activities take place?**

[ ] Yes   [ ] No   **Can I form questions correctly?**

[ ] Yes   [ ] No   **Can I differentiate between the uses of ESTAR vs SER?**

[ ] Yes   [ ] No   **Can I talk about how I am and where I am?**

[ ] Yes   [ ] No   **Can I talk about what I do presently?**

(At a novice learning level / new or beginner level)?

[ ] Yes   [ ] No   **Can I talk about what I will do?**

If you answered "No" to any of these questions, review those sections again and see your professor.

Vocabulary

Español	M/F	Inglés	Clasificación
¿Qué hora es?		What time is it?	Expresión
a la		at 1:00 or times related to one	Expresión
a las >2:00		at … >2:00 clock time	Expresión
abogado/a	El, La	lawyer	Sustantivo
abril	El	April	Sustantivo
abrir		to open	Verbo Regular
administración de empresas	La	business administration	Sustantivo
agosto		August	Sustantivo
año escolar	El	school year	Sustantivo
antropología	La	anthropology	Sustantivo
apartamento	El	apartment	Sustantivo
aprender		to learn	Verbo Regular
arquitecto/a	El, La	architect	Sustantivo
arte*	El, Las	art	Sustantivo
asistir		to attend	Verbo Regular
biblioteca	La	library	Sustantivo
biología	La	biology	Sustantivo
bolígrafo	El	pen	Sustantivo
cafetería	La	cafeteria	Sustantivo
calculadora	La	calculator	Sustantivo
ciencia	La	science	Sustantivo
ciencias políticas	Las	political science	Sustantivo
comer		to eat	Verbo Regular
comprender		to understand	Verbo Regular
contador/a	El, La	accountant	Sustantivo
contestar		to answer	Verbo Regular
correr		to run	Verbo Regular
creer		to believe	Verbo Regular
cuaderno	El	notebook	Sustantivo
curso	El	course	Sustantivo
de la madrugada		in the early morning	Expresión
de la mañana		in the morning	Expresión
de la noche		in the evening	Expresión
de la tarde		in the afternoon	Expresión
diciembre		December	Sustantivo

domingo(s)	El, Los	(on) Sunday/s	Sustantivo
edificio	El	building	Sustantivo
educación	La	education	Sustantivo
enero		January	Sustantivo
enfermero/a	El, La	nurse	Sustantivo
enseñar		to teach	Verbo Regular
es la... (1:00)		it is... 1:00 (time related to 1:00 o'clock)	Expresión
escribir		to write	Verbo Regular
español	El	Spanish language	Sustantivo
español	El	Spanish man	Sustantivo
español/a		Spanish	Adjetivo
española	La	Spanish woman	Sustantivo
esperar		to hope, wish, wait for	Verbo Regular
estadio	El	stadium	Sustantivo
estar		to be	Verbo Irregular
estudiante	El, La	student	Sustantivo
estudiar		to study	Verbo Regular
faltar		to miss, lack	Verbo Similar a Gustar
farmacéutico/a	El, La	pharmacist	Sustantivo
febrero		February	Sustantivo
fin de semana	El	(on) the weekend	Sustantivo
fines de semana	Los	(on) the weekends	Sustantivo
fracasar		to fail	Verbo Regular
geografía	La	geography	Sustantivo
gimnasio	El	gymnasium	Sustantivo
hablar		to talk, speak	Verbo Regular
hace buen tiempo		it's good weather	Expresión
hace frío		it's cold	Expresión
hace mal tiempo		it's bad weather	Expresión
hace sol		it's sunny	Expresión
hace viento		it's windy	Expresión
hacer (go)		to do, make	Verbo Irregular
historia	La	history	Sustantivo
idioma	El	language	Sustantivo
informática	La	computer science	Sustantivo

ingeniero/a	El, La	engineer	Sustantivo
invierno	El	winter	Sustantivo
ir		to go	Verbo Irregular
jueves	El, Los	(on) Thursday/s	Sustantivo
julio		July	Sustantivo
junio		June	Sustantivo
laboratorio	El	laboratory	Sustantivo
lápiz	El	pencil	Sustantivo
leer		to read	Verbo Regular
librería	La	bookstore	Sustantivo
libro	El	book	Sustantivo
literatura	La	literature	Sustantivo
llegar		to arrive	Verbo Regular
lunes	El, Los	(on) Monday/s	Sustantivo
maestro/a	El, La	teacher	Sustantivo
mapa	El	map	Sustantivo
martes	El, Los	(on) Tuesday/s	Sustantivo
marzo		March	Sustantivo
mas		but	Preposición
más		more	Adjetivo
matemáticas	Las	math	Sustantivo
mayo		May	Sustantivo
medicina	La	medicine	Sustantivo
médico/a	El, La	doctor	Sustantivo
miércoles	El, Los	(on) Wednesday/s	Sustantivo
nariz	La	nose	Sustantivo
necesitar		to need	Verbo Regular
noviembre		November	Sustantivo
octubre		October	Sustantivo
otoño	El	autumn/fall	Sustantivo
papel	El	paper	Sustantivo
pedagogía	La	education	Sustantivo
pluma	La	pen	Sustantivo
política	La	politics	Sustantivo
porque		because	Conjunción

preguntar		to ask (a question)	Verbo Regular
primavera	La	spring	Sustantivo
profesor/a	El, La	teacher/professor	Sustantivo
psicología	La	psychology	Sustantivo
público	El	people	Sustantivo
querer (e—ie)		to want/wish/love	Verbo Irregular
regresar		to return	Verbo Regular
residencia estudiantil	La	residence hall	Sustantivo
sábado (s)	El, Los	(on) Saturday/s	Sustantivo
saber (otros irregulares -yo)		to know	Verbo Irregular
sacar		to take	Verbo Regular
sacar (buenas/malas) notas		to get (good/bad) grades	Verbo Regular
semestre	El	semester	Sustantivo
septiembre		September	Sustantivo
si		if	Preposición
sí		yes	Adverbio
sociología	La	sociology	Sustantivo
son las… >2:00		it is… >2:00 clock time	Expresión
terminar		to finish	Verbo Regular
tienda	La	store	Sustantivo
tomar apuntes		to take notes	Verbo Regular
trabajar		to work	Verbo Regular
usar		to use	Verbo Regular
verano	El	summer	Sustantivo
vivir		to live	Verbo Regular
voz	La	voice	Sustantivo

En mi casa

Objectives

1. Codify the sounds in the Spanish alphabet.
2. Listen to the different Spanish accents.
3. Understand the Spanish intonation.
4. Learn about family and adjective vocabulary to be able to describe your family and home.
5. Identify objects in the home and discuss what you want in your home.
6. Expand your ability to speak about what you do presently.
7. Review grammar structures for more consistent usage in speech and writing.
8. Understand the concept of indirect objects and indirect object pronouns.
9. Differentiate clarifying, emphasizing and redundancy reduction with the indirect object pronouns.
10. Understand the concept of direct objects and direct object pronouns
11. Create sentences with both direct and indirect objects pronouns.
12. Express activities related to daily routines and personal care.
13. Speak and write Spanish avoiding redundancy.

Overview

1. Escuchemos los sonidos del alfabeto en español.

In class we have worked on dictation. What were you feeling when your professor read and you needed to write? It was a surprise for you when you were able to recognize the sounds in Spanish and could codify the sounds with symbols (letters). Identifying the sound can be tricky especially between the **Spanish** "i" and the **English** "e." Don't worry, with practice, we will be able to recognize the sounds. We are sure that you recognized the meaning of some words. In the moment that the words had meaning to you, you stopped hearing Spanish and you started listening to Spanish! As you know, hearing and listening are not the same. Hearing is simply the act of perceiving. You were doing that in class as you were listening to the dictation and you were codifying the sounds with their equivalent symbols, the letters. Listening requires concentration. It isn't only recognizing the sounds vs letters; it is understanding the meaning from the words and sentences. There is a huge difference.

To succeed in communicating in Spanish, we need to read and write Spanish, but speaking and listening is another challenge to conquer. We need to be very clear on two strategies that we must follow to succeed.

A) Make Spanish words part of you, almost as your native language, through study, practice and constant review of Spanish.

- **Use flashcards as a technique.**

- **Visualize, vocalize and understand:** by looking at images and reading aloud you will work on your ability to speak and to listen. Remember that you can visualize by imagination and vocalize like we studied in Unit 2.

- **Use the diglot weave method to communicate** in all your reports. In all your homework insert Spanish words in your English sentences. Keep working and soon your sentences will be 100% in Spanish.

B) Understand that language and culture are inextricably linked with one another. It is impossible to speak any language without knowing the culture. The theories about this relationship between culture and language have been argued and scrutinized by many linguists and scholars since the 19th Century. The Modern Language Association (MLA) that promotes the study and teaching of languages and literatures states the culture of a speaker is reflected in his or her speech. **The accent, vocabulary, style of speaking and structure of arguments identify a speaker as a member of a certain cultural group or society** (1). To be able to succeed in our Spanish communication, we need to gain awareness, appreciation and respect for the Spanish speakers' culture and understand cultural differences within the United States and between the different countries that speak Spanish.

 ¿Hispano o latino o hispanohablante?

It is very common in the United States to view all Spanish speakers as the same. We forget there are twenty-two different Spanish-speaking nations with a strong link between them that make them like brothers but with their own unique identity. The same happens with the English speaker. Imagine that if because we speak English the rest of the world did not acknowledge whether we are from Australia, England, Scotland, United States, etc. We are proud of our nationality and region. When someone asks us about our origin we answer I am from Kansas, I am from New York. The same happens with Spanish speakers. Mexican, Puerto Ricans, Dominicans, Argentinians, Spanish, each one is proud of their own unique culture.

As humans, we like to generalize. By doing so, we tend to create stereotypes which is a big cultural mistake.

Keep in mind the phrase:

"**To generalize is a lack of education**" *by Mary Carmen Alegre-Riesgo*

Because...

Not All Mexicans are illegals   *Not every US citizen eats just burgers*   *All Italians don't sing at their meals*

As we commented before, the Spanish language is approximately 60% derived from Latin. Remember "latino" means the language of a group of people was derived from Latin. The different countries that speak Italian, French, Romanian and Portuguese are Latinos. As we studied, culture and language are inextricably linked. That is the reason that we will find that they share some similarities; but that doesn't imply that they are all the same.

The other 40% of the Spanish Language comes from Arabic, Greek and the Native American cultures, also called pre-Hispanic or pre-Colombian cultures (before the arrival of the Hispanics or before Columbus arrived). Languages of those cultures were integrated in Spanish, as Nahuatl from México, Maya form México and Guatemala, Quechua form Peru and Southern Andes, Guarani from Paraguay, etc. Each country where Spanish is spoken has their unique patterns related to pronunciation, cadence, and the meaning of individual words, just as we found different patterns among English speakers. The difference with English is that the Native American cultures did not have a big influence on the language. The reason for this difference was that the Spanish and British conquerors had two very different visions for the new territories. While the two empires wanted the territories and wealth that was in them, the Spanish conquerors also had the objective to convert the native people to Christianity. The native cultures were destroyed in this process, but the people were included in the traditions of the Spanish ruling classes and marriages between groups were common. In contrast, the British colonization excluded and isolated the native people from participation in the economic and religious life of the colonies. In the Spanish territories a new culture was developed, the Mestizo culture, where the Spanish and pre-Hispanic cultures were integrated.

As we hear different Spanish accents, we will find different ways to say the same thing in each region and/or country. For example, bus: In Paraguay and México city is called a "**Micro**", in the north of México "**camión**", in Puerto Rico, the Dominican Republic and Cuba "**guagua**", in Uruguay "**ómnibus**", in Guatemala "**camioneta**", and in España "**bus**", in Ecuador "**colectivo**", in Colombia "**buseta**", in Nicaragua "**ruta**". When we learn another language, we forget these little characteristics. We have them in English in Minnesota you drink a pop, in New York you drink a soda.

Because language and culture are inextricably linked, we are integrating different topics in each unit to help you to understand some of the cultural differences. Answer the following questions. They are a review of some cultural facts that we studied. In case you don't remember you can review our last units. Use the diglot-weave method to write your answers.

1. ¿Qué es el seseo?_____

2. ¿Qué países son Norteamericanos?_____

3. ¿Cuántos continentes tenemos en español?_____

4. ¿Quiénes son latinos?_____

5. ¿Qué países son americanos?_____

6. ¿Cuántos países hablan español?_____

7. ¿Qué países son hispanoamericanos?_____

8. ¿Quiénes son hispanos?_____

9. ¿Do you think that all the countries that speak Spanish have the same culture? ____

Why/why not?_____

_____

_____

In class, we will talk about your answers.

2. Escuchemos los diferentes acentos en el español.

Observa los videos 1.4.1 and 1.4.2 on the online platform to listen to the different Spanish accents..

TAREA:

Answer the next question: Why does the accent, vocabulary, style of speaking and structure of arguments identify a speaker as a member to a certain country, if all of them speak Spanish? Document your answer on paper that you hand in the next class. Submit at least 5 different statements based on the two videos you watched. Additionally, indicate what regional differences you noticed from those who spoke per country.

Pay attention, in the first video you will listen to the actual characteristics of each nationality. With the second one, you will listen to the characteristics that differentiate each accent from the point of view of the copycat. Listen several times to these two videos; this will allow you to develop your listening and complete your homework.

Practiquemos nuestra pronunciación:

Building on the knowledge you gained of pronunciation in the previous unit; in this section we want you to be familiar with the pronunciation of new words. Remember the rules that we studied before so you have better control of Spanish phonetics. The next two charts are a summary of what we studied before: **the 10 syllabic rules and Irregular phonemes in Spanish**:

1. A simple consonant or consonant group goes with the following vowel.
2. Two consonants are separated; except when you have an S (goes with the syllable be-fore.)
3. Three consonants are usually divided after the first one, unless the second is an S.

4. Four consonants between vowels are always divided after the second.
5. Diphthongs or triphthongs are destroyed if the soft vowel is stressed.
6. The diphthong exists also with the h in the middle.
7. Words ending in vowel, n, or s are stressed on the next to the last syllable.
8. Words ending in any consonant except , n, or s are stressed on the last syllable.
9. When rules above are not followed, It is when we use the orthographic accent.
10. Diacritical accents are used to differentiate between same words with different mean-ing.

Sonido:	vocal a	vocal e	vocal i	vocal o	vocal u
K	ca	que	qui	co	cu
G	ga	gue	gui	go	gu
Gw	gua	güe	güi	guo	
H	**ja**	**ge, je**	**gi, ji**	**jo**	**ju**
Th, S	za	ce	ci	zo	zu
S	sa	se	si	so	su
silent	ha	he	hi	ho	hu

Using the charts that we just presented to you, you need to divide the following new words in syllables. The consonants with the vowel that have an irregular phoneme are marked in yellow; remember the ceceo or seseo as in how these are pronounced in Spain. After you divide the words in syllables, circle the stressed syllable. You need to write the sound that the consonant in yellow (irregular phoneme) needs to follow and the reason it has this sound. Follow the examples.

Remember the highlighted syllable is not the stressed or accented syllable. It is only showing you where the irregular phoneme is.

palabra	Sí – la - bas	sonido	razón
casa	ca - sa	K	Sound K ca, co,cu
gustar	gus - tar	G	Sound g gu, ga,go
cigüeña	ci –güe- ña	GW	Sound gw güe, güi
hacer	ha -cer	TH/S	Sound th/s ce, ci
adjetivos	Ad –je - ti - vos	H	Sound H ja,jo,je,ju
gigante			
acordar			
goma			
conseguir			
guerra			
pequeño			
guante			
pingüino			
anaranjado*			
sugerir			
izquierda			
jirafa			
ciencias			
espejo			
calor			
querer			
acuerdo			

Nota: anaranjado en España y el Caribe, naranja en gran parte de Hispanoamérica.

3. Comprendamos la entonación del idioma español.

The pattern or melody of rising or falling pitch changes in the voice when used in speaking is known as intonation. This pattern distinguishes kinds of sentences or speakers of different language cultures. Often people say that **English intonation has too many variations and Spanish intonation is more constant.** Let's examine the elements that comprise intonation to understand this variation. Intonation is the result of stress and tone.

Stress is when we give particular emphasis or importance to a letter, syllable or word. Here we find the first big difference between Spanish and English. As we studied, Spanish words have a stressed syllable (sílaba tónica). **The stress is on the vowel of the stressed syllable.** All words have stress. In English, we have a **stress on each word, but we also stress the content words in the sentence**; content words being nouns, verbs or adjectives.

Let's see the next example:

English stresses certain words: **Content words**

My mother has a new house.

My mother has a new house

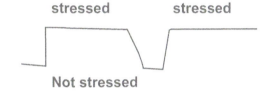

For Spanish all the words are stressed the same: Mi mamá tiene una casa nueva

In Spanish **we don't differentiate between the content and the function words**. That is the reason the intonation seems more consistent in Spanish.

Let's see the next example:

¡Mi mamá está feliz!   ¡Mi mamá está triste!

My mom is happy!   *My mom is sad!*

Tone, in general terms and to avoid confusion, is the musical sound when we speak that has different degrees from high to low. As in English, Spanish intonation depends directly on the type of sentence that we are saying. We have three types of sentences and each one of them has a specific tone pattern.

Declarative/declarativas are used in making a statement. Spanish intonation starts in a low tone, rises to a higher one on the first stressed syllable, maintains the tone until the last stressed syllable, and then goes back to the initial low pitch, dropping even lower at the very end. Mi mamá está feliz = My mother is happy.

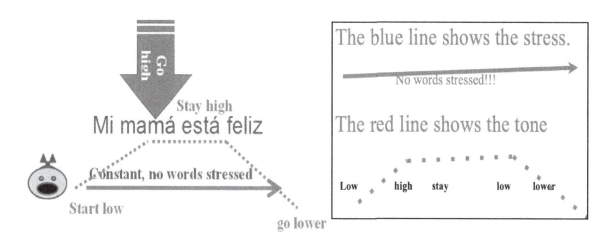

At this time, our objective is that you understand the difference in the tones. With practice it will become natural to you, as your native language tone. Keep in mind, declarative sentences in Spanish:

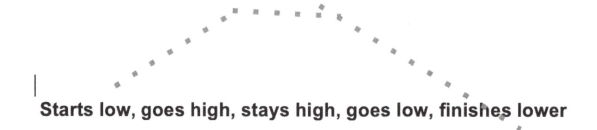

Starts low, goes high, stays high, goes low, finishes lower

Exclamatory/exclamativas are used in making a statement expressing excitement or emotion. When we write an exclamatory sentence we use the exclamation marks to represent the excitement or emotion. When we are speaking, it is the difference of the tone that tells us the excitement or the emotion that we are feeling. In English, we only use one exclamation mark at the end of the sentence, but in Spanish remember we open and we close the exclamation with exclamation marks at the beginning and end of the sentence. When we speak in Spanish, we follow the same pattern as the declarative sentences, but we start above the normal tone and quickly descend into below the normal pitch..

In red, we have the pattern of a declarative sentence: Mi mamá está feliz. In purple, we have the pattern in an exclamative sentence: ¡Mi mamá está feliz! Although they are the same words in English and Spanish, the difference is in the tone when we speak and in the exclamation marks when we write.

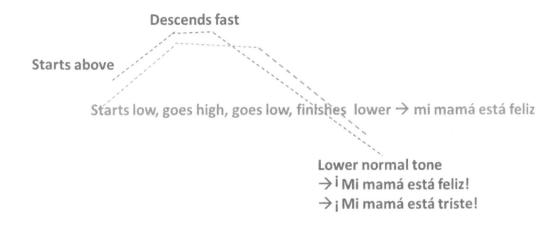

Descends fast

Starts above

Starts low, goes high, goes low, finishes lower → mi mamá está feliz

Lower normal tone
→ ¡ Mi mamá está feliz!
→ ¡ Mi mamá está triste!

Interrogative/interrogativas: are used to make questions. In Spanish, the interrogative sentences are declarative sentences with questions marks (opened and closed). In Spanish, you may change the structure like in English:

¿Mi mamá está feliz?   My mother is happy?

¿Está feliz mi mamá?   Is my mother happy?   The two options are correct!

That it is the reason why it is so important that you understand the change of tone when you ask a question when speaking. The only difference between a declarative and interrogative sentence is the tone when you are speaking or the opened and closed questions mark, when you are writing.

Oraciones declarativas:	¿Oraciones interrogativas?
Tú estudias español.	¿Tú estudias español?
You study Spanish.	Do you study Spanish?

The tone pattern in Spanish interrogative sentences starts as in the exclamatory sentences, above the normal tone. From here the following syllables are descending until the last syllable where the tone rises again. In green you can see how the tone pattern is in an interrogative sentence.

We have interrogative sentences that start with an interrogative word; these are never confused with the statements and follow almost the same pattern that we use in English interrogative sentences. The interrogative word in Spanish, as you remember always is stressed.

The last interrogative questions that we will study, are the tag questions. This is used when the person knows the answer or is trying to direct it. Your mom is happy, isn't she?

These are very simple because they are declarative sentences, followed by a word that implies the question. In Spanish frequently we use ¿verdad? right? ¿no? not (literally)? In other words, we use the intonation for declarative sentences and we use the intonation for the interrogative sentences only in the short tag: ¿verdad? right? ¿no? not?

Observa los videos 1.4.3 to be able to answer the following questions that we are going to discuss in class. Remember use all the words in Spanish that you can in your answers. (Diglot Weave Method)

1. The meaning of a sentence depends on what factor(s)? _____

_____

2. What types of intonation do we have in English? _____

3. What are the differences between Spanish and English Intonation: _____

_____

For now, you have some idea about intonation, stress and tone in the different sentences. With practice, you will see and hear the difference. If you are curious about other accents or to listen to Spanish dialogues to practice, you can visit the web site developed by "Unversitat Pompeu Fabra Barcelona, España."

Observa el website 1.4.4 Atlas interactivo de la entonación del español and start practicing.

4. Describamos nuestra familia y nuestra casa: Los adjetivos.

As you saw in the previous section the rules for authentic pronunciation of Spanish are organized for you in something similar to a hierarchy or order. It would seem if we compare them to a family, that stress and tone are like fraternal twins~different but equally important in the phonetics family. In this next section, we will talk about family members and their characteristics.

Leamos y repasemos

Let's read and review el diálogo entre Marta y José sobre sus familias   practicando el estrés y el tono/la intonación.

Marta:	Hola José, ¿Cómo estás?
José:	¡Qué gusto verte Marta! Estoy bien, ¿y tú?
Marta:	Bien gracias. ¿Cómo está tu familia? ¿Está tu familia aquí para las fiestas?
José:	Sí, vamos a celebrar la Navidad en la casa de mi hermano y su esposa. Mi hermano (Pedro) y su esposa Anita (mi cuñada) viven en un pueblo cerca de Salamanca.
Marta:	¿Cómo es Anita? ¿Es ella española también?
José:	No, amiga. Anita es colombiana. Ella es morena, simpática y habla con un acento muy diferente, pero bonito, de lo que estamos acostumbrados en España. Ellos están muy felices porque ella está embarazada.
Marta:	¡Qué bueno! ¡Vas a ser tío! ¡Enhorabuena! ¿Cómo están tus padres? Tienen que estar muy felices de ser abuelos pronto.

José:	Sí, mis padres están felices y los padres de mis padres, mis abuelos, están tan emocionados de ser bisabuelos.
Marta:	El bebé es muy afortunado de ser tu sobrino y va a ser un nieto muy mimado y amado por todos.
José:	Gracias amiga, pero dime de tu familia. ¿Estás en la boda de tu hermana?
Marta:	Sí, la boda ocurre en mayo pero los suegros, los padres del novio de mi hermana, no quieren tener la boda en la iglesia de nuestro pueblo. Ellos sugieren la iglesia de Toledo.
José:	Yo entiendo el problema, Marta. Ellos prefieren la compañía del famoso El Greco.
Marta:	Ja,ja,ja. En este momento, yo debo de buscar un vestido (dress) porque si siguen con el conflicto, mi hermana va a casarse mañana en nuestra iglesia en Salamanca sin la familia de su novio.
José:	¡Ay amiga!, tienes razón—es una solución posible. Recomiendo la tienda a la izquierda de la mueblería. Mi hermana y mi madre siempre compran allí. Buena suerte con todo.
Marta:	Gracias José. Oye amigo, espero las noticias del bebé.
José:	Sí, yo voy a llamarte inmediatamente.

Right now the important thing is to concentrate on your pronunciation. Review the dialogue for words you recognize. The words in bold are verbs we will study soon. For now, let's focus on the family words. Study the words below and re-read the dialogue above.

Your comprehension as well as strategies for explaining a word in other words, which is referred to as circumlocution, will grow. You probably experienced in your native language moments when you could not come up with the word that was on "the tip of your tongue". You worked around that by coming up with a different way to say what you were thinking. Notice above in the dialogue when José says "Mi hermano, Pedro, y su esposa, mi cuñada Anita..." If when you are speaking and cannot recall the word, sister-in-law in this case, think of another way to define that word. In this case, cuñada may be defined as the wife of my brother (my brother's wife = la esposa de mi hermano.)

In Spanish, we do not have an apostrophe " 's" to indicate possession. We use the word "de" meaning of or from to indicate possession. Therefore my grandmother is the mother of my mother. We would say "La madre de mi madre" instead of Mi madre's madre." Never say or write something with an apostrophe in Spanish.

On the vocabulary list below, identify the stressed syllable of the family related word in the first column, by highlighting where the natural stress of the word is located. This will help your pronunciation sound más auténticos.

¡Buena suerte!

La familia	Family
el (la) abuelo(a)	grandfather/grandmother
el (la) cuñado(a)	brother-in-law/sister-in-law
el (la) esposo(a)	husband/wife
el (la)hermano(a)	brother/sister
el (la) hijo(a)	son/daughter
la madre (mamá)	mother
el (la) nieto(a)	grandson/granddaughter
la nuera	daughter-in-law
el padre (papá)	father
los padres	parents
el (la) primo(a)	cousin
el (la) sobrino(a)	nephew/niece
el (la) suegro(a)	father-in-law/mother-in-law
el (la) tío(a)	uncle/aunt
el yerno	son-in-law
Los padrinos/la madrina/el padrino	the godparents/godmother/godfather
Los parientes	the relatives
El novio/la novia	boyfriend/girlfriend
Ser soltero (a)	To be single
Estar casado (a)	To be married
Estar divorciado (a) de	To be divorced
El padrastro	stepfather
la madrastra	stepmother
El (la) hermanastro (a)	stepsibling
El (la) hijastro (a)	stepchild
El (la) medio (a) hermano (a)	half siblings
El (la) perro(a)	dog
El (la) gato (a)	cat

Los adjetivos: Describiendo a otros

Describing others: When you want to describe someone or others, you will use adjectives that correspond to the gender and number of the person(s).

    If talking about a male (one person who is male):

Choose adjectives that end in o or e (singular and masculine.)

Ejemplo: El doctor es alto. El profesor Gómez es paciente.

 If talking about more than one male:

Choose adjectives that end in o or e and add "s" to indicate plurality and the masculine gender.

Ejemplo: Sus 4 hermanos son altos. Juan y José son irresponsables.

 If talking about a female (one person who is female):

Choose adjectives that end in a or e (singular and feminine.)

Ejemplo: Penélope Cruz es bonita. Su abuela es inteligente.

 If talking about more than one female:

Choose adjectives that end in a or e and add "s" to indicate plurality and the feminine gender.

Ejemplo: Nuestras amigas son perezosas. María, Lupe y Rosa son responsables.

Los adjetivos:

aburrido/a	boring
antipático/a	unpleasant
bueno/a	good
cómico/a	funny; comical
inteligente	intelligent
interesante	interesting
malo/a	bad
paciente	patient
perezoso/a	lazy
pobre	poor
responsable	responsible
rico/a	rich
simpático/a	nice
tonto/a	silly; dumb
trabajador/a	hard-working
alto/a	tall
bajo/a	short
bonito/a	pretty
débil	weak
delgado/a	thin
feo/a	ugly
fuerte	strong

gordo/a	fat
grande	big; large
guapo/a	handsome/pretty
joven	young
pequeño/a	small

Write 3 words that describe your best female friend.

1. _____

2. _____

3. _____

Write 3 words that describe your best male friend.

1. _____

2. _____

3. _____

Practiquemos

Contesta las preguntas sobre tu propia familia en español y con oraciones completas.

1. ¿Cuántas personas hay en tu familia? _____

2. ¿Cuántos hermanos tienes? _____

3. ¿Cómo se llaman tus padres? _____

4. ¿Tienes abuelos? _____

5. ¿Eres soltero (a) o estás casado (a)? _____

6. ¿Eres tío o tía? _____

7. ¿Cómo es tu madre? _____

8. ¿Tu madre es alta? _____

9. ¿Cómo es tu padre? _____

10. ¿Es tu padre fuerte? _____

11. ¿Cómo es el esposo de tu hermana? _____

12. ¿Cómo son los padres de tu mejor amigo? _____

Los colores

Colors are also adjectives since they describe an object. As in the adjective examples above colors will **agree** in **gender** and **number** with the object they describe.

Los colores	The colors	
amarillo (a)	yellow	
anaranjado (a)	orange	
azul	blue	
blanco (a)	white	
café	brown	
gris	gray	
marrón	brown	
morado (a)	purple	
negro (a)	black	
rojo (a)	red	
rosado (a)	pink	
verde	green	

¿Cuál es tu color favorito?

Mi color favorito es rosado.

La bandera de Los Estados Unidos es roja, blanca y azul.

El libro es negro.

Las novelas son negras y azules.

Tengo un coche verde.

Remember the gender can be masculine as with el coche blanco, feminine as with la casa blanca or neuter: el coche azul o la casa azul. Analyze the names of the colors in Spanish and write the colors that are neutral, in other words, write the colors that don't change to agree with a feminine or masculine noun:

_____

_____

Think about the examples above and respond to the following:

1. Is the word "color" masculine or feminine? _____

_____

2. From the vocabulary chart or the examples, how can you tell the gender of the word "color"?

_____

_____

3. What colors change for the feminine form? _____

_____

4. What colors don't change for the feminine form? _____

_____

Look at the example about la bandera de los Estados Unidos. Notice the words roja y blanca. These were changed to agree with the feminine gender of the word "bandera". Why was there no change to the word "azul"? _____

_____

5. How do you make a color that ends in a consonant, such as azul, plural? _____

_____

_____

6. ¿Cómo se dice, (How does one say) "My house is yellow"? _____

_____

8. ¿ Cómo se dice, "We have a red, green and black pen." ? _____

_____

9. Mi color favorito es _____ (fill in your preference.)

5. Nuestra casa, sus cuartos y los objetos.

As you remember from Unidad 2 you are able to provide your "domicilio" or "dirección". You can answer the questions:

¿Cuál es su dirección? ¿Cuál es tu dirección? ¿Dónde vive usted?" o ¿Dónde vives tú?

Remember the formula to answer these questions:

La dirección de la Universidad de SUNY Geneseo es: La calle **College Círculo** número 1, Geneseo

The formula has four components. Write the components in the following space. You can review Unidad 2 if you don't remember:

_____   +   _____   +   _____   +

_____

Translate to English the next questions:

¿Cuál es su dirección de correo electrónico? _____

_____

Look up the word for this symbol @? : _____ and for dot: _____ using Wordreference to choose the correct context.

El hogar—the home

Joe Melsha says "Home is wherever we gather with our family and friends. Houses get bought and sold; a home stays with you always." In the Spanish speaker's culture the home is their house and they love to share: "Mi casa es su casa" (formal) is Spanish for "My house is your house"; a common saying to invite someone into your house and allow them to make themselves at home.

Perhaps you have been looking for the ideal apartment or home, or you need to furnish an apartment or home. To do so, it is helpful to know how to say the rooms in a home. If you go to Corte Inglés or even Home Depot or Lowes in México, you will want to know which aisle has items for the bathroom versus the dining room.

Los cuartos de la casa	The rooms of the home
La casa	The house
El hogar	The home
El baño	The bathroom
El comedor	The dining room
La sala	The living room
La cocina	The kitchen
El cuarto	The bedroom
La recámara	(el dormitorio es más una residencia estudiantil)
El dormitorio	
La habitación	
El garaje	The garage
La oficina	The office
El sótano	The basement
El ático	The attic

Añadamos

Let's add some things to your house.

el sillón | el sofá | la silla | el cuadro | el DVD

la mesa | la chimenea | el salón | el teléfono | la televisión / el televisor

		el mando de la televisión	el radio	la lámpara
las cortinas	la estantería	el control de la televisión	la radio	

Hay otros cuartos en tu casa que necesitan cosas (objetos). In the last column, indicate the room(s) that would have these objects. Remember to include the article to help you recall if the gender of the word is masculine or feminine.

Las objetos de la casa		El cuarto en la casa
La cama	The bed	
El teléfono	The phone	
La silla	The chair /seat	
La mesa	The table	
La puerta	The door	
El piso	The floor	
La lámpara	The lamp	
El espejo	The mirror	
La radio	The radio	
El sofá	The sofa	
La basura	The trash	
El televisor	The tv set	
La ventana	The window	
El horno	The oven	
La estufa	The stove	
El refrigerador	The refrigerator	
El lavabo	The sink	
El microondas	The microwave	
La lavadora	The washing machine	
La secadora	The dryer	

Leamos

Read the passage aloud for pronunciation and comprehension.

Let's pretend you are working with your sister: tu hermana que es diseñadora. Ella va a las tiendas contigo para comprar.

Rosa: Gracias, Raquel, por venir a mi casa. **Tengo** ganas de decorar mi casa pero no **sé** qué necesito.

Raquel: **Es** un placer, hermana. Primero, **sugiero** los muebles para tu recámara y el baño. No **puedes** vivir y dormir aquí con solo la recámara y el baño.

Rosa: Siempre **eres** muy sensata. Yo **puedo** comer en tu casa o en la de mamá.

Raquel: **Quiero ir** a la mueblería, Inlab Muebles, y a Costco.

Rosa: (En Inlab Muebles) **Prefiero** una cama doble, una mesa de noche, unas lámparas y un sillón.

Raquel: ¿Qué color te gusta en tu recámara?

Rosa: **Quisiera** el color blanco para los muebles y en la pared, azul para la tranquilidad.

Raquel: Perfecto. Ahora compramos la cama, la mesa y el sofá. **Vamos** a Costco para las lámparas y las cosas del baño.

Rosa: (en Costco…) Por favor, ¿**Consigues** las lámparas? Yo busco las toallas y los adornos del baño. Voy a **poner** un tema tropical en el baño.

Raquel: Vale, Rosa, pero por favor, no **vayas a poner** la fruta en el baño…es para la cocina …ja,ja,ja.

Comprendamos:

Apply what you understood from the dialogue to the questions below:

1. ¿Qué color representa la tranquilidad según Rosa? _____

2. ¿Compran Rosa y Raquel una cama en Costco? _____

3. ¿Qué quiere Rosa en su recámara? _____

4. ¿Dónde no se pone la fruta? _____

5. ¿Qué es Inlab Muebles? _____

Repasemos: Let's review.

Observa el website 1.4.5 y contesta las preguntas siguientes (following). In these questions, we will practice providing responses to questions about addresses as well as items for the house.

1. ¿En cuál ciudad y país es Muebles Inlab? (Tienes que buscar la información en la primera página). _____

_____

2. ¿Cuál es el número de teléfono de esta tienda? (Hay dos). (Write the words for the numbers. In Spanish, phone numbers are provided in pairs. If there is an odd number of digits, then the first number would stand alone and then the rest of the numbers will be in pairs.)

_____

_____

3. ¿Qué tipos de preguntas muestran en la página como las preguntas que los clientes hacen frecuentemente? Escribe sobre 2 y sus respuestas.

_____

_____

_____

_____

Aprendamos un poco más: Let's learn a little more.

In previous units, we addressed some of the cultural norms that exhibit politeness and as a result of you incorporating them into your daily interactions; you will earn the respect of others from Spanish speaking cultures. Some of these aspects were the usage of Señor, Señora, Señorita, titles and usted when you meet someone for the first time or again with people of title throughout your conversations. Eye contact and physical proximity in conversations are also cultural norms that you should become accustomed to with people from Hispanic countries.

Expanding on the concept of respect, you may have noticed one of the words used in the dialogue with Rosa y Raquel is **"quisiera"**. Rosa says it when she wants to indicate that she would like white furniture. **Quisiera** means I would like (or he, she or usted would like) and is one of the most polite ways of requesting something anywhere whether it be at home, a store, restaurant or seeking information or assistance.

TAREA: For homework create 10 sentences in Spanish using **quisiera** and items that you would like in your ideal room. Be specific by adding the items and adjectives within your sentences. Remember place your assignment on the instructor's desk at the beginning of the class.

6. Expandamos nuestra habilidad de hablar: Conjugación de verbos.

In addition to understanding the general meaning of what you read and being able to answer questions about location and phone, you may have noticed again verbs that were highlighted in "morado" from this dialogue and the previous one. This section will show you how to conjugate verbs—that means taking the infinitive or non-specific verb and breaking it down to correspond or agree with each subject you will encounter in Spanish.

As a review, you learned that verbs tell you the _____ that someone is doing.

In Spanish, there are (hay) _____ types of verbs. These end in _____ _____

or _____.

Verbs ending in _____ _____ or _____ are known as _____ because they are not yet conjugated (broken out specifically by subject.)

Think of Buzz Lightyear:

to Infinity and Beyond

Infinity—unknown ending

Infinitive—unknown subject.

Each of the **3 verb types** has its own endings by person.

+ You will take off the infinitive ending→this gives you the ROOT or the STEM.

+ Take the root and add the subject specific ending to get your conjugated verb.

When you have a verb such as "Necesitar"→ to need, simply follow these steps:

1. Drop the infinitive ending (in this case, AR)

2. Take the root, "Necesit" ,and add the verb ending that corresponds to the subject.

3. If the subject is "**yo**", add the **yo ending** for an **AR verb** per the chart below (o).

The result → necesito—I need.

Persona ngular	Singular	AR	ER	IR	Persona plural	Plural	AR	ER	IR
1era.	yo	o	o	o	1era.	nosotros (as)	amos	emos	imos
2da.	tú	as	es	es	2da.	vosotros (as)	áis	éis	ís
3era.	él, ella, Ud.	a	e	e	3era.	ellos, ellas, Uds	an	en	en

This was a review of what you studied in the previous units. The verbs that follow the pattern above are known as regular verbs. They follow the 3 steps noted above and have no changes to them. Three of them were underlined in the conversation between Rosa y Raquel.

You may have noticed the verbs in morado in the dialogue above between Rosa y Raquel. Those verbs are referred to as irregular verbs because they do not follow the 3 steps above and require a bit more effort on the language learner's part to master them.

So far you have learned a few irregular verbs such as:

SER—to be **(soy, eres, es, somos, sois, son)**

TENER—to have **(tengo, tienes, tiene, tenemos, tenéis, tienen)**

VENIR—to come **(vengo, vienes, viene, venimos, venís, vienen)**

DECIR—to say/tell **(digo, dices, dice, decimos, decís, dicen)**

IR—to go **(voy, vas, va, vamos, vais, van)**

ESTAR—to be **(estoy, estás, está, estamos, estáis, están)**

You also learned a few verbs that change in the "**Yo**" **form** only. We referred to these as the "**go**" **verbs**; for example **poner**-**pongo**; **salir**-**salgo** (Unit 3). There are a few others that have a change in the "**Yo**" form for you to practice.

Verbs such as **Conducir**—to drive; **Traducir**—to translate; **Producir**—to produce have a pattern. Other verbs such as **Conocer**—to know or be acquainted with a person, place or familiarity with a person or place also fit in this group of "Yo" changers although they change in a different way than the "go" group. We will learn more about conocer in the next unit but for now you will gain experience in forming the verb conjugations.

Did you notice anything that **conducir**, **traducir** and **producir** have in common?

Personas	conducir	traducir	producir
1era singular	conduzco	traduzco	produzco
2 da singular	conduces	traduces	produces
3 era singular	conduce	traduce	produce
1 era plural	conducimos	traducimos	producimos
2 da plural	conducís	traducís	producís
3 era plural	conducen	traducen	producen

It is noted in the chart below for the "**YO**" form only:

If the inifinitive ends in **ucir**	then add a Z before the C in the root
If the infinitive ends in **cer** *	then add a Z before the C in the root

Please learn the patterns of the verbs that have the "**zc**" changes.*Remember "hacer" is **part of the "go" verb changers and the rule above** does not apply **to hacer.**

Please answer the questions in Spanish:

1. ¿Conduces a Geneseo? _____

2. ¿Qué días conduces a Geneseo? _____

3. ¿Traduces mucho en la clase de español? _____

4. ¿Traducen de inglés a español los estudiantes? _____

5. ¿Qué produce Apple o Dell? _____

6. ¿Conoces bien Geneseo? _____

7. ¿Reduces la cantidad de basura por reciclar las cosas plásticas? _____

_____

Many verbs have their unique changes. The best way to learn them is to create flashcards with the verb infinitive on one side and the meaning and if the verb is regular o irregular.

Another way to master the many irregular verbs in their infinitive is noted for you in the chart below. Take the verb **Acordar** for example and provide all the conjugations for it in the present tense. Repeat until you have mastered the fact that **Acordar** is an irregular verb.

So how are these verbs irregular and exactly what are does that mean?

IRREGULAR VERBS in the PRESENT TENSE in the INDICATIVE MOOD:

In order to succeed in conjugating verbs you need to know the **AR, ER** and **IR** verb endings well. They apply to the irregular verbs as well as the regular verbs. One factor that makes an irregular verb **"irregular"** is that the "root" or "stem" changes but the endings are the same as they would be for **AR, ER or IR** verbs.

Let's see an example:

Singular		Plural	
yo	o	nosotros (as)	amos
tú	as	vosotros (as)	áis
él, ella, Ud	a	ellos, ellas, Uds	an

Empezar (to begin) is an irregular verb. The root or stem is "empez" and the ending is "**AR**". The **endings** for the "**AR**" verbs that you already know are:

Singular		Plural	
yo	empiezo	nosotros (as)	empezamos
tú	empiezas	vosotros (as)	empezáis
él, ella, Ud	empieza	ellos, ellas, Uds	empiezan

Empezar is an irregular verb because it has a change in the root or stem: "EMPEZ" → the second "E" changes to "IE."

The change in the root or stem applies to all forms except nosotros and vosotros. To provide you with a visual for this concept, think of this verb as a "boot verb".

Persona del singular	Conjuagación	Persona del plural	Conjugación
primera	empiezo	primera	empezamos
segunda	empiezas	segunda	empezáis
tercera	empieza	tercera	empiezan

Notice that nosotros and vosotros forms are outside of the boot. This means all forms change in the stem EXCEPT nosotros and vosotros.

Remember that as you study the vocabulary after this section practice conjugating all forms several times to master the stem changing verbs. Hint: Many dictionaries indicate a verb is a stem changing verb by placing the vowel pattern in parenthesis after the word. This may prompt you to recall the correct conjugations.

Pensar (e → ie) —to think

Singular		Plural	
yo	pienso	nosotros (as)	pensamos
tú	piensas	vosotros (as)	pensáis
él, ella, Ud.	piensa	ellos, ellas, Uds.	piensan

Comenzar (e → ie) —to begin

Singular		Plural	
yo	comienzo	nosotros (as)	comenzamos
tú	comienzas	vosotros (as)	comenzáis
él, ella, Ud.	comienza	ellos, ellas, Uds.	comienzan

Querer (e → ie) —to want, wish, love

(Notice that this is an **"ER"** verb so use the **"ER"** endings.)

Singular		Plural	
yo	quiero	nosotros (as)	queremos
tú	quieres	vosotros (as)	queréis
él, ella, Ud.	quiere	ellos, ellas, Uds.	quieren

The following irregulars change the "o" to ue" in the root. Again the endings are all the same as your regular **AR, ER, IR** endings. Let's start with poder (to be able to.) You are already an expert on this verb in the "yo" form—**yo puedo.**

Poder (o → ue) —to be able/can

Singular		Plural	
yo	puedo	nosotros (as)	podemos
tú	puedes	vosotros (as)	podéis
él, ella, Ud.	puede	ellos, ellas, Uds.	pueden

Practice with the following verbs; ACORDAR, VOLVER and DORMIR. As you do so, pay attention to the type of verb each of these represents and, of course, to their stem change.

ACORDAR DE (o → ue) —to remember

Notice that "acordar" always is followed by the preposition de

Singular		Plural	
yo		nosotros (as)	
tú		vosotros (as)	
él, ella, Ud.		ellos, ellas, Uds.	

VOLVER (o → ue) —to return

Singular		Plural	
yo		nosotros (as)	
tú		vosotros (as)	
él, ella, Ud.		ellos, ellas, Uds.	

DORMIR (o → ue) —to sleep

Singular		Plural	
yo		nosotros (as)	
tú		vosotros (as)	
él, ella, Ud.		ellos, ellas, Uds.	

Observe el video 1.4.6 and listen to the song about stem changing verbs. It may help you recall the patterns. Now conjugate Jugar and Servir.

JUGAR A (u → ue) —to play a game or sport.

*Notice that Jugar always is followed by the preposition a when speaking about a game or sport only; not when playing with a person.

Singular		Plural	
yo		nosotros (as)	
tú		vosotros (as)	
él, ella, Ud.		ellos, ellas, Uds.	

SERVIR (e → i) —to serve

Singular		Plural	
yo		nosotros (as)	
tú		vosotros (as)	
él, ella, Ud.		ellos, ellas, Uds.	

Practiquemos: Let's practice

Observa el website 1.4.7 to practice the conjugations by writing them while using the program to verify your answers. Complete the chart repeatedly to gain mastery. You will later be able to apply this knowledge to the in-class practices.

Use this list of verb related vocabulary for the unit on the next page. Print and fold the list in half and quiz yourself by writing and speaking the answers to the expressions. (A master list of the vocabulary in this format may be found at the end of each unit.) Unfold the list, to check your answers. Place a checkmark next to the ones you have mastered well and practice again those that you did not recall easily.

With a partner, you can ask the expressions and place a checkmark by the ones your partner has mastered on his or her practice sheet. This will help them identify the verbs they have mastered and those they need to practice more.

	EN ESPAÑOL	EN INGLÉS	What are the conjugations of the verb?	1	2	3
1	*Acordar de (o—ue)					
2	Acostar (o—ue)					
3	Buscar					
4	Consegir (e—i)					
5	Construir					
6	*Deber de					
7	Decir (e—i)					
8	Desear					
9	Despedir (e—i)					
10	Despertar (e—ie)					
11	Devolver (o—ue)					
12	Dormir (o—ue)					
13	Esperar					
14	Gustar					
15	*Jugar a (u—ue)					
16	Mentir (e—ie)					
17	Morir (o—ue)					
18	Necesitar					
19	Preferir (e—ie)					
20	Querer (e—ie)					
21	Recomendar (e—ie)					
22	Romper					
23	Seguir (e—i)					
24	Sentir (e—ie)					
25	Servir (e—i)					
26	Sugerir (e—ie)					
27	Temer					
28	Volar (o—ue)					
29	Volver (o—ue)					

*Acordar de y jugar a always necesitan la preposición, deber de puede llevar o no la preposición dependiendo del uso.

Take this list one step further and practice the conjugations of each of the verbs. Say aloud all of the present tense conjugations for the verb. This means, say the yo form, tú form, etc through the ellos, ellas, ustedes form. **This may seem redundant but it is the best way to recall the verbs that have stem changes in the present tense in the indicative mood.**

7. Recordemos las estructuras verbales.

As you remember from Unit 3, Spanish has diferent kinds of grammatical structures to help us express a thought. The structures that we studied can be classified as follows:

+ The two verb rule.

+ Present progressive.

+ Ir + a + infinitive.

+ Tener + que + infinitive.

+ Deber + infinitive.

+ Gustar and similar verbs.

a) The two verb rule

These structures are formed by the combination of two verbs. If two verbs are used consecutively without a break in the subject or a conjunction (and, but, or), the first verb is conjugated and the second one stays in the infinitive. **When two verbs are walking, the first does the talking.** The verb that tells you the most is the first one because it is broken out by the subject. (The first verb means more in a sense.)

Think about the whole point of this book. **Yo puedo hablar** en español. **Yo puedo escribir** en español. **Yo puedo comprender** español. **Yo puedo entender** otras culturas.

¡Yo puedo tener muchas oportunidades siendo bilingüe!

Also we studied some structures where the verbs require a preposition between the conjugated verb and the infinitive such as:

+ **Vamos a estudiar** en casa de Juan.

+ **Tiene que estar** en casa.

+ **Debe esperar** a su hermano.* Notice: Deber can use or not the preposition de.

To the list of verbs above we will add one more verb for now that always needs a preposition. The first one that we will study is "**jugar**". In the next section we will study the other one.

Juego al (a el) fútbol todas las mañanas.

Juego a las muñecas *(dolls)* con mi amiga Beth.

Jugar always is followed by the prepositon a. The contraction of the preposition a and the article "el" = "a + el"= "al". This helps separate the sounds and is similiar to English when we say a bird vs an owl.

b) Present progressive

Do you remember the progressive form of the verbs? In English, we have the present progressive and past progressive. In Spanish, we have the progressive form in all the tenses. The progressive forms in Spanish are only used for emphasis, for instance, to emphasize that an action is taking place at a particular moment, as opposed to another time, or to stress continuity of the action. In English, the progressive tenses are used far more frequently and they are used for habitual actions, to state general truths, or to indicate that an action is happening at a specific moment.

The formula for the Spanish progressive forms is:

Auxiliar verb estar (conjugated in the tense needed) + **the gerund** (The "ing" form equivalent

¡**Estamos saliendo** ahora mismo! → We are leaving right now!

The gerund cannot stand alone as it is not a conjugated verb. To form the **gerund**, take the root + "ando" in AR verbs. Take the root + iendo in the ER and IR verbs: hablar → hablando. beber → bebiendo, vivir → viviendo.

To express the concept of an action in progress you need the verb "estar" conjugated in the tense that the action is happening (present, past, future) plus the gerund. Again we are applyng the two verb rule: **when two verbs are walking, the first does the talking**. In the progressive forms the first always is **"estar"** and the second part is a **gerund**.

When a verb is not conjugated it is called a verbal in English or verboide in Spanish. Until now we know two different types of **verboides**: gerund and infinitive. Later we will study the third one.

The **progressive forms** work as a structure: Estar (conjugated) + (gerund).

He is **running**.　　　　　　　　　She is **walking**.

Él está **corriendo**.　　　　　　　Ella está **caminando**.

c) Ir + a + Infinitive

As you recall, in Spanish, there are two ways **to express the future**. One is conjugating the verb in the future tense, and the other, more basic form used mostly in spoken Spanish, expresses plans **(future actions)**. The structure **"ir + a + infinitive"** will help us express **the future**, using the verb conjugation in present tense.

So far we've been learning conjugations in the indicative mood, at the present time. The construction **"ir + a + infinitive"** is extremely useful since you know the conjugation of the **verb to go** in the indicative mood in the present tense. With this knowledge **we can express any action in the future**, without knowing the conjugations for the true future tense.

Voy a nadar en la tarde.　　　　→ I'm going to swim in the afternoon.

Pedro y Dulce **van a** bailar hoy.　→ Pedro and Dulce are going to dance today.

¿Qué **van a** hacer hoy?　　　　　→ What are you going to do?

¡Claro que **vamos a** la fiesta!　　→ Of course we are going to the party!

Rosa **va al** cine.　　　　　　　　→ Rosa is going to the movies.

*Notice that the preposition "a" **comes after** ir when you want to say that someone is going to a place. When a is followed by the masculine definite article→ a + el (definite article) the **contraction al is mandatory**.

d) Tener + que + Infinitive

Sometimes adding a preposition after the conjugated verb changes the meaning significantly. An example is the verb "have" that we already studied: TENER:

Yo **tengo** 20 años.

Mi hermano **tiene** una casa.

Nuestros hijos **tienen** muchos juguetes (toys).

If we use Tener + que + Infinitive, the meaning is **HAVE TO**. In English and in Spanish we use this structure to express the idea of it being necessary to do something. **It is a responsibility.**

Tengo que estudiar las estructuras en español. → I **have to** study the Spanish structures.

Vosotros **tenéis que leer** la novela. → You (all) **have to** read the novel.

¡No **tengo que hacer** tarea hoy!. → I do not **have to** do homework today!

e) Deber + Infinitive

Spanish also has another structure to express obligation, but in this case it is a DUTY. We use the verb Deber + infinitive. As with the verb **tener**, the verb **deber** changes in meaning with or without the preposition. The verb **deber** without the preposition means **to owe**; an example is:

Juan **debe** el dinero a Pedro. → Juan **owes** the money to Pedro.

Deber has a completely different meaning when coupled with an infinitive as in must or should as a duty or moral obligation.

Margarita **debe ser honesta con** el doctor. → Margarita **must** be honest with the doctor.

Juan **debe** pagar la mátricula. . → Juan **must** pay the tuition.

Nosotros **debemos** llamar al 911. → We **must** call 911.

Deber de + infinitive is more for an expression or supposition. María debe de ser la persona más simpática del mundo. María **must be or has to be** the nicest person in the World.

f) Gustar and similar verbs

Another structure that we already studied is GUSTAR to indicate something or someone is pleasing to a person. As you recall, it has 4 components:

Person that is pleased (Indirect object -optional)	Indirect Object Pronoun	Gustar* Conjugated in Third person	Something or Action That is pleasing
A mí	me	gusta	el libro
A ti	te	gustan	los libros
A él, a ella, a usted	le	gusta	cantar
A nosotros	nos	gusta	cantar y bailar
A vosotros	os	gustan	las clases
A ellos, a ellas, a ustedes	les	gusta	el chocolate

*Remember: for **actions** or **singular** things we use gusta; for plural things we use gustan.

To analyze the structure gustar and how it works, remember some basic grammar elements. A **sentence** is the expression of a thought formed by the **subject** and the **predicate**. The predicate is formed by the **core** (conjugated verb) and the **complement** (extra information).

Sentence: **Noah speaks Spanish to Trevor.**

Sentence:	Noah	speaks	Spanish	to Trevor.
Subject:	person, animal or thing that does the action (conjugated verb): **Noah**			
Predicate: Core:		speaks Spanish to Trevor **speaks → action (conjugated verb)**		
Complement:			Extra information: **Spanish to Trevor**	

Sometimes it is not so simple to find the subject in a sentence at first glance. Look for the verb to help you determine **who?** or **what?** does the action.

Verb (core of the predicate): speaks

Who speaks Spanish? Noah is the answer!

Noah is the **subject** of our sentence.

Noah is doing the action.

The complement in the predicate is the **extra information.** The extra information is a word (or words) that are needed to complete the meaning of a sentence. Now we will study the direct and indirect complements, also known as direct or indirect objects.

The **Indirect Object** tells to whom or for whom something is done. To identify the **indirect object** we only need to ask "**to/for whom**" or "**to/for what**" the action is done:

To whom does Noah **speaks**? **To Trevor**

Trevor is the **indirect object.**

The **Direct Object** receives the action of a verb. It answers the questions "**what or whom**" about the verb.

What does Noah **speak**? **Spanish**

Spanish is the **direct object.**

Let's see more examples:

John and Karla	watch	TV	
Subject: who watches? John and Karla			
	Predicate: watch TV.		
	Core: watch.		
		Complement: TV.	
		Direct Object: what do they watch? TV.	
			Indirect Object: there is no indirect object.

As you see, not all sentences need to have a direct and indirect object. You find sentences with none, both, or only with one. Let's see other examples:

John	writes	his brother	
Subject: Who writes? John.			
	Predicate: writes his brother.		
	Core: writes.		
		Complement: his brother.	
		Direct Object: what does he write? There is no direct object	
			Indirect Object: to whom does he write? To his brother .

Now it is your turn: Identify the elements by dissecting the sentences and noting the parts that correspond below.

John	gives	his sister	a gift
Subject:			
Predicate:			
	Core:		
	Complement:		
		Direct Object:	
		Indirect Object:	

John	sees	the house	
Subject:			
Predicate:			
	Core:		
	Complement:		
		Direct Object:	
		Indirect Object:	

John	sings	a song	to his baby
Subject:			
Predicate:			
	Core:		
	Complement:		
		Direct Object:	
		Indirect Object:	

Bearing in mind the components of a sentence, let's review the structure gustar. This structure indicates some activity or activities (with the verb in infinitive) or a thing(s) that is/are pleasing to a person. This structure doesn't have a conventional formation: **sujeto + predicado (verbo + complement).** We start with the indirect object pronoun that agrees with whom is receiving joy or pleasure.

Sentence: **Me gusta el chocolate.**

We can start the sentence with the Indirect Object Pronoun, or we have the **option to start by emphasizing or clarifying** who is the Indirect Object. We will review this point later. For now we are going to start with the Indirect Object Pronoun, which is a pronoun that receives the action of the verb.

GUSTA means **something is pleasing.**

What is pleasing? **The chocolate!**

The subject is the chocolate, the thing which **provokes pleasure.**

Notice the **subject** for the verb "**gustar**" is after the verb. This is what was meant by looking at the verb to determine who your subject is. With the verbs that work like "gustar", the subject is after the conjugated verb.

To find an Indirect Object we need to answer "to/for WHOM" or "to/for WHAT" the subject is pleasing.

To whom **the chocolate** is pleasing?

¿A quién le gusta el chocolate? A mí → indirect object.

Notice the Indirect Object Pronouns represent the Indirect Object in the sentence; who receives the consequences of the actions of the subject.

(A mí) me gusta el chocolate.

Indirect Object Pronouns	
Me	**Nos**
(me)	(us)
Te	**Os**
(you, informal)	(you all, informal) [Spain only]
Le	**Les**
(him, her, or you formal)	(them or you all formal)

Remember the structure "gustar" is not following the conventional form **sujeto + predicado (verbo + complement)** → **the structure is backwards:** (predicado (complement verb) + subject.)

Oración:	(a mí)	me gusta	el chocolate
Predicado:	(a mí)	me gusta	
Core:		gusta	
Complement:	(a mí)	me	
Objeto Indirecto: ¿A quién gusta el chocolate?	(a mí)		
Pronombre de Objeto Indirecto		me	
Sujeto			el chocolate

If we would like to use the conventional form writing **sujeto + predicado (verbo + complement)**, we need to change the sentence **Me gusta el chocolate** to El chocolate me place. The meaning doesn't change, we are expressing the same idea with another verb, and in this case the sentence follows the conventional form.

Oración:	El chocolate	me place	(a mí)
Sujeto	el chocolate		
Predicado:		me place	(A mí)
Core:		place	
Complement:		me	(A mí)
Objeto Indirecto: ¿A quién place el chocolate?			a mí
Pronombre de Objeto Indirecto		me	

Estructura del verbo "gustar"				Hace la acción
Complemento (opcional)	(negacion)	obligatorio	Verbo	sujeto
(a mí)		me	gusta	• nombre singular • infinitivo (accion) • infinitivos (acciones)
(a tí)		te		
(a él / ella / usted)	(no)	le		
(a nosotros / nosotras)		nos	gustan	• nombre plural
(a vosotros / vosotras)		os		
(a ellos / ellas / ustedes)		les		

Pronombres de objeto indirecto recibe la consecuencia de la acción

Me **gusta** el chocolate.

El chocolate me **place**.

Indirect Object Pronouns	
Me (me)	**Nos** (us)
Te (you, informal)	**Os** (you all, informal) [Spain only]
Le (him, her, or you formal)	**Les** (them or you all formal)

In the sentence,"**Me gusta el chocolate**," I have the option to emphasize to whom the chocolate is pleasing using the optional part of the structure: a mí me **gusta el chocolate.**

As you can see in the sentence, we have the indirect object pronoun "me" and also have the indirect object "a mí". That is the reason why it is optional, we really don't need to have the **indirect object pronoun** and the indirect object, but we use the indirect object for **emphasis**.

In the case of the third persons in the singular or in the plural, we use the indirect object pronoun and the indirect object to **clarify...** let's see the following example:

Le **gusta el chocolate**

To whom is the chocolate pleasing?

¿A quién provoca placer el chocolate? le → Indirect Object Pronoun

Who is the indirect object**?**

I don't know who the indirect object is. It can be "ella, él or usted." Who is it?

I need to clarify. I need to use the optional section of the structure to specify who it is:

A ella le gusta el chocolate, a Juan le gusta el chocolate o a usted le gusta el chocolate.

In summary, with **the structure gustar and similar verbs,** use always the indirect object pronoun before the verb. In case we want to **emphasize** we can use the optional part of the structure, which is the indirect object as with the first and second persons (singular and plural). For the third person (singular and plural) the optional section has the function to **clarify** who the indirect object is.

Do you remember what other verbs use the structure gustar? _____

_____

The verbs that we studied are regular verbs, but now we will study an irregular one "DOLER". It changes the "o" to ue" in the root. Again the endings are all the same as the regular **ER** endings. Let's see the following examples:

Doler: to hurt, to ache: **¿A ustedes les duele correr y caminar?**

                                        A ellos les duelen los pies (feet).

As you notice "doler" is irregular. It changes the "o" to ue" in the root, the endings are all the same as the regular **ER** endings. Like "poder or dormir".

With all this information you can complete the following chart using the structure gustar and similar verbs with the verb: DOLER. **Don't forget for actions or singular things we use DUELE, for** plural **things we use** DUELEN. The structure DOLER indicates something or someone is hurting a person and has the four components as a similar verb that follow the structure GUSTAR.

Complete the following chart of components for the structure DOLER as in the example:

Person that is pleased (optional) Indirect Object	Indirect Object Pronoun	DOLER* Conjugated in Third person Duele or duelen	Something(s) or Action(s) that is/are hurting or aching Subject
A mí	me	duele	el brazo

TAREA: For homework apply what you learned about the new verbs and write 10 questions in Spanish using the "tú" form that you might use to get to know your future roommate better. You may include things like, "Do you sleep late? "Do you prefer to study in the dorm room or in the library?" "What things do you have for the dorm room or apartment?" What will you do on the weekend? Do you have to work? What are your duties? And also what he or she likes to do. Think about how you would answer these questions for yourself so you are prepared to answer these questions in partner activities. Remember to hand in your homework at the beginning of the next class.

8. Los pronombres de objeto indirecto (POI).

As you remember, **the subject and the predicate** are two parts of the sentence. **The subject** is who is doing the action. **The predicate** has the *core:* conjugated verb and the *complement* (extra information). An Indirect Object is part of the complement, it is extra information. The function of the Indirect Object is to indicate to whom or for whom an action is done. You have already learned the Indirect Object Pronouns with **"La estructura gustar y verbos similares".** The Indirect Object Pronouns are not exclusive of this structure. We can find indirect objects in several situations, for example:

Sentence:	Marie	reads	to her baby
Subject:	Marie		
Predicate:		reads to her baby	
Core (conjugated verb):		reads	
Complement (extra information):			to her baby
Indirect object (Marie reads to or for whom?):			to her baby

Indirect Object Pronouns	
Me	**Nos**
(me)	(us)
Te	**Os**
(you, informal)	(you all, informal) [Spain only]
Le	**Les**
(him, her, or you formal)	(them or you all formal)

The Indirect Object Pronoun precedes a conjugated verb **or** follows attached to the verboide (an infinitive or a gerund). The two options are correct.

María le **lee**	→ POI before conjugated verb **"lee".**
María le **tiene** que leer	→ POI before conjugated verb **"tiene".**
María tiene que leerle	→ POI attached to infinitive "leer".
María le está leyendo	→ POI before conjugated verb **"está".**

Está leyendo is in present progressive.

María está leyéndole   → POI attached to the gerund "leyendo".

Está leyendo is in present progressive.

Are you wondering why there is a written accent mark (an orthographic accent)? → leyéndole.   It is because the natural stress on the word leyendo is on the second "e", since the word ends in a vowel (Review Unit 1.2: La acentuación en español). When we add the extra syllable "le", we need to indicate where the natural stress was on the original word with el acento ortográfico → leyéndole.

Veamos otros ejemplos:

For each one of the following examples write the **subject of the sentence** (who is doing the action), **the action** (core of the predicate) and the Indirect Object (to whom or for whom the action is done).

Yo le canto una canción.

Sujeto:_____

Verbo:_____

Objeto Indirecto: _____

Pronombre de objeto indirecto: _____

Ella os enseña español.

Sujeto:_____

Verbo:_____

Objeto Indirecto: _____

Pronombre de objeto indirecto: _____

Juan les lee un cuento.

Sujeto:_____

Verbo:_____

Objeto Indirecto:_____

Pronombre de objeto indirecto: _____

Geneseo nos prepara para ser bilingües.

Sujeto:_____

Verbo:_____

Objeto Indirecto:_____

Pronombre de objeto indirecto: _____

Unfortunately the English verbs that require an indirect object pronoun, are not always the same in Spanish.

The following verbs are commonly used with indirect object pronouns (IOP).

Español	Inglés	Español	Inglés
contar (o-ue)	To tell	hablar	to speak
contestar	To answer	mandar	to send
dar*	To give	ofrecer	to offer
escribir	To write	pagar	to pay
explicar	To explain	preguntar	to ask a question
gritar	To shout, scream	regalar	to give a present

Dar irregular verb

Practiquemos: Write complete sentences using five of the verbs above with the different POI.

1._____

2._____

3._____

4._____

5._____

An **Indirect Object Pronoun (IOP)** can be emphasized or clarified by using a phrase introduced by the preposition **"a",** just as we studied with the structure "gustar". As you remember, the emphasis or clarification is optional.

for emphasis or clarification	IOP
a mí	me
a ti	te
a él, a ella, a usted	le
a nosotros/as	nos
a vosotros/as	os
a ellos, a ellas, a ustedes	les

Some examples:

Le escribo un email **a Juan**.

Tengo que escribirle un email **a Juan**.

¡Nos va a escribir un autógrafo **a nosotras**!

Debe de escribirnos un autógrafo **a nosotras**.

Quiero escribirte una carta **a ti**.

Te quiero escribir una carta **a ti**.

Now you use five other verbs from above and write complete sentences but clarify or emphasize the **IOP.**

1._____

2._____

3._____

4._____

5._____

9. En español evitamos la redundancia.

As you know conjugations in Spanish often let us know who the subject is. We can use the conjugated verb without the personal pronoun and still know who the subject is. That is not possible in English:

In Spanish these are clear.	In English, there are many possibilities for the subject.
Corres → the subject is "tú"	**run** → I run, **you** run, **they** run, **we** run ….
Bebo → the subject is "**yo**"	**drink** → I drink, **you** drink, **they** drink, **we** drink…
Bailáis → the subject is "**vosotros**"	**dance** → I dance, you dance, they dance…

Notice how in English "run, drink, dance" cannot stand alone. Many of the verbs in Spanish can stand alone and from them you know who is doing the action.

Spanish speakers do not like redundancy. It is a cultural aspect. When you use the personal pronouns all the time, Spanish speakers can interpret it as pretentious: **yo** corro, **yo** hablo, **yo** bebo, **yo, yo, yo**.

Let's read the next email with personal pronouns and without them:

Hola Mariana:

*¿Cómo estás **tú**? **Yo** estoy muy contenta. **Yo** tengo una gran noticia para ti. **Yo** estoy siguiendo tu consejo. **Yo** empiezo mis clases de español. **Yo** quiero ser una doctora bilingüe. **Tú** tienes razón, es importante que un doctor pueda hablar con todos sus pacientes. **Yo** sé que en los Estados Unidos el español es el segundo idioma más hablado. **Tú** eres mi ejemplo. **Tú** estudias negocios, tus padres son de Chile y **tú** estudias una especialización en español. **Nosotras** vivimos en un mundo global, **nosotras** debemos de ser bilingües o trilingües. ¿**Tú** puedes imaginar estudiar francés o árabe?*

*¿**Tú** qué piensas, a ti te gusta la idea de ser trilingüe?*

Un abrazo:

Beth

Hola Mariana:

*¿Cómo estás? Estoy muy contenta. Tengo una gran noticia para ti. Estoy siguiendo tu consejo. Empiezo mis clases de español. Quiero ser una doctora bilingüe. Tienes razón, es importante que un doctor pueda hablar con todos sus pacientes. Sé que en los Estados Unidos el español es el segundo idioma más hablado. **Tú** eres mi ejemplo. Estudias negocios, tus padres son de Chile y estudias una especialización en español. Vivimos en un mundo global, debemos de ser bilingües o trilingües. ¿Puedes imaginar estudiar francés o árabe?*

¿Qué piensas, a ti te gusta la idea de ser trilingüe?

Un abrazo:

Beth

Answer the following questions after analyzing the two emails:

1. ¿Cuántos pronombres personales se pueden evitar escribir? _____

2. En el segundo correo electrónico qué uso tiene "tú" y "a ti", ¿**Son utilizados para enfatizar o para clarifi**car?_____ ¿Por qué?_____

3. En la oración: "Ella necesita estudiar otros idomas" ¿El pronombre personal se utiliza para enfatizar o para clarificar?_____ ¿**P**or qué?_____

In conversations we frequently use Indirect Object Pronouns and Direct Object Pronouns to avoid redundancy, but before we can apply these terms, let's study what is a Direct Object.

Comprendamos los pronombres de objeto directo en el video 1.4.8. In this video we will understand how the direct object pronouns work in English and in Spanish.

---

10. Los pronombres de objeto directo (POD).

After studying the video, we now know what a direct object pronoun is in English and in Spanish. Recognizing the direct object pronouns, now we realize how often we use them in English. With this concept clear we are able to analyze the function of the direct object in the sentence. The direct object indicates who or what receives the action. The direct object is the person or thing that is directly affected by the action of the verb. It is part of the predicate. It answers the question **what** or **whom** receives the action.

Sentence:	Josefina	writes	a letter.
Subject:	Josefina		
Predicate:		writes a letter	
Core (conjugated verb):		writes	
Complement (extra information):			
Direct object (What does Josefina write?)			a letter

In the following chart, you will see the **personal pronouns**, the **indirect object pronouns (IOP)** and the **direct object pronouns (DOP)** for each one of the grammatical persons. As you can see the **IOP** and **DOP** are the same except in the 3rd person.

Person	Personal Pronouns	Indirect Object Pronouns	Direct Object Pronouns
1era singular	yo	me	me
2da singular	tú	te	te
3ra singular	**él, ella, usted**	le (se)	lo* / la
1era plural	nosotros/as	nos	nos
2da plural	vosotros/as	os	os
3ra plural	ellos, ellas, ustedes	les (se)	los* / las

The DOP identifies the gender of the direct object in the third person. That is the reason why we find two Direct Object Pronouns for the 3rd person singular: lo (masculine) or la (feminine) and two for the 3rd person plural: los (masculine) or las (feminine).

The difference between the Direct and the Indirect Object Pronouns is in the third person:

Direct Object Pronouns: Identify gender: " lo or la" and number: "los or las"

Indirect Object Pronouns: identify only number: "le or les"

Indirect Object Pronouns	Direct Object Pronouns
me	me
te	te
le	lo* / la
nos	nos
os	os
les	los* / las

Oración:	Josefina	escribe	una carta
Sujeto	Josefina		
Predicado:		escribe una carta	
Núcleo (verbo conjugado):		escribe	
Complement (Información extra):			
Objeto Directo: ¿Que escribe Josefina?			una carta ← **Gender: feminine**

Podemos usar el Pronombre de Objeto Directo: Josefina la escribe.

In this case, the gender of "carta" is feminine, but imagine that Josefina writes a book:

What is the gender of the word "libro"? _____.

Now re-write the sentence using the correct direct object pronoun that corresponds to "libro": _____

The following verbs in Spanish frequently take a direct object: The Direct Object Pronouns follow the same placement rules as the Indirect Object Pronouns, before the conjugated verb or attached to the verbal (el verboide en español.)

   Josefina lo tiene que escribir.

   Josefina tiene que escribirlo.

   Josefina lo está escribiendo.

   Josefina está escribiéndolo.

Remember, why do we use the orthographic stress? Write the reason here:_____

_____

The following verbs in Spanish can frequently take a direct object:

Español	Inglés	Español	Inglés
amar	to love	odiar	to hate
ayudar	to help	querer	to want; to love
detestar	to detest	respetar	to respect
esperar	to wait for*	ver	to see
invitar	to invite	visitar	to visit
necesitar	to need	golpear	to hit

*Esperar also can mean to hope, in that case we don't need a DOP.

In conversations we frequently use direct object pronouns to avoid redundancy, as in the next examples:

   Pedro: Hola Juan, ¿Está todo listo para la fiesta de tu hermano? **¿Tienes las invitaciones?**

   Juan: Sí, acabo de enviarlas

   Pedro: ¿Sabes si Laura va a la fiesta?

   Juan: No sé, la voy a invitar esta noche. La voy a ver en casa de mis padres.

   Pedro: ¿Tienes el regalo para tu hermano?

   Juan: Sí, lo tengo aquí.

   Pedro: ¡Aquí está mi regalo! ¿Lo puedo poner con el tuyo?

   Juan: ¡Claro!

Practiquemos los pronombres de objeto directo en el video 1.4.9. After you have viewed the video and understand the concept examine the following email sent by Miguel and Marimar to their friends Noah and Trevor. In this case Miguel and Marimar avoid redundancy by not using the subject pronouns, but they were not able to use **Direct Object Pronouns**. In purple you will find the **Direct Objects,** please apply the **Direct Object Pronouns** to avoid redundancy. Re-write the message in the lines below replacing the direct objects with the direct object pronouns.

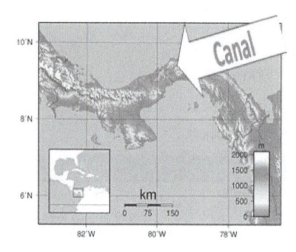

Queridos Noah y Trevor:

Estamos muy contentos en Panamá. Vimos el Canal de Panamá. Visitamos **el Canal de Panamá** por la tarde y es increíble. Esta obra impresionante une el océano Atlántico con el océano Pacífico es todo un símbolo de la ingeniería humana. Queremos sacar una foto del **Canal de Panamá**; Vamos a sacar **la foto** mañana. Vamos a enviar **la foto** a ustedes. Cuando ustedes vean **la foto** estamos seguros que van a venirnos a visitar en Panamá.

Un abrazo:

Marimar y Migue

_____
_____
_____
_____
_____
_____
_____

Practiquemos: Replace the direct object with the direct object pronouns when you rewrite the sentence.

¡Tienes una **canción nueva** en tu celular! ¿Puedo escuchar **la canción nueva**? <u>La puedo escuchar o puedo escucharla</u>_____

¿Cuándo vas a pintar **el baño de azul**? Mañana voy a pintar **el baño**. _____
_____

¿Dónde quieres poner **el sofá**? Quiero poner **el sofá** en la sala._____
_____

Tienes **tu teléfono**. ¿Puedo usar **tu teléfono**? _____
_____

¡Hace frío! ¿Por qué no cierras **la ventana**? Quiero **la ventana** abierta. _____
_____

¿Compras **un microondas hoy**? No, voy a comprar **un microondas** mañana. _____
_____

¿Quieres una **nueva televisión**? ¡Claro que quiero una **nueva televisión**! _____
_____

¡Amo* a **mi novio**! Amo tanto a **mi novio** que no puedo vivir sin él._____
_____

*El verbo amar en español. In Spanish, we use the verb "amar" only with people: ¡Amo a mi novio! In English it is common to use the verb love with objects or concepts: I love Spanish! I love chocolate! In these cases in Spanish, we use the structures that work like gustar: **¡Me fascina el español! ¡Me encanta el chocolate!**

You studied how to use the indirect and the direct object pronouns separately. Let's study how we can use the **direct and the indirect object pronoun** in the same sentence.

11. Las oraciones con objeto directo e indirecto.

A sentence always has a subject and a verb (core). It may contain a complement (extra information: direct object or indirect object or both). It is not mandatory to have direct and indirect objects. In the following example, the sentence has both the **direct and the indirect object**. Analyze each one of the components of the sentence:

The **subject** is **who** is doing the action.

The **indirect object** tells **to whom or to what or for whom or for what** the action is done.

The **direct object** is the person or thing that is directly affected by the action and answers the question **what or whom receives the action.**

Canto una canción a ti*

* *Never use* "a yo" *or* "a tú" *we use* "a mí" *or* "a ti".

Núcleo: **canto**
Sujeto: **¿Quién canta?** Yo

Complemento: Objeto Indirecto: ¿A quién canto una canción? A ti.

   Pronombre O. I. : te → se refiere a ti.

Objeto Directo: ¿Qué canto? Una canción.

   Pronombre O. D.: la → se refiere a una canción.

Indirect Object Pronouns	Direct Object Pronouns
me	me
te	te
le (se)	lo / la
nos	nos
os	os
les (se)	los / las

When we use both an **indirect and a direct object pronoun** in the same sentence, the **indirect object pronoun** goes first and then the **direct object pronoun**:

Canto **una canción** a ti → Te la canto.

Leo **un libro** a vosotros → Os lo leo.

Although the real-life application of this concept occurs via answers to questions, practice the concept by rewriting the sentences using the direct and indirect object pronouns. We intentionally left out the indirect and direct object pronouns although typically you would see the indirect object pronouns in the sentence along with the indirect object that is noted for emphasis or clarity. In class, we will practice with questions.

1. Juan escribe una carta a mí. _____

2. Rosario compra un regalo a ti. _____

3. La profesora enseña el objeto directo a Rosa._____

4. Ellos ayudan a estudiar el vocabulario a nosotros. _____

5. Yo vendo mi coche a vosotros. _____

6. Eduardo compra el café a ustedes. _____

Let's analyze your answers for sentences 3 and 6:

3. La profesora enseña los pronombres a Rosa.

Núcleo: enseña

Sujeto: ¿Quién enseña? La profesora

Complemento:

Objeto Indirecto: ¿A quién enseña? A Rosa

Pronombre O. I. : le

Objeto Directo:**¿Qué enseña?** los pronombres

Pronombre O.D. : los

La profesora le los* **enseña** (That does not sound right—keep reading to find out why.)

6. Eduardo compra el café a ellas.

Núcleo: **compra**

Sujeto: **¿Quién compra?** Eduardo

Complemento:

Objeto Indirecto: **¿A quién compra?** A ellas

Pronombre O. I. : les

Objeto Directo:**¿Qué compra?** el café

Pronombre O.D. : lo

Eduardo les lo* **compra** (That does not sound right either.—Keep reading to find out why.)

*The word "lelo" in Spanish means stunned, slow, or loony! We don't want to call any one "lelo!"

To avoid this problem when you use both the indirect and direct object pronouns with the 3rd person (singular o plural), the indirect object pronoun "le" and "les" becomes "se".

La profesora se los **enseña. Eduardo** se lo **compra.**

¡ Nunca use LELO o LELOS o LELA o LELAS ! Always use "SE" when you have an indirect object pronoun (LE or LES) and direct object pronoun (LO, LOS, LA or LAS) in the same sentence. ¡ No queremos tener LELOS! ☺

Don't forget that the direct and the indirect object pronouns either precede a conjugated verb or are attached to a verbal (verboide--infinitivo o gerundio).

La profesora se los **enseña.**	**Eduardo** se las **compra.**
La profesora se los **va a enseñar.**	**Eduardo** se las **va a comprar.**
La profesora va a enseñárselos.	**Eduardo va a comprár**selas.

When we use the indirect and direct object pronouns before the conjugated verb we have **two words**. When we use them attached to the infinitive, it is only **one word**. When we attach the indirect and direct object pronouns to the infinitive an **orthographic stress** is required on the syllable before the combined direct and indirect object pronouns:

Enseñár**selo**,   compr**ár**selo, regal**ár**selo, prepar**ár**selo…

Practiquemos los pronombres de objeto indirecto y directo en el **video 1.4.10**. After this video you will be ready to do your homework

TAREA: Write a dialogue between you and your best friend in Spanish about what school and home by including questions and answers with the goal of using the indirect and direct object pronouns, but also to apply all your Spanish knowledge. Use the different verbs that take a direct or indirect object, practice the structures, use your vocabulary and review your question words. The dialogue needs to have 20 questions with answers. You need to print your dialogue double spaced.

12. Expresemos actividades relacionadas al cuidado personal y la rutina diaria: Los pronombres reflexivos.

In the following paragraph let's review the grammar structures that are related to the 2 verb rule, verbs that require a preposition between the 2 verbs and also the present progressive form.

Yo **quiero** caminar en el parque, pero mi hermano **prefiere** caminar en el gimnasio. A él no **le gusta** el parque porque hace calor, pero yo **quiero** caminar en el lago (lake). No **quiero** caminar en el gimnasio porque soy entrenador (coach). ¡**Quiero** salir del gimnasio! **Tengo que** estar en el gimnasio todos los días de la semana y cuando **quiero** hacer ejercicio con mi hermano los fines de semana, ¡él **quiere** ir al gimnasio! **Debo de** buscar otro trabajo. **Necesito** trabajar fuera (out) del gimnasio. **Espero** tener un nuevo trabajo muy pronto (very soon) ¡**Voy a estar** muy feliz en mi nuevo trabajo! En este momento (in this momento), **estoy escribiendo** mi renuncia (resignation) para no trabajar más en el gimnasio.

All the conjugated verbs in this paragraph are actions that a subject (yo, mi hermano or él) is doing. The subjects are performing an action. There are actions related to personal care that often take another grammar element. Let's examine the following examples where the subjects are the recipient of the action:

She bathes herself.

The subject is performing the action for herself → **She bathes** herself.

 Me ducho en la mañana.

*I shower (**myself**) in the morning.*

Te **peinas** el pelo.

You brush your hair (**yourself**).

Se habla.

He/she is talking to (**himself**).

Me veo en el espejo.

I see (**myself**) *in the mirror.*

When the subject is performing the action toward or for him or herself, the action is called **reflexive**. In Spanish, many actions related to personal care or daily routines are **reflexive**. To indicate a **reflexive action** you need to use the **reflexive pronouns**. Compare the sentences below:

Ella baña al perro.

She bathes the dog. The *dog* is the object of *bathe*.

Ella se baña

She bathes **herself**. **She (herself)** is the object of *bathe*.

In both examples the verbs in Spanish follow the same conjugation. To make the action reflexive we need to use the **reflexive pronouns**. Pay attention that in Spanish the **reflexive pronouns** go before the **conjugated verb for an action that one does to oneself.**

When the object of the verb is the same person as the subject, you will need to use a reflexive pronoun that agrees with the subject of the verb in number (singular, plural) and in person (1st, 2nd, 3rd).

+ **Me** baño.   *I bathe myself.*

+ **Te** bañas.   *You bathe yourself.*

+ **Se** baña.   *He/She/formal You bathe(s) himself/ herself/ yourself.*

+ **Nos** bañamos. *We bathe ourselves.*

+ **Os** bañais.   *You wash yourselves.*

+ **Se** bañan.   *They wash themselves./You wash yourselves.*

In the following chart, you will find the **personal pronouns**, the **indirect object pronouns**, **the direct object pronouns** and the reflexive pronouns for each one of the grammatical persons.

Persona	Pronombres personales	Pronombres de objeto indirecto	Pronombres de objeto directo	Pronombre reflexivos
1era del singular	yo	me	me	me
2da del singular	tú	te	te	te
3era del singular	él, ella, usted	le (se)*	lo / la	se
1era del plural	nosotros/as	nos	nos	nos
2da del plural	vosotros/as	os	os	os
3era del plural	ellos, ellas, ustedes	les (se)*	los / las	se

***Don't forget** to avoid an insult lelo, lela, lelos or lelas; we use "se" instead of the "le" or "les".*

Reflexive pronouns have almost the same forms as indirect and direct object pronouns except "se" is used for the third person. The reflexive pronoun will always be the same person (1st, 2nd, 3rd) and number (singular, plural) as the subject of the sentence.

You already know how to use the reflexive pronouns, only you did not know their name! Remember when you started studying Spanish and you learned one of the ways to introduce yourself?

"me **llamo**",   "te **llamas**",   "se **llama**",

"nos **llamamos**",   "os **llamáis**",   "se **llaman**"

You can add reflexive pronouns to almost any verbs in order to make them reflexive. As we studied before in Spanish many actions related to personal care or daily routines are reflexive. To help to identify the most common Spanish verbs that require a reflexive pronoun, you will see attached to the infinitive the pronoun "se".

Notice that the reflexive pronoun corresponds to the same person as the verb ending. (Agreement)

Lavarse	(to wash one's self)	Yo me lavo las manos (hands.)
Dormirse (o→ue)	(to fall asleep)	Nos dormimos a las 9:00 de la noche.
Despertarse (e→ie)	(to wake up)	Ellos se despiertan tarde (late) todos los días.
Despedirse (e→i)	(to bid farewell to)	Tú te despides de mamá con un beso (kiss.)

Servirse	(e→i)	(to serve one's self)	Vosotros **os** servís la sopa (soup.)
Acostarse	(o→ue)	(to put one's self to bed)	Ustedes **se** acuestan a las 10:00 de la noche.
Romperse		(to break a part of one's body)	Juan **se** rompió la mano (*Juan broke his hand.*)

As you see, in the examples above the **reflexive pronouns** are placed immediately before the conjugated verb. There are grammar structures when you can attach the **reflexive pronoun** to the unconjugated verb (verboide), as we studied before with the indirect and direct object pronouns such as in the following examples:

Me voy a dormir. or **Voy a** dormirme.

Me tengo que despertar. or **Tengo que** despertarme.

Me debo de despedir. or **Debo de** despedirme.

Me estoy bañando. or **Estoy** bañándome.*

* Remember the orthographic stress

Notice: the two options are correct, the meaning is the same.

In the next list you have verbs related to personal care or daily routines that require a reflexive pronoun. Most are regular in the indicative mood, in the present tense, which you have already learned.

Verbos relativos al cuidado personal o rutina diaria.

Reflexion

afeitarse	to shave
bañarse	to bathe
cepillarse el pelo	to brush one's hair
cepillarse los dientes	to brush one's teeth
ducharse	to shower
lavarse (las manos)	to wash (one's hands)
maquillarse	to put on makeup
peinarse	to comb one's hair
ponerse la ropa	to put on clothes
quitarse la ropa	to take off clothes

Complete the following sentences with the appropriate form of the indicated reflexive verb: lavarse, maquillarse, afeitarse, peinarse, despertarse (e→ie).

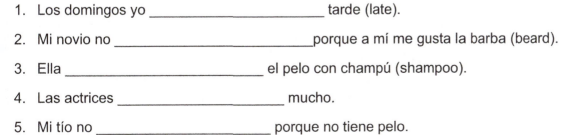

1. Los domingos yo _____ tarde (late).

2. Mi novio no _____porque a mí me gusta la barba (beard).

3. Ella _____ el pelo con champú (shampoo).

4. Las actrices _____ mucho.

5. Mi tío no _____ porque no tiene pelo.

Write the following sentences a different way by changing the position of the reflexive pronoun, but without changing their meaning. You will move the placement of the reflexive pronouns according to the examples we have shown you in the lesson.

1. Voy a lavarme el pelo._____

2. Ella no tiene que maquillarse. _____

3. Pedro se va a afeitar. _____

4. Tenéis que acostaros temprano. _____

Previously, we studied some irregular verbs related to the grammatical structures. We talked about verbs that always need a preposition and we studied "jugar a" as one of them. Also we already studied "acordarse de". As you remember these grammatical structures help us express ourselves correctly. In this case the verb "acordar" without the preposition means: **to agree; BUT** with the preposition "de" the meaning changes "to remember" and remember it is also a verb that requires a **reflexive pronoun: "ACORDARSE DE"**. Now you have all the elements to practice this versatile verb. Now you know that when a Spanish verb in the infinitive has the letters "se" attached, it is showing that it is a verb that requires a reflexive pronoun.

TAREA: Write 10 sentences related to personal care or daily routines. Don't forget to use the reflexive pronouns. Include when you do these activities or how often you do them to expand your skills. You will hand in your paper in the next class.

13. Evitando la redundancia por el uso de los pronombres de objeto directo e indirecto.

In all languages redundancy is not very accepted. When writing or speaking you should avoid redundancy. Languages have so many words that you can express similar thoughts using different words. This simple tactic will help you make your speech or your writing more pleasing.

In Spanish, as in English, writers frequently use pronouns to avoid redundancies using subject pronouns, direct object pronouns, indirect object pronouns and reflexive pronouns. As you recall the direct, indirect and reflexive pronouns only change in the third person.

Persona	Pronombres personales	Pronombres de objeto indirecto	Pronombres de objeto directo	Pronombre reflexivos
1era del singular	yo	me	me	me
2da del singular	tú	te	te	te
3era del singular	él, ella, usted	le (se)	lo / la	se
1era del plural	nosotros/as	nos	nos	nos
2da del plural	vosotros/as	os	os	os
3era del plural	ellos,ellas,ustedes	les (se)	los / las	se

The big difference between the three pronoun types is:

The **direct object pronouns** identify gender and number:

María escribe una carta. → María la escribe. → **una carta:** singular, femenino → la

María escribe unos emails. → María los escribe. → **unos emails:** plural, masculino → los

The **indirect object pronouns** identify only number:

María canta a su mamá. → María le canta. → **a su mamá:** singular → le

María canta a sus hermanos. → María les canta. → **a sus hermanos:** plural → les

The **reflexive pronouns do** not identify anything (no gender, no number), except that the subject receives the action or does the action to itself:

Laura se ve ,   Paco se cepilla,   Lupita se baña.

Remember the following rules:

Position 	Before the conjugated verb or attached to the infinitive or gerund (if it exists): Ella se **baña.** Ella se **tiene que** bañar. Ella **tiene que** bañarse. NEVER: ~~Ella tiene se que bañar.~~ ~~Ella tiene que se bañar.~~
Two pronouns	When we use two pronouns we always use first the indirect object pronoun and then the direct object pronoun. José me lo **debe de** regalar. ← Indirect + Direct José **debe de** regalármelo. ← Indirect + Direct NEVER separate them: ~~José me debe de regalarlo~~ . ← Keep the Indirect+Direct pronouns together. NEVER lelo, lelos, lela, lelas: Lelo, lelos, lela, lelas are words that can be interpreted as an insult: stunned, slow, or loony. Always change the indirect object pronoun "le" or "les" for "se" to avoid this situation when there is a direct object pronoun beginning with "L". ~~Laura le la tiene que mandar~~ → Laura se la **tiene que** mandar. ~~Laura tiene que mandárlela~~ → Laura **tiene que** mandársela.

Number of words	Before the conjugated verb each pronoun is a word.
	When they are attached to the infinitive or gerund, it is only one word that also needs an orthographic stress: **comérselo.**
	Él se lo está dando. ← 2 words → se lo
	Él está dándoselo. ← 1 word + orthographic stress
	NEVER:
	~~Él selo está dando.~~
	~~Él está dando se lo.~~

In the following paragraph the redundancy was not avoided. Write the paragraph again using the different pronouns to correct the redundancy:

La madrastra de Cenicienta (Cinderella), Lady Tremaine no es simpática con Cenicienta. Lady Tremaine tiene dos hijas llamadas Griselda y Anastasia. Griselda y Anastasia son muy feas y gritonas (screamers). Griselda y Anastasia no están bien educadas. Lady Tremaine les da a Griselda y a Anastasia todo. Griselda y Anastasia hacen la vida muy difícil para Cenicienta. Cenicienta está muy triste. Cenicienta trabaja todo el día y además Cenicienta tiene que servir a Anastasia y a Griselda. Cenicienta tiene que lavar la ropa de Anastasia y Griselda. Anastasia y Griselda son egoistas.

_____

_____

_____

_____

_____

_____

_____

_____

_____

_____

The Spanish language has another peculiarity, because the conjugated verbs indicate the subject of the sentence in Spanish it is preferable to **avoid the personal pronouns**, except when we want to clarify or emphasize. In English it is the opposite. We need to indicate who the subject of the sentence is. In Spanish we know who the subject is by the conjugated verb.

When we use the subject several times in the same paragraph, it can be interpreted as pretension.

Nosotras somos muy bonitas, **nosotras** somos elegantes, **nosotras** somos bellas, **nosotras** somos … **nosotras**… **nosotras**…

¡No queremos ser como las hermanastras de Cenicienta!

The follow conversation has too much repetition, please fix the conversation making it more natural in the space after each sentence.

Federico: ¿Piensas comprarle un regalo a tu hermano para su cumpleaños?

Since this first sentence establishes the setting you don't need to change anything.

Laura: Sí, el sábado, pienso comprarle un regalo a mi hermano para su cumpleaños.

_____

Federico: Pero tu hermano está viviendo en Madrid ahora ¿verdad?

_____

Laura: Sí, mi hermano está viviendo en Madrid, yo pienso mandarle el regalo a mi hermano a Madrid.

_____

Federico: ¡Mandar el regalo a tu hermano a Madrid va a costarte mucho dinero a ti!

_____

Laura: ¡Yo sé, pero es una sorpresa que yo quiero darle a mi hermano.

_____

Federico: ¡Caray! Tú debes de querer mucho a tu hermano.

_____

Laura: Mi hermano es mi mejor amigo, yo quiero mucho a mi hermano.

_____

Federico: Entonces tú sabes qué regalo vas a comprarle a tu hermano.

_____

Laura: ¡Claro! Voy a comprarle a mi hermano una tarjeta de regalo del Corte Inglés.

_____

Federico: ¿Dónde vas a comprar la tarjeta de regalo del Corte Inglés?

_____

Laura: Yo voy a comprar la tarjeta del Corte Inglés por internet.

_____

Federico: Entonces… ¿tú no vas a mandarle un regalo a tu hermano desde Estados Unidos?

_____

Laura: ¡Claro que yo no voy a mandarle un regalo desde E.U.A.! ¡Yo no tengo tanto dinero!

_____

You've just studied many concepts that permit you to speak and write with more style in Spanish. You possess quite a bit of knowledge in a short period of time. As we move into the next unit, you will learn how to express possession and have opportunities to review all that you have learned thus far. Before that though, please answer the following questions:

[ ] Yes [ ] No **Can I hear Spanish and sometimes am able to listen and understand?**

[ ] Yes [ ] No **Can I recognize cultural differences between the Spanish speaking countries?**

[ ] Yes [ ] No **Can I use correct the sound of consonants C, G, J and H with each vowel?**

[ ] Yes [ ] No **Can I understand the differences between Spanish and English intonation?**

[ ] Yes [ ] No **Can I ask and talk about family members and their characteristics?**

[ ] Yes [ ] No **Can I exchange personal information including home and email addresses?**

[ ] Yes [ ] No **Can I talk about my home and label items in rooms?**

[ ] Yes [ ] No **Can I identify familiar people, places and objects?**

[ ] Yes [ ] No **Can I use Spanish expressions to indicate responsibilities, duties, likes and future intentions?**

[ ] Yes [ ] No **Can I understand the function of the indirect objects in a sentence?**

[ ] Yes [ ] No **Can I understand the function of the direct objects in a sentence?**

[ ] Yes [ ] No **Can I use correctly the direct object, indirect object and reflexive pronouns?**

[ ] Yes [ ] No **Can I talk about activities related to personal care or daily routines?**

[ ] Yes [ ] No **Can I speak and write more succinctly by avoiding redundancy in Spanish?**

If you answered "No" to any of these questions, review those sections again and see your professor.

Vocabulary

Español	M/F	Inglés	Clasificación
¿Qué hay de nuevo?		What's new?	Expresión
a la derecha		to the right	Adverbio
a la izquierda		to the left	Adverbio
abuelo/a	El, La	grandfather/grandmother	Sustantivo
aburrido/a		bored	Adjetivo
acordar (o—ue)		to remember	Verbo Irregular
acostar (o—ue)		to put in bed	Verbo Irregular
afortunado/a		fortunate/lucky	Adjetivo
alto/a		tall	Adjetivo
amarillo/a		yellow	Adjetivo
anaranjado/a		orange	Adjetivo
antipático/a		unpleasant	Adjetivo
asiento	El	chair	Sustantivo
ático	El	attic	Sustantivo
azul		blue	Adjetivo
bajo/a		short	Adjetivo
baño	El	bathroom	Sustantivo
barato/a		inexpensive, cheap	Adjetivo
basura	La	trash	Sustantivo
blanco/a		white	Adjetivo
boda	La	wedding	Sustantivo
buscar		to look for	Verbo Regular
café		brown	Adjetivo
cama	La	bed	Sustantivo
caro/a		expensive	Adjetivo
casa	La	house	Sustantivo
cocina	La	kitchen	Sustantivo
comedor	El	dining room	Sustantivo
cómico/a		funny; comical	Adjetivo
conseguir (e—i)		to get, obtain	Verbo Irregular
construir (i—y)		to build	Verbo Regular
cuñado	El	brother-in-law	Sustantivo
cuñada	La	sister-in-law	Sustantivo
debajo		under	Preposición
deber		to owe	Verbo Regular
deber (followed by an infinitive)		to have to/must	Verbo Regular
débil		weak	Adjetivo

decir (e—i)		to say/tell	Verbo Irregular
delgado/a		thin	Adjetivo
desear		to want/wish	Verbo Regular
despedir (e—i)		to say good-bye	Verbo Irregular
despertar (e—ie)		to wake up	Verbo Irregular
devolver (o—ue)		to return/give back	Verbo Irregular
dormir (o—ue)		to sleep	Verbo Irregular
dormitorio	El	bedroom	Sustantivo
encima		above/on top	Adverbio
enhorabuena		congratulations	Expresión
espejo	El	mirror	Sustantivo
esposa	La	wife	Sustantivo
esposo	El	husband	Sustantivo
estar casado/a		to be married	Expresión, Verbo Irregular
estar divorciado/a de		to be divorced	Expresión, Verbo Irregular
estoy de acuerdo		I agree	Expresión
estufa	La	stove	Sustantivo
feo/a		ugly	Adjetivo
fuerte		strong	Adjetivo
garaje	El	garage	Sustantivo
gato/a	El, La	cat	Sustantivo
girlfirend	La	girlfriend	Sustantivo
gordo/a		fat	Adjetivo
grande		big; large	Adjetivo
gris		gray	Adjetivo
guapo/a		pretty	Adjetivo
hermana	La	sister	Sustantivo
hermanastro/a	El, La	step-sibling	Sustantivo
hermano	El	brother	Sustantivo
hermoso/a		beautiful	Adjetivo
hija	La	daughter	Sustantivo
hijastro/a	El, La	step-child	Sustantivo
hijo	El	son	Sustantivo
hogar	El	home	Sustantivo
horno	El	oven	Sustantivo
inteligente		intelligent	Adjetivo
interesante		interesting	Adjetivo

joven		young	Adjetivo
jugar (u—ue)		to play a sport or game	Verbo Irregular
lámpara	La	lamp	Sustantivo
lavabo	El	sink	Sustantivo
lavadora	La	washing machine	Sustantivo
lo siento		I am sorry	Expresión
madrastra	La	step-mother	Sustantivo
madre (mamá)	La	mother	Sustantivo
madrina	La	god-mother	Sustantivo
marrón		brown	Adjetivo
mayor		older	Adjetivo
menor		younger	Adjetivo
mentir (e—ie)		to lie	Verbo Irregular
mesa	La	table	Sustantivo
microondas	El	microwave	Sustantivo
morado/a		purple	Adjetivo
morir (o—ue)		to die	Verbo Irregula
naranja		orange	Adjetivo
negro/a		black	Adjetivo
nieto/a	El, La	grandson/granddaughter	Sustantivo
no mucho		not much	Expresión
no muy bien		not very well	Expresión
novia	La	girlfriend	Sustantivo
novio	El	boyfriend	Sustantivo
nuera	La	daughter-in-law	Sustantivo
nuevo/a		new	Adjetivo
oficina	La	office	Sustantivo
olvidar(se)		to forget	Verbo Regular
paciente	El, La	patient	Sustantivo
paciente		patient	Adjetivo
padrastro	El	step-father	Sustantivo
padre	El	father	Sustantivo
padres	Los	parents	Sustantivo
padrino	El	god-father	Sustantivo
padrinos	Los	god-parents	Sustantivo
papá	El	father	Sustantivo
parientes	Los	relatives	Sustantivo
pase		come in	Expresión
pequeño/a		small	Adjetivo

perezoso/a		lazy	Adjetivo
perro/a	El, La	dog	Sustantivo
piso	El	floor	Sustantivo
pobre		poor	Adjetivo
preferir (e—ie)		to prefer	Verbo Irregular
primero/a		first	Adjetivo
primo/a	El, La	cousin	Sustantivo
pronto		soon	Expresión
puerta	La	door	Sustantivo
quisiera (querer)		I would like (very polite request)	Expresión
recomendar (e—ie)		to recommend	Verbo Irregular
refrigerador	El	refrigerator	Sustantivo
responsable		responsible	Adjetivo
rico/a		rich	Adjetivo
rojo/a		red	Adjetivo
romper (se)		to break	Verbo Regular
rosado/a		pink	Adjetivo
sala	La	living room	Sustantivo
secador	El	drier	Sustantivo
seguir (e—i)		to follow/continue	Verbo Irregular
segundo/a	El, La	second	Adjetivo, Sustantivo
sentir (e—ie)		to feel, regret, to be sorry	Verbo Irregular
ser soltero/a		to be single	Expresión, Verbo Irregular
servir (e—i)		to serve	Verbo Irregular
silla	La	seat	Sustantivo
sobrino/a	El, La	nephew/niece	Sustantivo
sofá	El	sofa	Sustantivo
sótano	El	basement	Sustantivo
suegra	La	mother-in-law	Sustantivo
suegro	El	father-in-law	Sustantivo
sugerir (e—ie)		to suggest	Verbo Irregular
teléfono	El	phone	Sustantivo
televisión	La	TV	Sustantivo
televisor	La	tv (actual electronic)	Sustantivo
temer		to fear	Verbo Regular

tener calor (go + e—ie)		to be hot	Expresión, Verbo Irregular
tener celos (go + e—ie)		to be jealous	Expresión, Verbo Irregular
tener éxito (go + e—ie)		to be successful	Expresión, Verbo Irregular
tener frío (go + e—ie)		to be cold	Expresión, Verbo Irregular
tener ganas de... (go + e—ie)		to feel like...(doing something)	Expresión, Verbo Irregular
tener hambre (go + e—ie)		to be hungry	Expresión, Verbo Irregular
tener miedo (de) (go + e—ie)		to be afraid (de)	Expresión, Verbo Irregular
tener paciencia (go + e—ie)		to be patient	Expresión, Verbo Irregular
tener prisa (go + e—ie)		to be in a hurry	Expresión, Verbo Irregular
tener razón (go + e—ie)		to be right	Expresión, Verbo Irregular
tener sed (go + e—ie)		to be thirsty	Expresión, Verbo Irregular
tener sueño (go + e—ie)		to be tired / sleepy	Expresión, Verbo Irregular
tener...años (go + e—ie)		to...years old	Expresión, Verbo Irregular
tercer/a		third	Adjetivo
tercero	El	third	Sustantivo
tío/a	El, La	uncle/aunt	Sustantivo
tome asiento		sit down	Expresión
tonto/a		silly; dumb	Adjetivo
trabajador/a		hard-working	Adjetivo
ventana	La	window	Sustantivo
verde		green	Adjetivo
viejo/a		old	Adjetivo
volar (o—ue)		to fly	Verbo Irregular
volver (o—ue)		to return	Verbo Irregular
yerno	El	son-in-law	Sustantivo

En la comunidad

Objectives

1. Learn and use various manners to show possession
2. Learn and apply the concepts for Spanish phonics that lead to spelling changes.
3. Learn the differences between "conocer vs saber".
4. Review Spanish language characteristics.
5. Fluency through linking words.
6. Learn the rules for Spanish punctuation and capitalization.
7. Review some of the more challenging grammar concepts to date.
8. Progress in reading comprehension and gain exposure to another mood in Spanish.

Contents

*"Give your mind a chance to travel
through foreign languages."*

Neil Simon

As you reflect on your journey in Spanish you may realize:

+ You can appreciate Spanish culture, while also valuing your own culture.

+ Knowing another language will expand your opportunities, improving your employment potential.

+ You have grown as a global citizen.

+ You possess a great deal of knowledge for a beginning level student of a second language. It takes much practice to maintain and improve language skills so we will start this chapter with a new concept to give you more time to really take ownership of it.

1. Expresando posesiones: Adjetivos posesivos cortos, largos y preposición "de".

There are a few ways to express possession or describe to whom or what something pertains. Remember in Spanish, we do not use " 's" to show possession but rather **the object is of the person** as in some of the examples above "**el arte de Pablo Picasso**" or "**al profesor de inglés.**

Possessive expression in Spanish	Definition	Placement	Example
De	Of /from	Object of the possession • verb "ser" • de • possesor	El libro es de Marisa*. El libro es de la profesora*. El libro es de él.

__Notice__ proper names don't need the article "__de__ Marisa", common names need the article "__de__ la profesora".

We can use the preposition **"de"** with all the personal pronouns except with **"yo"** and **"tú"**. Below we will study other options to express possession accurately.

We have also used throughout your studies other forms of possession called **possessive adjectives = adjetivos posesivos.** You know them in terms of **"mi nombre", "tu número de teléfono", "su dirección"** or **"nuestra casa", "vuestra familia", "sus profesiones", "nuestra clase",** etc.

Like subject pronouns, possessive adjectives are identified according to the person they represent:

Singular		Plural	
First person	my	First person	our
Second person	your	Second person	your
Third person	his, her, your	Third person	their/your

A possessive adjective identifies the possessor, instead of the objects possessed:

Is that **Pedro's** car? Yes, it is **his** car.

Is that **Mercedes's** car? Yes, it is **her** car.

In Spanish we have two sets of possessive adjectives: stressed and unstressed, also known as short and long possessive adjectives. Let's start with the short ones, because they are very common. The difference in Spanish is that possessive adjectives not only identify the possessor as in English, but also need to agree with the number of the possessed noun (possession), as do all **Spanish adjectives.**

Mi nombre es María	Mis nombres son José María
Possesor = YO	Possesor = YO
Possesion = nombre	Possesion = nombres
Número = singular	Número = plural
Adjetivo posesivo = mi	Adjetivo posesivo = mis
Verbo Ser = **singular**	Verbo Ser = **plural**

Adjetivos posesivos cortos: Need to agree with the number of the possession, except the plural of the first and second person. In these persons, the possessive adjectives need to agree in number (singular) and in gender (masculine/feminine).

Possesor	Gender	Possession singular	Possession plural
My		mi	mis
Your (tú form)		tu	tus
His,her, your (usted form)		su	sus
		su	sus
Our	Masculine	nuestro	nuestros
	Feminine	nuestra	nuestras
Your (vosotros/as form)	Masculine	vuestro	vuestros
	Feminine	vuestra	vuestras
Their, your (ustedes form)		su	sus

possesor :   possession: libro (singular y masculine)

Josefina tiene mi libro.   → Josefina has my book.

Josefina tiene tu libro.   → Josefina has your book.

Josefina tiene su libro.   → Josefina has her (his,your,their) book.

Josefina tiene **nuestro** libro. → Josefina has our book. → nuestro possessor 1st person plural

nuestro (possession singular y masculine) = libro

What happens if the possessions are some novels → novelas plural y femenino

Josefina tiene **mis** novelas. → Josefina has my novels.

Josefina tiene **tus** novelas. → Josefina has your novels.

Josefina tiene **sus** novelas. → Josefina has her (his, your, their) novels.

Josefina tiene **nuestras** novelas. → Josefina has our novels. → nuestras possessor 1st person plural.

nuestras possession plural y femenino=novelas

Keeping in mind that the possessive adjectives agree with the possession and not the subject of the sentence necessarily, use the table and follow the logic of the examples above to complete the following examples:

possesor   **possession:** libros (plural y masculine)

Josefina tiene _____ libros.   → Josefina has my books.

Josefina tiene _____ libros.   → Josefina has your books *(tú form)*.

Josefina tiene _____ libros.   → Josefina has her (his, your, their) books.

Josefina tiene _____ libros.   → Josefina has our books.

Josefina tiene _____ libros.   → Josefina has your (vosotros form).

Josefina tiene _____ libros.   → Josefina has their books.

It's very important that you pay attention to the placement of the possessive short adjectives!

Possessive Adjectives			
Mi/mis	My		Es mi libro.
Tu/tus	Your	**Before the noun**	¿Tienes tus cuadernos?
Su/sus	His, her, your		¿Cuál es su nombre?
Nuestro (a) (os) (as)	Our		Nuestras clases son divertidas.
Vuestro (a) (os) (as)	Your (Spain)		Vuestros estudiantes son inteligentes.
Su/sus	Their, your		Sus amigos son simpáticos.

We already studied the orthographic stress; with this knowledge in mind, we would like you to identify which is the correct sentence and why?

¿Es mi libro? or ¿Es mí libro? _____

¿Tienes tu cuaderno? Or ¿Tienes tú cuaderno? _____

If you don't know the difference review "el acento diacrítico" in unit 2.

Now analyze the next sentences and write the three possible possessors.

Su coche es nuevo.   Who is the possessor? _____

Su casa es vieja.   Who is the possessor? _____

Sus libros son caros.   Who is the possessor? _____

Because the possessive adjective "su/sus" has many meanings, we prefer to use the possessive expression that we studied above "DE" and a reference to the owner by name or pronoun.

Su coche es nuevo.   →   El coche de ella es nuevo.

Su casa es vieja.   →   La casa de él es vieja.

Sus libros son caros. →   Los libros de usted son caros.

Remember:

+ Possessive adjectives are identified according to the person they represent

+ Short possessive adjectives are placed before the noun.

+ Short possessive adjectives need to agree with the possession (noun) not with the possessor

Agreguemos: In Spanish we have another set of possessive adjectives called stressed or long possessive adjectives. They are used to add emphasis to the possessor and correspond to the English "of mine", "of yours", etc. One of the differences is that the long possessive adjectives have four forms to agree in gender and number for each person. Singular-masculine, singular-feminine, plural-masculine, plural-feminine. As with the short possessive adjectives, the gender and the number agree with the possession (noun possessed).

The next chart deals with possessive long or stressed possessives. You learned much about stress in Spanish already so this application will be easy for you.

Possessive adjectives in Spanish	Definition	Placement	Example
Mío(s) / mía(s)	My, of mine	After an object to show more emphasis than the possessive adjectives noted above.	El libro es mío. → It's my book.
Tuyo(s) / tuya(s)	your		La casa es tuya. → It's your house.
Suyo(s) / suya(s)	His, her, your	Your tone will indicate the difference when using the nuestro and vuestro forms.	La novela es suya. → It's her novel.
Nuestro(s) / nuestra(s)	Our		La comida es nuestra. → It is ours.
Vuestro(s) / vuestra(s)	Your (Spain)		No es vuestra. → No, it's yours.
Suyo(s) / suya(s)	Their, your		Los exámenes son suyos. → The exams are yours.

Hay un dicho: **Mi casa, es su casa**.
Ahora con los adjetivos largos: **la casa mía, es la casa suya**.

Notice: the different structures if we use the preposition "de" to express possession, the short possessive adjectives or the long possessive adjectives.

Artículo + Posesión **+ verbo ser (singular/plural) + de + possessor** → El coche **es de Juan**.

Verbo ser (singular/plural) **+ posesivo corto +** posesión → **Es su coche**

Artículo + Posesión **+ verbo ser (singular/plural) + posesivo largo** → El coche **es suyo**.

As you remember, the possessive adjectives for the third persons are ambiguous; we don't know who the possessor really is: she, he or you (formal). Then, it is better to use the preposition **de** to clarify:

La casa es **suya**.	or	Es **su** casa.	→	**La casa es** de ella.
El coche es **suyo**.	or	Es **su** coche.	→	**El coche es** de él.
Las novelas son **suyas**.	or	Son **sus** novelas.	→	**Las novelas son** de usted.
Los libros son **suyos**.	or	Son **sus** libros.	→	**Los libros son** de ellos.

Also we can use a proper name: La lámpara es de Beth. Here we are being very specific!

We can use the preposition "de" with all the personal pronouns except with **"yo" and "tú"**.

La cama es **nuestra**.	or	Es **nuestra** cama.	→	**La cama es** de nosotros.
El gato es **vuestro**.	or	Es **vuestro** gato.	→	**El gato es** de vosotros.
La novelas son **suyas**.	or	Son **sus** novelas.	→	**Las novelas son** de usted.

But NEVER: La silla es de tú or la mesa es de yo. ¡NUNCA!-->NEVER

¡Practiquemos!

Here you have a possession and a possessor, you need to write one sentence using the short possessive adjectives, one sentence using the long possessive adjectives and one more using the preposition "de". Pay attention to the gender and number of the objects and use the correct article as you need it.

Example:

Possession: televisiones.   Possessor: Juan y Paco.

a) Las televisiones son suyas. b) Son sus televisiones. c) Las televisiones son de ellos (Juan y Paco).

2. Possession: dormitorio.   Possessor: nosotras.

_____

_____

3. Possession: espejo.   Possessor: mi mamá.

_____

_____

4. Possession: basura   Possessor: vosotros.

_____

_____

5. Possession: microondas.   Possessor: El Doctor Pérez.

_____

_____

6. Possession: secador.   Possessor: yo.

_____

_____

7. Possession: oficina.   Possessor: el director y la secretaria.

_____

_____

8. Possession: perro.   Possessor: tú.

_____

_____

9. Possession: boda.   Possessor: mi novia y yo.

_____

_____

10. Possession: bolígrafo   Possessor: tu hermana

_____

_____

2. Tomando posesión de la fonética—un repaso y un poco más.

Several times we said that Spanish is phonetic, that we write it as it sounds. If we have good control of the vowels sounds, we can have a very good control of the Spanish pronunciation. We also studied that knowing the sound of each consonant or consonant group with each vowel is key. Here is a chart about the sounds of the vowels and the consonants that have changes.

	Sonido Inglés:	vocal a	vocal e	vocal i	vocal o	vocal u
Fonética irregulares: Consonante - vocal	K	ca	que	qui	co	cu
	G	ga	gue	gui	go	gu
	Gw	gua	güe	güi	guo	
	H	**ja**	**ge,je**	**gi,ji**	**jo**	**ju**
	Th, S	za	ce	ci	zo	zu
	S	sa	se	si	so	su
	silent	ha	he	hi	ho	hu

Let's revisit the verb **conducir (to drive)**, an **"IR" verb as it relates to the above chart.** Write the conjugation of the verb in the indicative mood in the present time:

yo   _____   nosotros/as   _____

tú   _____   vosotros/as   _____

él, ella, usted   _____   ellos, ellas, ustedes _____

Now read aloud the conjugation that you just wrote, did you note it correctly or does something sound wrong?

Remember the sound   K   with the letter **C**   is with the vowels a, o, u

the sound th/s   with the letter **C**   is with the vowels i, e

The verb condu**c**ir has **th/s** sound with the "I" but when we change the ending to conjugate the verb, we take off the" **ir**" and we use the ending "**o**". Then we are using the sound **K** with the vowel "**o**".

Can you hear the incorrect sound? ->   **yo condu**co   **nosotros/as condu**cimos

tú conduces   **vosotros/as condu**cís

él, ella, Ud. conduce   **ellos, ellas, Uds. condu**cen`

All the endings are the **th/s,** except in the first person (yo), where the **"co"** creates the sound **K**. To avoid this inconsistency, we add a **Z** before the last syllable co, to have the soft sound of **th/s** and then the **K** sound with the **o**.

yo conduz**co**   **nosotros/as condu**cimos

tú conduces   **vosotros/as condu**cís

él, ella, Ud. conduce   **ellos, ellas, Uds. condu**cen

Although we studied this pattern in the previous unit, we want to reinforce the concept of sound rules. By making this minor change, we keep the soft sound "th/s" along with the endings of the conjugation of the **infinitive verbs ending with "ir".** Go back to your conjugations above, note the difference in a different color pen to make it stand out.

There are several verbs that have this "phonetic irregularity" in the first person. In the next chart write the conjugation for the first person, in the indicative mood in the present, making the phonetic adjustment:

Verbo en infinitivo	Significado en inglés	Conjugación primera persona
conducir	To drive/ to lead	*yo conduzco*
deducir	To deduct	
introducir	To introduce	
producir	To produce	
reducir	To reduce/ to cut back	
reproducir	To reproduce	
seducir	To seduce	
traducir	To translate	

Let's see another example, conocer (to know). Following what we just studied, write the conjugation for the first person of the next verbs. Pay attention to the fact that the infinitive ends in "er".

Verbo en infinitivo	Significado en inglés	Conjugación primera persona
conocer	To know/ to meet	*Yo conozco*
crecer	To grow up	
establecer	To establish	
nacer	To be born	
obedecer	To obey	
parecer	To appear	

After this exercise, we recommend you make your flashcards: You don't need to write all the conjugations. In this case, you can write (reg with **ZC**) to help you remember the change that the verb has based on phonetics. Now you understand why it changes; **when you understand, you know!**

¡Hola!

Yo puedo hablar español

Below are other verbs that have some phonetic irregularities. You will be able to understand these irregularities if you remember the table:

Fonética irregulares: Consonante - vocal	Sonido Inglés:	vocal a	vocal e	vocal i	vocal o	vocal u
	K	ca	que	qui	co	cu
	G	ga	gue	gui	go	gu
	Gw	gua	güe	güi	guo	
	H	**ja**	**ge,je**	**gi,ji**	**jo**	**ju**
	Th, S	za	ce	ci	zo	zu
	S	sa	se	si	so	su
	silent	ha	he	hi	ho	hu

3. Las diferencias entre saber y conocer.

Since you just learned the present tense indicative conjugations for conocer, let's learn the differences between "conocer" and "saber".

> **Observa el video 1.5.1**, on the online platform and you will learn that both verbs mean **"to know"** but they are not the same.

Just as when you learned that ser/estar mean the same thing: **"to be"**, saber and conocer have their varying reasons for usage for "to know".

yo cono**zco**	nosotros conoc**emos**
tú conoc**es**	vosotros conoc**éis**
él, ella, Ud. conoc**e**	ellos, ellas, Uds. conoc**en**

Conocer: to know a person

to be acquainted with a person, place or object.

(In the past tense, it also means to have met someone for the first time.)

Remember when we talked about Celia Cruz and you listened to some of her music. ¿Conoces **la música de Celia Cruz?** Are you familiar with Celia Cruz's music? **Sí, yo conozco la música de Celia Cruz.**

Since you have not met her, you would say, **"Yo no conozco a Celia Cruz."** I do not know Celia Cruz.

Are you familiar with Cuba? Have you traveled there and know the area? **¿Conoces Cuba? Sí, conozco Cuba.**

Knowing information about Cuba such as the capital is Havana or that Celia Cruz is from Cuba requires a different verb indicating knowledge: "saber".

Saber: to know a fact, information, skill or talent.

(The opposite is true when used with no saber; meaning one is lacking in knowledge or ignorant of a fact, information, skill or talent.)

to know something by memory or by heart.

The conjugations for saber in the present indicative were in a previous unit. As in conocer, just the **"yo"** form is irregular.

yo sé	**nosotros sab**emos
tú sabes	**vosotros sab**éis
él, ella, Ud. sabe	**ellos, ellas, Uds. sab**en

Sabes que Celia Cruz es de Cuba. Sabes que la capital de Cuba es Habana.

Think about if you just arrived at Geneseo and you needed directions. You can ask:

"¿Sabe Ud. dónde está la biblioteca? ¿Sabe Ud. dónde puedo comprar los libros?

The answer would be, **"Sí, yo sé. La biblioteca está al lado del edificio Erwin.**

"Sí, yo sé. La librería está en la unión.

Practiquemos conocer y saber.

Write the conjugation for the verb that fits best with the sentence given and be prepared to indicate why you chose your answer.

1. Yo _____ a Juan. Somos muy buenos amigos.

2. Busco el libro. ¿ _____ usted dónde está?

3. Tengo que llamar a María. ¿ _____ (tú) su número de teléfono?

4. Pablo es joven. No _____ conducir.

5. ¿Quiere hablar bien el español? Es necesario_____ la fonética española.

6. La chica es muy popular. _____ a muchas personas en la universidad.

7. Nosotros _____ los cuadros (paintings) de Picasso. Nos gustan mucho.

8. Ud. y Humberto no _____ bien Acapulco. Es su primera vez en México.

9. Son bilingües. _____ hablar español e inglés.

10. Mis amigos y yo _____ esquiar bien.

11. ¿_____ tú al muchacho rubio?

12. La señora _____ Santo Domingo.*

13. Yo _____ donde está la República Dominicana.*

14. Yo no _____ al profesor de inglés.

15. Yo _____ que Madrid está en España.

*__Notice__ the difference between being familiar with a place (having traveled there perhaps) versus where it is located.

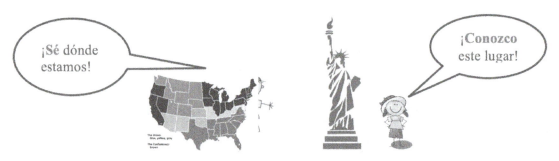

¡Sé dónde estamos!

¡Conozco este lugar!

¡Sabes mucho español ya (already)!

Aprendamos lugares en la comunidad:

Let's learn some more places in the community and some adjectives to describe these places. As you practice these, think of how you would answer the questions in your community for ¿**Sabes** dónde está _____(la biblioteca por ejemplo)? o ¿**Conoces** un buen restaurante? Remember knowing where a place is would require the use of "**saber**" vs being familiar with a place would require "**conocer**."

Unos lugares en la comunidad	Some places in the community
el apartamento	apartment
el banco	bank
la biblioteca	library
el cuerpo de los bomberos	fire department
la cafetería	cafeteria
el centro comercial	shopping center/mall
el cine	movie theatre
el consultorio	doctor's office
el corte	court
el estadio	stadium
el gimnasio	gymnasium
el hospital	hospital
la iglesia	church
la librería	bookstore
la oficina	office
la panadería	bakery
la peluquería	hairdresser
la plaza mayor	the main plaza/center of town
la policía	police department
la residencia	dormitory
el supermercado	supermarket
el teatro	theatre
la tienda	store

Los adjetivos	The adjectives
barato (a)	inexpensive, cheap
caro (a)	expensive
grande	big
pequeño (a)	small
hermoso (a)	beautiful
nuevo (a)	new
viejo (a)	Old
mayor	Older
menor	younger

menor   hermosa

Practiquemos con los **artículos indefinidos** y los lugares en la comunidad. Fill in the blank with the **indefinite article** and the type of place according to the community vocabulary above.

1. Wegmans es _____ _____.

2. _____ _____ son San José y San Patricio en la ciudad de Nueva York.

3. Strong y Rochester General son _____ _____.

4. El Doctor San Bernard ayuda a los perros. Trabaja en _____ _____ _____.

5. El lugar donde puedo guardar o sacar mi dinero es ____ _____ _____.

Contestemos: Answer in complete sentences to practice the community related words.

1. ¿Sabes dónde se puede ver la película "El Hobbit"?_____ _____.

2. ¿Cómo se llaman las residencias en Geneseo? _____ _____.

3. ¿Cuál es su supermercado favorito? _____ _____.

4. ¿En qué tipo de tienda se venden los libros?_____ _____.

5. ¿Qué número marco yo para la policía? _____ _____.

6. ¿Es grande o pequeño, el centro comercial Marketplace? _____ _____.

7. ¿Es hermosa la Plaza Mayor de Madrid? _____
_____.

Although we briefly touched upon some of the places in the community and a few new concepts, we will revisit these concepts in your next course. Having said that though, think of how far you have come in your first Spanish course. With practice and persistence you are able to discuss and write about yourself, your family and friends, your school life and home and your community. Some of the concepts we studied are below. Review them and take ownership of the information. Complete the extra practices on websites we have recommended and of course, consult your instructor if you would like additional assistance.

4. Recordemos las características del idioma español.

Let's review and summarize the different facts that define the Spanish language that we have studied. If any of these are unfamiliar or need review, review the previous units and see your instructor for help.

1. **The Spanish language is synonymous with Castilian = castellano.**

2. **Until March 1994, the Spanish alphabet had 30 letters**. Today the Spanish alphabet has 27 letters. After 1994, Spanish renamed the letters LL, CHE, and RR as consonant groups and the Ñ became an additional letter (Notice the ñ always has a tilde.)

3. **The Spanish alphabet is divided into vowels and consonants.**

4. **Spanish emphasizes the vowels**, which are always pronounced clearly.

5. **Vowel groups (diphthongs and triphthongs) cannot be divided into syllables.** Diphthongs are combinations of strong vowels (a, e, o) and soft vowels (i, u), while triphthongs are the next combinations: (iai / iei / uai / uei / uau).

6. **Consonant groups (as ch, ll, rr, br, gl, tr, pl, etc...) cannot be divided into syllables.**

7. **Spanish has only two double consonants: NN and CC** (*Since 1992).

8. **Spanish words are divided into syllables.** There are specific rules for the syllabic division.

9. **Spanish words always have a stressed syllable = sílaba tónica.** The stress is always on the vowel of the stressed syllable and there are specific rules to follow. If a word does not follow one of the rules, an orthographic stress (written accent) is required. An orthographic stress on the soft vowel breaks a diphthong or triphthong.

10. **Spanish is phonetic: you write Spanish according to what you hear.** There are a few silent letters such as "h" at the beginning of a word and "u" when it is used with "g" to make a soft sound with "i" and "e" as in **Mi**g**uel** or g**uitarra**. "U" is also silent with "q" to make a strong sound with the "i" and "e" as q**ué** or qui**én**.

11. **As in English, Spanish has many dialectal variations in the pronunciation of some sounds,** the "el seseo" in the north of Spain and the south of Spain and Hispano-America is an example.

12. **Spanish and English have cognates,** words that have a common etymological origin that may look and sound the same.

13. **Spanish is a language of emotions,** we use our body at the same time that we speak: hands, head, arms, etc. It is passionate; we use any element that is in our power to show our feelings and emphasize the meaning of our words.

14. **Spanish accentuates a negative answer:**

¿Estudias italiano?	**No**, yo **no** estudio italiano.
¿Te gusta Enrique Iglesias?	**No, no** me gusta.
¿Tienes mi libro?	**No, no** tengo tu libro / **No**, yo **no** tengo tu libro.

15. **Spanish punctuation** includes opened and closed question and exclamation marks. Spanish has a tilde over some vowels to represent the orthographic stress. Spanish has double dots only on the vowel "**ü**" called dieresis to break the silence of the "**u**" with g**ue** and g**ui** as "verg**ü**enza".

16. **All words have stress in a Spanish sentence.** This means that unlike English, no single word stands apart from the others in terms of emphasis.

17. **Spanish tone is different for each type of statement. Declarative:** low, goes high, maintains, goes back, finishes lower. **Exclamatory**: follows the same pattern as the declarative sentences, but we start above the normal tone and quickly descend below the normal pitch. **Interrogative**: starts as in the exclamatory sentences, above the normal tone, from here the following syllables descend until the last syllable where the tone rises again.

5. Frecuencia y encadenamiento de palabras.

Spanish has a special way to make the transition from one word to another word when you are speaking. This is one of the two challenges that we face when we are learning a new language. It is very different to understand the words individually than to be able to understand a bunch of words in several sentences with natural speed. When you are talking with one of your friends, you don't stop until you finish your idea. Perhaps you want to emphasize what you just said, or your friend interrupts you to tell you something. During this time, all the words are continually linked together until there is a reason to stop. We can master the grammar and the vocabulary of the new language, but it is difficult for us to hear the sounds of the words that the native speakers put together and divide these sounds in the way that we can understand each word. The good news is that the ability to understand linking words is something that comes naturally.

The second challenge is the ability to speak while linking the words like native speakers. Linguistic experts think that the ability to speak as native speakers by linking the words doesn't come in a natural way. The challenge for us is to develop this skill through proper pronunciation. Incorrect pronunciation leads to miscommunication. Linking the words incorrectly doesn't cause miscommunication.

You may ask yourself: why we are studying this? One of the objectives of any language student is to become fluent. The flow or fluidity of speech via the ability to link words affords one the ability to be termed fluent in a language. Fluency in another language is a desirable skill sought by global-minded employers and tends to give the speaker opportunities to build relationships with heritage speakers.

Encadenamiento = Spanish Linking. In short, it refers to the lack of a phonetic border between words in a sentence or question. This makes us feel that Spanish is spoken very fast. As always, Spanish has very simple but rigid rules that help us understand this concept and start working on our skills to link words.

Spanish language philosophy: The musicality of the Spanish language is based on the fact that most of the syllables begin with a consonant sound and end with a vowel sound. In other words, Spanish doesn't tend to have syllables begin with vowels or end in consonants. In the next four rules you will be able to see how the final sound is linked onto the word that follows it.

Regla uno: The final vowel of one word is pronounced with the initial vowel of the next word.

Example: La escuela   abre la puerta   a las ocho → **La- es-cue-la-bre-la-puer-ta-las-o-cho**

Regla dos: This rule often creates diphthongs and triphthongs by joining the final vowel of one word and the initial vowel of the next word, when they are different.

Example: La escuela   abre la puerta   a las ocho → **Laes-cue-la-bre-la-puer-ta-las-o-cho**

Regla tres: Sometimes the final consonant of a word is pronounced together with the initial vowel of the next word.

Example: El doctor es una buena persona → **El-doc-to-res-una-bue-na-per-so-na**

Regla cuatro: When the final consonant of one word is the same as the initial consonant of the following word, only one sound is made but with longer duration.

Example: comemos sabroso → **Co-me-mo-sa-bro-so**

In the next video you will hear and see how we apply these rules. The video is all in Spanish. Remember, we are **introducing the Spanish word linking** concept to you. We want you to be **familiar with the concept, to know it exists, understand the mechanics, and notice these elements when you listen to Spanish**. The more conscious you are of this phonetic phenomenon, **the easier it will be for you to develop faster your understanding and also your skills in linking Spanish words.** Now, listen to the next video and try to identify the concepts that we just studied. Repeat aloud all the words and how they are linked.

Observa el video 1.5.2, on the online platform to practice these concepts.

6. Las reglas de puntuación y el uso de mayúsculas en español.

English grammar defines punctuation as a group of rules and conventions. When we speak, we use pauses and voice pitch to be understood. Punctuation plays a similar role in writing, making it easier to read. As we were studying intonation, tones, etc., we needed to study punctuation to be able to write and make the meaning clear.

Spanish punctuation is the same as English punctuation with some exceptions, some of them we already studied. Complete the exceptions that we have in Spanish punctuation:

First: What happens with questions marks in Spanish? _____ _____

Second: What do the Spanish exclamation and question marks have in common? _____

Third: The dash (-). In quotations, a dash is generally used to indicate a change in the speaker instead of quotation marks. La profesora dijo: - ¿Qué hora es?- The professor said: "What time is it?"

We can use **"<< >>"** to indicate quoted speech and dialogue: <<Yo amo el español>> "I love Spanish"

English	Símbolos de puntuación	Español
apostrophe	' '	apóstrofe
asterisk	*	asterisco
braces	{ }	llaves
brackets	[ ]	corchetes
colon	:	dos puntos
comma	,	coma
dash	—	raya
dieresis	ü	diéresis
exclamation mark	¡!	¡abre, cierra!
hyphen	-	guion
parentheses	( )	paréntesis
period	.	punto
question mark	¿?	¿abre, cierra?
quotation marks	" " << >>	comillas, doble comilla
semicolon	;	punto y coma
suspension points	...	puntos suspensivos

As we studied, English and Spanish punctuation are the same excluding the three cases above: question marks (opened and closed), exclamation marks (opened and closed) and the dash. When we talk about capital letters, it is a different story. Spanish doesn't use capital letters as frequently as used in English. The rule is very simple: **Only proper nouns are capitalized or the word at the beginning of the sentence.**

As you progress in your knowledge of Spanish, you can incorporate the tips above and belo w in your written communication.

In Spanish, the following are not capitalized when not starting the sentence:

1. The pronouns are not capitalized. Except usted y ustedes if abbreviated as Ud. Uds.

2. The days of the week or months of the year.

3. Names of political parties, languages and titles

4. Nationalities

5. BUT abbreviations are capitalized:

usted → Ud.   ustedes → Uds.   → you (formal)

señor → Sr.   señora → Sra.   señorita → Srta.   → Mr., Mrs., Miss

doctor → Dr.   doctora → Dra.   → Dr.

The following nouns are always capitalized:

1. Titles or nicknames to designate specific people: Juana La Loca → Joan the Mad

2. Titles that are equivalent to proper names:

El Rey → The King

El rey Juan Carlos I → Juan Carlos I King

El Presidente → The President

El presidente Washington → President Washington

3. Certain collective nouns: La Nación → the Nation

El Reino → the kingdom

4. Divine Attributes: Creador → Creator   Redentor → Redeemer

Something interesting about Spanish speakers is their frequent references to God in daily speech. It is acceptable to use expressions like "Si Dios lo permite = If God permits" or "Con el permiso de Dios" = With the permission of God". Remember: "Generalizing is lack of education", most of the Spanish speakers are Apostolic Roman Catholic, **but not all!** Understanding the behaviors and values is equally important to succeed in communication as learning the grammar and phonetic rules of the language.

Practiquemos lo aprendido: Rewrite the following passages, inserting proper punctuation and capitals.

1. quien es cristóbal colon? el descubrió américa en 1492.

_____

2. me gusta comer tacos mexicanos los lunes.

_____

3. qué inteligente! siempre tiene buenas notas en español.

_____

4. en agosto voy a ir de vacaciones a el salvador un país hispanohablante.

_____

5. el presidente habla por la televisión a todos uds.

_____

6. el flaco es su apodo (nickname), todos lo llaman "el flaco"

_____

In Spanish, we use nicknames frequently as a way to show affection to the person, but when a Spanish speaker uses your full name, you can be sure you're in trouble. The names of Spanish speakers normally include four elements: the first name, a second first name and two second names or last names. One is the second/last name of the father and the next one is the mother's second name or last name. A common first name for females is María for religious traditions, but normally they use the second name on a daily basis.

Example: **¡María Guadalupe López Velázquez!**

Everybody will call her Guadalupe, not María. The nickname (apodo) for people called Guadalupe is "Lupita or Lupe". Her father is Juan José López Torres which is the reason why she has the last name López appear prior to her mother's last name. Her mom is Mary Carmen Velázquez Riesgo. Lupita's second last name is Velázquez. But if her mom calls her:

"María Guadalupe" ¡ven aquí!...,

then Lupita knowns she is in trouble! (¡pobrecita Lupita!)

1. ¿Cuántos nombres tienes?_____ y ¿Cuántos apellidos?_____

2. ¿Tienes un apodo?_____ ¿Cuál es?_____

3. ¿Qué piensas de esta costumbre latina?_____

_____.

Sabes que algunos países latinos, como Italia, quieren cambiar el orden de los apellidos. Quieren que primero sea el apellido de la madre y después el apellido del padre.

4. ¿Qué piensas sobre este cambio en el orden de los apellidos?, ¿Estás de acuerdo con el cambio? Si /no y por qué.

_____

_____

_____

_____

7. Tres grandes cuestiones del español.

Hasta este momento en tus estudios del español has aprendido tres de los grandes interrogativos del español:

¿Ser o Estar?

¿Conocer o Saber?

¿Requiere un pronombre directo o indirecto o los dos? (Direct or Indirect Object Pronouns)

Como siempre, el dominar y poder aplicar correctamente estos conceptos requiere práctica, requiere que los utilices una y otra vez, hasta que sean parte tuya. Para ayudarte con este objetivo hemos seleccionado tres videos con música rap. Diviértete escuchando cada uno de ellos, pon mucha atención pues deberás de escribir los elementos que resumen el uso correcto de cada una de estas cuestiones.

Mira el video 1.5.3 ¿Ser o Estar? En la siguiente tabla escribe los elementos que el video presenta para el uso correcto de estos dos verbos.

Ser	Estar

Mira los videos 1.5.4 and 1.5.5 ¿Saber vs Conocer? En la siguiente tabla escribe los elementos que el video presenta para el uso correcto de estos dos verbos.

Saber	Conocer

> **Mira el video 1.5.6 and 1.5.7 ¿Indirect or direct object pronouns?** En la siguiente tabla escribe los elementos que el video presenta para el uso correcto de pronombres de complementos indirectos y directos.

Indirectos	Directos
What verbs always require an IOP?	

Practiquemos ser y estar: Nuestra amiga Mónica va a estudiar en Lima, va de viaje en un par de días y por ello les escribe el siguiente correo electrónico a su futura familia peruana. Completa los espacios con los verbos ser o estar.

Queridos Señores Ramírez:

Mi nombre _____ Mónica, _____ estadounidense, del estado de Nueva York. Yo _____ estudiante en SUNY, Geneseo. Geneseo _____ una villa univer-sitaria que _____ al norte del estado de Nueva York, en Rochester. ¡Geneseo _____ a solo tres horas de Canadá! La villa _____ muy pequeñita, todos los bares y restau-rantes _____ en la calle principal, podemos ir y regresar a la universidad cam-inando. Mi especialidad _____ antropología. _____ muy interesada en la cultura inca. _____ impresionada por sus obras arqueológicas, me encantará poder visitar Machu Picchu, su ciudad sagrada. Sé que _____ en los Andes a una gran altura, he visto algunas fotografías, estar en Machu Picchu será un sueño hecho realidad para mí.

Mi familia _____ pequeña, _____ hija única. Mi padre _____ arqui-tecto, mi madre _____ secretaria en una escuela secundaria. Ellos _____ en Puerto Rico de vacaciones en este momento.

_____ alta, _____ morena y mis ojos_____ color azul. _____buena

persona y _____ muy trabajadora. _____ muy contenta de poder hacer

este viaje a vuestro país.

Vivo en los dormitorios de la universidad_____ muy cerca de la calle principal de

Geneseo.

Hoy tenemos una fiesta por el fin de clases, la fiesta_____ en casa de mi amiga

Beth. Ella _____ muy preocupada, _____ horneando mi pastel favorito. Mis amigos

me han regalado un vestido para mi viaje a Lima _____ de algodón, _____ muy bo-

nito, _____ rosado y tiene lunares blancos.

Hoy _____ domingo, 28 de mayo y _____ mediodía, en dos días más voy a _____

con vosotros.

Mis más respetuosos saludos:

Mónica

Practiquemos el saber y conocer en el presente del modo indicativo: Completa la de-
scripción de la vida de Mónica sobre sus planes en Lima, Perú. Llena los espacios con la
forma correcta de saber o conocer. Tienes que decidir primero si la oración requiere saber o
conocer. Después conjuga el verbo en el presente del indicativo.

Como yo no _____ nada de Perú voy a la biblioteca. La bibliotecaria, Rocío,

es mi amiga.

Yo la _____ bien. Ella _____ donde están to-

dos los libros porque ella es muy lista. Su familia es de Perú entonces ella no solamente

_____

Lima pero muchos lugares como Cuzco también. Me pregunta ¿_____tú

que las ruinas de Machu Picchu son de los incas, gente indígena de la región? Los es-

pañoles no las descubrieron por no _____ (infinitive form) su ubicación por la

vegetación que las cubrieron.

La pregunto, ¿_____ tú cómo llegar a Machu Picchu? Ella _____

que existen viajes en tren, autobús y hasta en helicóptero, pero yo quiero _____

el camino como los incas del pasado.

También debo de _____ la ciudad de Arequipa, conocida como la Ciudad Blanca. Su centro histórico es declarado Patrimonio Cultural de la Humanidad por la arquitectura de sus construcciones coloniales.

Otro fin de semana voy a _____ la Selva Amazona. Yo _____ que viajar es muy caro pero _____ (tú) que solamente vives una vez y hay que experimentar todo.

Nuestro último ejercicio: los pronombres de complementos indirectos y directos. A continuación se te presenta una de las páginas del diario de Mónica justamente cuando regresó de Lima y planea su próximo viaje a España. Llena los espacios los pronombres de complementos indirectos y directos.

Querido Diario:

Acabo de regresar de Perú. No sabes cuánto _____ gusta Lima. _____ encanta conocer ese fabuloso país. Solamente _____ llevo algunos recuerditos a mis padres y a mis amigos más cercanos, pero estoy feliz de compartir_____ con ellos.

Al regresar a Geneseo me encuentro con muchas sorpresas. Mi amigo Emilio está trabajando para un banco en su pueblo. _____ pregunta a mí si quiero un trabajo. A él _____ digo que no. No _____ quiero (referente al trabajo). Tengo ganas de irme a España entonces voy a solicitar un trabajo en la oficina de estudios internacionales porque ellos _____ pagan mejor a mí. ¿Cuánto va a costar un boleto a Madrid? No _____ sé pero voy a buscar_____ hoy. Tengo unas amigas que quieren ir conmigo. A ellas, _____ fascina todo de España. Entonces ahora mismo busco los boletos para nosotras.

¡Qué ganga! En el internet, _____ _____ compro por $500 ida y vuelta (round trip). Tengo que irme para decir_____ (what happens when both an indirect and direct object pronoun are needed?)

Mónica

8. La comprehension de la lectura.

Leamos sobre lo que Mónica y sus amigos pueden ver en Madrid.

Read aloud the passage below for pronunciation. There is much to do and see in Madrid. Let's see what one of Madrid's most popular tour guides, **Señor Viajes** has to share with us.

Bienvenidos a todos. Soy el Señor Viajes, me gusta mucho trabajar como guía de turistas. Me encanta enseñar las bellezas de Madrid, voy a ser su guía en este viaje. Primero, sugiero que Uds pasen por El Paseo del Arte. Como ya saben ustedes donde está el Prado por el metro, recomiendo que Uds. vayan al Prado para ver las obras (works) de los artistas famosos como Goya, Zurbarán, Picasso, Velazquez, Murillo, Dega y muchos más y de diferentes países. Es posible que ustedes necesiten un par de días para ver todo lo que el museo ofrece.

Muy cerca al Prado hay otros dos museos, el Thyssen-Bornemisza y el Museo Nacional Centro de Arte Reina Sofía. Es necesario que ustedes visiten este museo por el arte de Dalí, Miró y la obra maestra de Pablo Picasso: La Guernica. La Guernica demuestra el sufrimiento de la gente de un pueblo, Guernica, en el norte de España en la región del País Vasco cuando El General Franco dio (gave) permiso a los alemanes a bombardear la ciudad.

Es importante durante sus días explorando Madrid que disfruten los parques. La Casa de Campo y El Parque de Retiro son unos parques muy famosos. También yo quiero que ustedes descansen y tomen unas tapas y unos refrescos en los diferentes restaurantes que existen en Madrid y especialmente en la Plaza Mayor. Siempre es interesante observar la vida en la Plaza.

Deseo que ustedes vean el cambio de la guardia enfrente del Palacio Real. Dudo que los monarcas estén allí porque ahora solamente se usa el palacio para las ceremonias especiales. Los monarcas tienen otra residencia pero durante nuestra visita, es posible que ustedes se sientan como parte de la familia real con toda la belleza que tiene el Palacio Real. Vamos a visitar muchas atracciones durante sus vacaciones.

Now that you have read for pronunciation, re-read for comprehension. You will see various verbs and expression throughout the reading that are in bold either in black (in the present indicative—what you have studied throughout this course) or purple (known as the present subjunctive—a mood that you will study with us next semester.) Did you notice the verbs in the second half of the sentence are conjugated with different vowels than what you may have been accustomed to seeing? You will learn more about that next semester but for now read the questions below and find the answers in the reading above.

1. ¿Qué país estamos visitando? _____

_____

2. ¿Cómo se llama el guía de turistas? _____

_____

3. ¿En cuál museo, se puede ver la Guernica? _____

_____

4. ¿Quién dio su permiso de bombardear el pueblo Guernica? _____

5. ¿Para qué se usa el Palacio Real ahora? _____

6. ¿Viven en el Palacio Real el Rey Felipe y la Reina Leticia de España? _____

TAREA: Ahora es el momento en que incorporas todo que has aprendido. Tu profesor(a) va a crear situaciones en las cuales vas a aplicar todo que has estudiado. Estudia todo. Vas a hablar sobre las introducciones y presentaciones a otras personas, tu vida en casa, tu vida en la escuela, las acciones que haces en tu vida con descripciones. Piensa lógicamente del progreso natural de una conversación para responder y para crear preguntas y oraciones habladas. Estudia y practica enfrente de un espejo la pronunciación, el vocabulario, las frases para conocer a otra persona.

Despedida/Goodbye: In the Spanish world we need to say hello to each other when we arrive and goodbye when we part. This book will not be the exception, but before we say goodbye, we would like to share with you a very common saying in Spanish: "QUERER ES PODER" The meaning is: **"to want is to be able."**

You can achieve whatever the goal is if you really want to ...

if you put the time and effort into it.

Yo puedo
hablar español

See all the achievements that you have made in your first Spanish semester. Look at how many things **you** CAN DO in Spanish now, just for this unit:

[ ] Yes   [ ] No   **Can I express possession in different ways? Three to be precise.**

[ ] Yes   [ ] No   **Can I apply the concepts for Spanish phonics which will help me identify spelling changes?**

[ ] Yes   [ ] No   **Can I define, differentiate and apply "conocer" and "saber"?**

[ ] Yes   [ ] No   **Can I apply the rules for Spanish punctuation and capitalization?**

[ ] Yes   [ ] No   **Can I link words to gain fluency?**

[ ] Yes   [ ] No   **Can I identify some of the common errors made by beginning Spanish students?**

[ ] Yes   [ ] No   **Can I write short paragraphs or brief dialogues in Spanish?**

[ ] Yes   [ ] No   **Can I understand simple spoken and written Spanish?**

[ ] Yes   [ ] No   **Can I converse with a non-native and native-speaker of Spanish with simple sentences and questions?**

If you answered "No" to any of these questions, review those sections again and see your professor.

Consider the overall course goals that you have achieved:

Interpersonal Communication: I can communicate and exchange information about familiar topics using phrases and simple sentences, sometimes supported by memorized language. I can usually handle short social interactions in everyday situations by asking and answering simple questions.

Presentational Speaking: I can present basic information on familiar topics using language I have practiced using phrases and simple sentences.

Presentational Writing: I can write short messages and notes on familiar topics related to everyday life.

Interpretive Listening: I can often understand words, phrases, and simple sentences related to everyday life. I can recognize pieces of information and sometimes understand the main topic of what is being said.

Interpretive Reading: I can understand familiar words, phrases, and sentences within short and simple texts related to everyday life. I can sometimes understand the main idea of what I have read.

Vocabulary

Español	M/F	Inglés	Clasificación
(a)fuera de		outside of	Preposición
a		to; at	Preposición
a la derecha		to the right	Adverbio
a la izquierda		to the left	Adverbio
acerca de		about	Preposición
adjetivo	El	adjective	Sustantivo
afuera de		outside	Adverbio
al lado de		next to	Preposición
alquilar		to rent	Verbo Regular
antes de		before (time/space)	Preposición
apagar		to turn off	Verbo Regular
ayudar		to help	Verbo Regular
cambiar		exchange in terms of currency	Verbo Regular
cambiar		to change	Verbo Regular
cancelar		to cancel	Verbo Regular
centro comercial	El	shopping center/mall	Sustantivo
cerca de		near	Preposición
cine	El	movie theatre	Sustantivo
cobrar		to charge (a bill)	Verbo Regular
conducir (c—zc)		to drive	Verbo Regular
conocer (c—zc)		to know/to be familiar	Verbo Regular
consultorio	El	doctor's office	Sustantivo
cortar		to cut	Verbo Regular
corte	La	court	Sustantivo
costar (o—ue)		to cost	Verbo Irregular
cuerpo de bomberos	El	fire department	Sustantivo
cuidar		to care / to take care of	Verbo Regular
debajo de		under; underneath	Preposición
delante de		in front	Preposición
dentro de		inside of	Preposición
derecho		straight	Adjetivo, Adverbio
desde		from	Preposición
después de		after	Preposición
detrás de		behind	Preposición
doblar		to turn/flip	Verbo Regular
en		in	Preposición
encima de		on top of	Preposición
encontrar (o—ue)		to meet/encounter	Verbo Irregular

enfrente de		across from; facing	Preposición
entre		among; between	Preposición
fuera de		except	Preposición
funcionar		to function	Verbo Regular
girar		to turn	Verbo Regular
hacia		toward	Preposición
hasta		until	Adverbio
iglesia	La	church	Sustantivo
lejos de		far from	Adverbio
limpiar		to clean	Verbo Regular
lugar en la comunidad	El	place in the community	Sustantivo
mantener (irreg yo)		to maintain	Verbo Irregular
mujer policía	La	policewoman	Sustantivo
pagar		to pay	Verbo Regular
para		for; in order to	Preposición
pasar (pasar por)		to pass/to pass by	Verbo Regular
pedir (e—i)		to ask for	Verbo Irregular
peluquería	La	hairdresser	Sustantivo
plaza mayor	La	main plaza/center of town	Sustantivo
poder (o—ue)		to be able/can	Verbo Irregular
policía	La	police department	Sustantivo
policía	El	policeman	Sustantivo
poner (go)		to put	Verbo Irregular
por		for; through; by; because of	Preposición
posesivo	El	possessive	Sustantivo
prestar		to borrow; to loan; to lend	Verbo Regular
quedar		to be located	Verbo Regular
recto		straight	Adjetivo, Adverbio
residencia	La	dormitory	Sustantivo
según		according to	Adverbio, Preposición
sin		without	Preposición
sobre		about	Preposición
supermercado	El	supermarket	Sustantivo
teatro	El	theatre	Sustantivo
veterinario/a	El, La	veterinarian	Sustantivo

Verbs: Spanish to English

Español	Inglés	Clasificación
abrir	to open	Verbo Regular
aburrir	to bore	Verbo Regular
acordar (o—ue)	to remember	Verbo Irregular
acostar (o—ue)	to put in bed	Verbo Irregular
agregar	to add	Verbo Regular
almorzar (o—ue)	to have lunch	Verbo Irregular
alquilar	to rent	Verbo Regular
analizar	to analyze	Verbo Regular
andar	to walk	Verbo Regular
apagar	to turn off	Verbo Regular
aparcar	to park	Verbo Regular
aprender	to learn	Verbo Regular
arreglar	to fix	Verbo Regular
asistir	to attend	Verbo Regular
averiguar	to find out	Verbo Regular
ayudar	to help	Verbo Regular
batir	to mix/beat	Verbo Regular
beber	to drink	Verbo Regular
buscar	to look for	Verbo Regular
cambiar	exchange in terms of currency	Verbo Regular
cambiar	to change	Verbo Regular
cancelar	to cancel	Verbo Regular
cenar	to have dinner	Verbo Regular
cobrar	to charge (a bill)	Verbo Regular
cocer (o —ue) z*	to cook (in terms of how something is cooked)	Verbo Irregular
cocinar	to cook	Verbo Regular
combinar	to combine	Verbo Regular
comer	to eat	Verbo Regular
comprar	to buy	Verbo Regular
comprender	to understand	Verbo Regular
conducir (c—zc)	to drive	Verbo Irregular
congelar	to freeze	Verbo Regular

conocer (c—zc)	to know/to be familiar	Verbo Irregular
conseguir (e—i)	to get, obtain	Verbo Irregular
construir (i—y)	to build	Verbo Irregular
contener (go + e—ie)	to contain	Verbo Irregular
contestar	to answer	Verbo Regular
correr	to run	Verbo Regular
cortar	to cut	Verbo Regular
coser	to sew	Verbo Regular
costar (o—ue)	to cost	Verbo Irregular
creer	to believe	Verbo Regular
cubrir	to cover	Verbo Regular
cuidar	to care / to take care of	Verbo Regular
deber	to owe/must	Verbo Regular
deber (followed by an infinitive)	to must be as in probability	Verbo Regular
decir (e—i)	to say/tell	Verbo Irregular
derretir	to melt, thaw	Verbo Regular
desayunar	to have breakfast	Verbo Regular
desear	to want/wish	Verbo Regular
despedir (e—i)	to say good-bye	Verbo Irregular
despertar (e—ie)	to wake up	Verbo Irregular
desvestir(se) (e—i)	to undress	Verbo Irregular
devolver (o—ue)	to return/give back	Verbo Irregular
disgustar	to dislike	Verbo similar a gustar
dividir	to divide	Verbo Regular
doblar	to turn/flip	Verbo Regular
doler (o--ue)	to hurt	Verbo Similar a Gustar
dormir (o—ue)	to sleep	Verbo Irregular
elegir (g—j)	to choose	Verbo Regular: Cambio Fonético
encantar	to really like or be pleasing	Verbo Similar a Gustar
encender (e—ie)	to turn on (stove for example)	Verbo Irregular
encontrar (o—ue)	to meet/encounter	Verbo Irregular
enseñar	to teach	Verbo Regular
escoger (g—j)	to choose	Verbo Regular: Cambio Fonético
escribir	to write	Verbo Regular
escurrir	to drain	Verbo Regular
esperar	to hope, wish, wait for	Verbo Regular
estar	to be	Verbo Irregular

estar casado/a	to be married	Expresión, Verbo Irregular
estar divorciado/a de	to be divorced	Expresión, Verbo Irregular
estudiar	to study	Verbo Regular
faltar	to miss, lack	Verbo Similar a Gustar
fascinar	to be fascinated by	Verbo Similar a Gustar
fracasar	to fail	Verbo Regular
freír (e—i)	to fry	Verbo Irregular
funcionar	to function	Verbo Regular
girar	to turn	Verbo Regular
guisar	to cook/stew	Verbo Regular
gustar	to be pleasing (like)	Verbo Regular (Requires IOP)
hablar	to talk, speak	Verbo Regular
hacer (go)	to do, make	Verbo Irregular
hacer falta	to need; to be lacking	Verbo Similar a Gustar
hervir (e—ie)	to boil	Verbo Irregular
hornear	to bake	Verbo Regular
importar	to be of importance, to matter	Verbo similar a gustar
intercambiar	to exchange/give/ receive	Verbo Regular
interesar	to be of interest	Verbo Regular
ir	to go	Verbo Irregular
jugar (u—ue)	to play a sport or game	Verbo Irregular
leer	to read	Verbo Regular
limpiar	to clean	Verbo Regular
llegar	to arrive	Verbo Regular
llenar	to fill in	Verbo Regular
llevar	to wear; to take; to carry	Verbo Regular
mantener (irreg yo)	to maintain	Verbo Irregular
mentir (e—ie)	to lie	Verbo Irregular
merendar	to have a snack	Verbo Regular
mezclar	to mix	Verbo Regular
molestar	to bother	Verbo Regular, Verbo Similar a Gustar
morir (o—ue)	to die	Verbo Irregular
mostrar (o—ue)	to show	Verbo Irregular
necesitar	to need	Verbo Regular
no gustar	to dislike	Verbo Similar a Gustar
olvidar(se)	to forget	Verbo Regular
pagar	to pay	Verbo Regular
pasar	to pass	Verbo Regular
pasar (pasar por)	to pass/to pass by	Verbo Regular

pedir (e—i)	to ask for	Verbo Irregular
pegar	adhere to/stick/hit	Verbo Regular
poder (o—ue)	to be able/can	Verbo Irregular
poner (go)	to put	Verbo Irregular
poner(se) (go)	to put/to put on	Verbo Irregular
preferir (e—ie)	to prefer	Verbo Irregular
preguntar	to ask (a question)	Verbo Regular
preparar	to prepare	Verbo Regular
prestar	to borrow; to loan; to lend	Verbo Regular
promover (o—ue)	to promote	Verbo Irregular
quedar	to be located	Verbo Regular
quedar(se) bien/mal	to fit well/poorly	Verbo Regular
quemar	to burn	Verbo Regular
querer (e—ie)	to want/wish/love	Verbo Irregular
recibir	to receive	Verbo Regular
recomendar (e—ie)	to recommend	Verbo Irregular
reducir (c—zc)	to reduce	Verbo Irregular
regresar	to return	Verbo Regular
relajar(se)	to relax	Verbo Regular
remover (o—ue)	to remove	Verbo Irregular
reparar	to repair	Verbo Regular
repetir (e—i)	to repeat	Verbo Irregular
reservar	to reserve	Verbo Regular
revisar	to revise/check	Verbo Regular
romper (se)	to break	Verbo Regular
saber (otros irregulares -yo)	to know	Verbo Irregular
sacar	to take	Verbo Regular
sacar (buenas/malas) notas	to get (good/bad) grades	Verbo Regular
salar	to add salt	Verbo Regular
sazonar	to season	Verbo Regular
seguir (e—i)	to follow/continue	Verbo Irregular
señalar	to signal	Verbo Regular
sentar(se) (e—ie)	to sit	Verbo Irregular
sentir (e—ie)	to feel, regret, to be sorry	Verbo Irregular
ser (muy irregular)	to be	Verbo Irregular
ser soltero/a	to be single	Expresión, Verbo Irregular
servir (e—i)	to serve	Verbo Irregular
sugerir (e—ie)	to suggest	Verbo Irregular
temer	to fear	Verbo Regular

tener (go + e—ie)	to have	Verbo Irregular
tener calor (go + e—ie)	to be hot	Expresión, Verbo Irregular
tener celos (go + e—ie)	to be jealous	Expresión, Verbo Irregular
tener éxito (go + e—ie)	to be successful	Expresión, Verbo Irregular
tener frío (go + e—ie)	to be cold	Expresión, Verbo Irregular
tener ganas de… (go + e—ie)	to feel like…(doing something)	Expresión, Verbo Irregular
tener hambre (go + e—ie)	to be hungry	Expresión, Verbo Irregular
tener miedo (de) (go + e—ie)	to be afraid (de)	Expresión, Verbo Irregular
tener paciencia (go + e—ie)	to be patient	Expresión, Verbo Irregular
tener prisa (go + e—ie)	to be in a hurry	Expresión, Verbo Irregular
tener razón (go + e—ie)	to be right	Expresión, Verbo Irregular
tener sed (go + e—ie)	to be thirsty	Expresión, Verbo Irregular
tener sueño (go + e—ie)	to be tired / sleepy	Expresión, Verbo Irregular
tener…años (go + e—ie)	to…years old	Expresión, Verbo Irregular
terminar	to finish	Verbo Regular
tomar apuntes	to take notes	Verbo Regular
trabajar	to work	Verbo Regular
traer (igo)	to bring	Verbo Irregular
usar	to use	Verbo Regular
vestir(se) (e—i)	to dress	Verbo Irregular
visitar	to visit	Verbo Regular
vivir	to live	Verbo Regular
volar (o—ue)	to fly	Verbo Irregular
volver (o—ue)	to return	Verbo Irregular

Glosario Español

Español	M/F	Inglés	Clasificación
(a)fuera de		outside of	Preposición
(muchas) gracias		thank you (very much)	Expresión
(muy) bien, gracias.		(very) well thank you	Expresión
¡Qué chévere!		How great!	Expresión
¿adónde?		where?	Adverbio
¿Cómo está Usted (Ud.)?		How are you? (formal)	Expresión
¿Cómo estás tú?		How are you? (informal)	Expresión
¿Cómo se llama Ud.?		What is your name?	Expresión
¿Cómo te llamas tú?		What is your name?	Expresión
¿cómo? ¡cómo!		how? How!	Adverbio
¿cómo? ¡cómo!		what? What!	Adverbio
¿cuál?		which?	Pronombre
¿cuáles?		which ones?	Pronombre
¿cuándo?		when?	Pronombre
¿cuánto?		how much?	Pronombre
¿cuántos?		how many?	Pronombre
¿de dónde?		from where?	Preposición
¿dónde?		where?	Adverbio
¿por qué?		why?	Pronombre
¿Qué hay de nuevo?		What's new?	Expresión
¿Qué hora es?		What time is it?	Expresión
¿Qué tal?		How is it going? (informal)	Expresión
¿qué?		what?	Pronombre
¿quién?		who?	Pronombre
¿quiénes?		who? (pl.)	Pronombre
a		to	Preposición
a		to; at	Preposición
a la		at 1:00 or times related to one	Expresión

a la derecha		to the right	Adverbio
a la izquierda		to the left	Adverbio
a las >2:00		at … >2:00 clock time	Expresión
abogado/a	El, La	lawyer	Sustantivo
abril	El	April	Sustantivo
abrir		to open	Verbo Regular
abuelo/a	El, La	grandfather/grandmother	Sustantivo
aburrido/a		bored	Adjetivo
accidente	El	accident	Sustantivo
acerca de		about	Preposición
acordar (o—ue)		to remember	Verbo Irregular
acostar (o—ue)		to put in bed	Verbo Irregular
actor	El	actor	Sustantivo
actriz	La	actress	Sustantivo
adiós		good bye	Expresión
adjetivo	El	adjective	Sustantivo
administración de empresas	La	business administration	Sustantivo
afortunado/a		fortunate/lucky	Adjetivo
africana		African	Adjetivo
africana	La	African woman	Sustantivo
africano		African	Adjetivo
africano	El	African man	Sustantivo
afuera de		outside	Adverbio
agosto		August	Sustantivo
al lado de		next to	Preposición
alemán		German	Adjetivo
alemán	El	German language	Sustantivo
alemán	El	German man	Sustantivo
alemana		German	Adjetivo
alemana	La	German woman	Sustantivo
alquilar		to rent	Verbo Regular
alto/a		tall	Adjetivo
amarillo/a		yellow	Adjetivo
analizar		to analyze	Verbo Regular
anaranjado/a		orange	Adjetivo
ángel	El	angel	Sustantivo
año escolar	El	school year	Sustantivo
antes de		before (time/space)	Preposición

antipático/a		unpleasant	Adjetivo
antropología	La	anthropology	Sustantivo
apagar		to turn off	Verbo Regular
apartamento	El	apartment	Sustantivo
aprender		to learn	Verbo Regular
arquitecto/a	El, La	architect	Sustantivo
arte*	El, Las	art	Sustantivo
artístico/a		artistic	Adjetivo
así, así		so, so	Expresión
asiento	El	chair	Sustantivo
asistir		to attend	Verbo Regular
ático	El	attic	Sustantivo
auto	El	car	Sustantivo
ayudar		to help	Verbo Regular
azul		blue	Adjetivo
bajo/a		short	Adjetivo
balance	El	balance	Sustantivo
banana	La	banana	Sustantivo
banco	El	bank	Sustantivo
baño	El	bathroom	Sustantivo
barato/a		inexpensive, cheap	Adjetivo
basura	La	trash	Sustantivo
bello/a		beautiful	Adjetivo
biblioteca	La	library	Sustantivo
bien		well	Adjetivo, Adverbio
biología	La	biology	Sustantivo
blanco/a		white	Adjetivo
boda	La	wedding	Sustantivo
bolígrafo	El	pen	Sustantivo
bonito/a		pretty	Adjetivo
buenas noches		good evening	Expresión
buenas tardes		good afternoon	Expresión
bueno/a		good	Adjetivo
buenos días		good morning	Expresión
buscar		to look for	Verbo Regular
cabina	La	cabin	Sustantivo
café		brown	Adjetivo
cafetería	La	cafeteria	Sustantivo
calculadora	La	calculator	Sustantivo

cama	La	bed	Sustantivo
cambiar		exchange in terms of currency	Verbo Regular
cambiar		to change	Verbo Regular
canal	El	channel	Sustantivo
cancelar		to cancel	Verbo Regular
caro/a		expensive	Adjetivo
carro	El	car	Sustantivo
casa	La	house	Sustantivo
catorce		14	Adjetivo
centro comercial	El	shopping center/mall	Sustantivo
cerca de		near	Preposición
cero		0	Adjetivo
chao		goodbye	Expresión
china	La	Chinese woman	Sustantivo
chino	El	Chinese language	Sustantivo
chino	El	Chinese man	Sustantivo
chino/a		Chinese	Adjetivo
cien		100	Adjetivo
ciencia	La	science	Sustantivo
ciencias políticas	Las	political science	Sustantivo
ciento >101…199		100 > 101…199	Adjetivo
cinco		5	Adjetivo
cincuenta		50	Adjetivo
cine	El	movie theatre	Sustantivo
cobrar		to charge (a bill)	Verbo Regular
coche	El	car	Sustantivo
cocina	La	kitchen	Sustantivo
colección	La	collection	Sustantivo
colega (used for male or female)	El, La	colleague	Sustantivo
combinar		to combine	Verbo Regular
comedor	El	dining room	Sustantivo
comer		to eat	Verbo Regular
cómico/a		funny; comical	Adjetivo
como		like, as	Preposición
comprender		to understand	Verbo Regular
con permiso		excuse me, when you need to physically move	Expresión
concierto	El	concert	Sustantivo
conducir (c—zc)		to drive	Verbo Regular

conocer (c—zc)		to know/to be familiar	Verbo Regular
conseguir (e—i)		to get, obtain	Verbo Irregular
construir (i—y)		to build	Verbo Regular
consultorio	El	doctor's office	Sustantivo
contador/a	El, La	accountant	Sustantivo
contestar		to answer	Verbo Regular
correr		to run	Verbo Regular
cortar		to cut	Verbo Regular
corte	La	court	Sustantivo
costar (o—ue)		to cost	Verbo Irregular
creer		to believe	Verbo Regular
cuaderno	El	notebook	Sustantivo
cuarenta		40	Adjetivo
cuatro		4	Adjetivo
cuerpo de bomberos	El	fire department	Sustantivo
cuidar		to care / to take care of	Verbo Regular
cultura	La	culture	Sustantivo
cumpleaños	El, Los	birthday	Sustantivo
cuñado	El	brother-in-law	Sustantivo
cuñada	La	sister-in-law	Sustantivo
curioso/a		curious	Adjetivo
curso	El	course	Sustantivo
de		of / from	Preposición
de la madrugada		in the early morning	Expresión
de la mañana		in the morning	Expresión
de la noche		in the evening	Expresión
de la tarde		in the afternoon	Expresión
de nada		you're welcome	Expresión
debajo		under	Preposición
debajo de		under; underneath	Preposición
deber		to owe	Verbo Regular
deber (followed by an infinitive)		to have to/must	Verbo Regular
débil		weak	Adjetivo
decir (e—i)		to say/tell	Verbo Irregular
delante de		in front	Preposición
delgado/a		thin	Adjetivo
delicado/a		delicate	Adjetivo
dentista (used for male or female)	El, La	dentist	Sustantivo

dentro de		inside of	Preposición
derecho		straight	Adjetivo, Adverbio
desde		from	Preposición
desear		to want/wish	Verbo Regular
despedir (e—i)		to say good-bye	Verbo Irregular: E-I
despertar (e—ie)		to wake up	Verbo Irregular
después de		after	Preposición
detalle	El	detail	Sustantivo
detrás de		behind	Preposición
devolver (o—ue)		to return/give back	Verbo Irregular
diciembre		December	Sustantivo
diez		10	Adjetivo
diez y nueve / diecinueve		19	Adjetivo
diez y ocho / dieciocho		18	Adjetivo
diez y seis / dieciséis		16	Adjetivo
diez y siete /diecisiete		17	Adjetivo
distancia	La	distance	Sustantivo
dividir		to divide	Verbo Regular
doblar		to turn/flip	Verbo Regular
doce		12	Adjetivo
doctor/a	El, La	doctor	Sustantivo
domingo(s)	El, Los	(on) Sunday/s	Sustantivo
Don/Doña		title of respect (usually with elders)	Sustantivo
dormir (o—ue)		to sleep	Verbo Irregular
dormitorio	El	bedroom	Sustantivo
dos		2	Adjetivo
doscientos		200	Adjetivo
edificio	El	building	Sustantivo
educación	La	education	Sustantivo
Él or él		he	Pronombre
El gusto es mío.		The pleasure is mine.	Expresión
ella		she	Pronombre
ellas		they (all women)	Pronombre
ellos		they (all men or neuter)	Pronombre
en		in	Preposición
encantado/a		pleased to meet you	Adjetivo
encima		above/on top	Adverbio
encima de		on top of	Preposición

encontrar (o—ue)		to meet/encounter	Verbo Irregular
enero		January	Sustantivo
enfermero/a	El, La	nurse	Sustantivo
enfrente de		across from; facing	Preposición
enhorabuena		congratulations	Expresión
enorme		enormous	Adjetivo
enseñar		to teach	Verbo Regular
entre		among; between	Preposición
es la… (1:00)		it is… 1:00 (time related to 1:00 o'clock)	Expresión
escribir		to write	Verbo Regular
esencial		essential	Adjetivo
español	El	Spanish language	Sustantivo
español	El	Spanish man	Sustantivo
español/a		Spanish	Adjetivo
española	La	Spanish woman	Sustantivo
especial		special	Adjetivo
espejo	El	mirror	Sustantivo
esperar		to hope, wish, wait for	Verbo Regular
esposa	La	wife	Sustantivo
esposo	El	husband	Sustantivo
Esta es mi amiga, Ana.		This is my friend, Ana.	Expresión
estadio	El	stadium	Sustantivo
Estados Unidos	Los	United States	Sustantivo
estadounidense	El, La	United States citizen	Adjetivo, Sustantivo
estar		to be	Verbo Irregular
estar casado/a		to be married	Expresión, Verbo Irregular
estar divorciado/a de		to be divorced	Expresión, Verbo Irregular
estoy de acuerdo		I agree	Expresión
estructura	La	structure	Sustantivo
estudiante	El, La	student	Sustantivo
estudiar		to study	Verbo Regular
estufa	La	stove	Sustantivo
excelente		excellent	Adjetivo
expreso/a		express	Adjetivo
extremo/a		extreme	Adjetivo, Sustantivo

faltar		to miss, lack	Verbo Similar a Gustar
familia	La	family	Sustantivo
famoso/a		famous	Adjetivo
fantástico/a		fantastic	Adjetivo
farmacéutico/a	El, La	pharmacist	Sustantivo
febrero		February	Sustantivo
feo/a		ugly	Adjetivo
fin de semana	El	(on) the weekend	Sustantivo
fines de semana	Los	(on) the weekends	Sustantivo
foto	La	photo	Sustantivo
fracasar		to fail	Verbo Regular
francés		French	Adjetivo
francés	El	French language	Sustantivo
francés	El	French man	Sustantivo
francesa		French	Adjetivo
francesa	La	French woman	Sustantivo
fuera de		except	Preposición
fuerte		strong	Adjetivo
funcionar		to function	Verbo Regular
garaje	El	garage	Sustantivo
gato/a	El, La	cat	Sustantivo
general		general	Adjetivo, Sustantivo
geografía	La	geography	Sustantivo
gimnasio	El	gymnasium	Sustantivo
girar		to turn	Verbo Regular
gordo/a		fat	Adjetivo
grande		big; large	Adjetivo
gris		gray	Adjetivo
guapo/a		handsome	Adjetivo
guapo/a		pretty	Adjetivo
guía	El, La	guide	Sustantivo
gustar		to be pleasing (like)	Verbo Regular (Requires IOP)
hablar		to talk, speak	Verbo Regular
hace buen tiempo		it's good weather	Expresión
hace frío		it's cold	Expresión
hace mal tiempo		it's bad weather	Expresión
hace sol		it's sunny	Expresión

hace viento		it's windy	Expresión
hacer (go)		to do, make	Verbo Irregular
hacia		toward	Preposición
hasta		until	Adverbio
hasta luego		see you later	Expresión
hasta mañana		see you tomorrow	Expresión
hermana	La	sister	Sustantivo
hermanastro/a	El, La	step-sibling	Sustantivo
hermano	El	brother	Sustantivo
hermoso/a		beautiful	Adjetivo
hija	La	daughter	Sustantivo
hijastro/a	El, La	step-child	Sustantivo
hijo	El	son	Sustantivo
historia	La	history	Sustantivo
hogar	El	home	Sustantivo
horno	El	oven	Sustantivo
hospital	El	hospital	Sustantivo
hotel	El	hotel	Sustantivo
idioma	El	language	Sustantivo
iglesia	La	church	Sustantivo
igualmente		likewise, it's mutual	Adverbio
ilusión	La	illusion	Sustantivo
importante		important	Adjetivo
imposible		impossible	Adjetivo
individual		individual	Adjetivo
infinito/a		infinite	Adjetivo
informática	La	computer science	Sustantivo
ingeniero/a	El, La	engineer	Sustantivo
inglés		English	Adjetivo
inglés	El	English language	Sustantivo
inglés	El	English man	Sustantivo
inglesa		English	Adjetivo
inglesa	La	English woman	Sustantivo
inteligente		intelligent	Adjetivo
interactivo/a		interactive	Adjetivo
interesante		interesting	Adjetivo
invención	La	invention	Sustantivo
invierno	El	winter	Sustantivo

ir		to go	Verbo Irregular
isla	La	island	Sustantivo
joven		young	Adjetivo
jueves	El, Los	(on) Thursday/s	Sustantivo
jugar (u—ue)		to play a sport or game	Verbo Irregular
julio		July	Sustantivo
junio		June	Sustantivo
laboratorio	El	laboratory	Sustantivo
lámpara	La	lamp	Sustantivo
lápiz	El	pencil	Sustantivo
lavabo	El	sink	Sustantivo
lavadora	La	washing machine	Sustantivo
leer		to read	Verbo Regular
lejos de		far from	Adverbio
león	El	lion	Sustantivo
letra	La	letter	Sustantivo
librería	La	bookstore	Sustantivo
libro	El	book	Sustantivo
limpiar		to clean	Verbo Regular
literatura	La	literature	Sustantivo
llegar		to arrive	Verbo Regular
lo siento		I am sorry	Expresión
lugar en la comunidad	El	place in the community	Sustantivo
lunes	El, Los	(on) Monday/s	Sustantivo
madrastra	La	step-mother	Sustantivo
madre (mamá)	La	mother	Sustantivo
madrina	La	god-mother	Sustantivo
maestro/a	El, La	teacher	Sustantivo
malo/a		bad	Adjetivo
mantener (irreg yo)		to maintain	Verbo Irregular
mapa	El	map	Sustantivo
máquina	La	machine	Sustantivo
marrón		brown	Adjetivo
martes	El, Los	(on) Tuesday/s	Sustantivo
marzo		March	Sustantivo
mas		but	Preposición
más		more	Adjetivo
matemáticas	Las	math	Sustantivo

material	El	material	Sustantivo
mayo		May	Sustantivo
mayor		older	Adjetivo
me llamo …(José)		my name is… (José)	Expresión
medicina	La	medicine	Sustantivo
médico/a	El, La	doctor	Sustantivo
melodía	La	melody	Sustantivo
memoria	La	memory	Sustantivo
menor		younger	Adjetivo
mentir (e—ie)		to lie	Verbo Irregular
mesa	La	table	Sustantivo
mexicana	La	Mexican woman	Sustantivo
mexicano	El	Mexican man	Sustantivo
mexicano/a		Mexican	Adjetivo
México		Mexico	Sustantivo
mi (mis)		my	Adjetivo
mi apellido es … (Ramos)		my last name is …(Ramos)	Expresión
microondas	El	microwave	Sustantivo
miércoles	El, Los	(on) Wednesday/s	Sustantivo
miserable		miserable	Adjetivo
momento	El	moment	Sustantivo
morado/a		purple	Adjetivo
moreno/a		brunette	Adjetivo
morir (o—ue)		to die	Verbo Irregular
mucho gusto		pleased to meet you	Expresión
mujer policía	La	policewoman	Sustantivo
música	La	music	Sustantivo
muy bien		very well	Adjetivo, Adverbio
nación	La	nation	Sustantivo
naranja		orange	Adjetivo
nariz	La	nose	Sustantivo
necesidad	La	necessity	Sustantivo
necesitar		to need	Verbo Regular
negro/a		black	Adjetivo
nieto/a	El, La	grandson/granddaughter	Sustantivo
no mucho		not much	Expresión
no muy bien		not very well	Expresión
nosotros/as		we	Pronombre

nota	La	note	Sustantivo
noventa		90	Adjetivo
novia	La	girlfriend	Sustantivo
noviembre		November	Sustantivo
novio	El	boyfriend	Sustantivo
nuera	La	daughter-in-law	Sustantivo
nuestro/a		our	Adjetivo
nueve		9	Adjetivo
nuevo/a		new	Adjetivo
números	Los	numbers	Sustantivo
objetivo	El	objective	Sustantivo
océano	El	ocean	Sustantivo
ochenta		80	Adjetivo
ocho		8	Adjetivo
octubre		October	Sustantivo
oficina	La	office	Sustantivo
olvidar(se)		to forget	Verbo Regular
once		11	Adjetivo
opción	La	option	Sustantivo
opinión	La	opinion	Sustantivo
orden	La	order	Sustantivo
original		original	Adjetivo
otoño	El	autumn/fall	Sustantivo
paciente	El, La	patient	Sustantivo
paciente		patient	Adjetivo
padrastro	El	step-father	Sustantivo
padre	El	father	Sustantivo
padres	Los	parents	Sustantivo
padrino	El	god-father	Sustantivo
padrinos	Los	god-parents	Sustantivo
pagar		to pay	Verbo Regular
papá	El	father	Sustantivo
papel	El	paper	Sustantivo
para		for; in order to	Preposición
parientes	Los	relatives	Sustantivo
parque	El	park	Sustantivo
pasar (pasar por)		to pass/to pass by	Verbo Regular
pase		come in	Expresión
pedagogía	La	education	Sustantivo
pedir (e—i)		to ask for	Verbo Irregular

peluquería	La	hairdresser	Sustantivo
pequeño/a		small	Adjetivo
perdón		excuse me; when you cough or sneeze	Expresión
perezoso/a		lazy	Adjetivo
perro/a	El, La	dog	Sustantivo
personal		personal	Adjetivo
pino	El	pine	Sustantivo
piso	El	floor	Sustantivo
planta	La	plant	Sustantivo
plaza mayor	La	main plaza/center of town	Sustantivo
pluma	La	pen	Sustantivo
pobre		poor	Adjetivo
poder (o—ue)		to be able/can	Verbo Irregular
policía	La	police department	Sustantivo
policía	El	policeman	Sustantivo
política	La	politics	Sustantivo
poner (go)		to put	Verbo Irregular
por		for; through; by; because of	Preposición
por favor		please	Expresión
porque		because	Conjunción
posesivo	El	possessive	Sustantivo
posibilidad	La	possibility	Sustantivo
posible		possible	Adjetivo
preferir (e—ie)		to prefer	Verbo Irregular
preguntar		to ask (a question)	Verbo Regular
presidente	El, La	president	Sustantivo
prestar		to borrow; to loan; to lend	Verbo Regular
primavera	La	spring	Sustantivo
primero/a		first	Adjetivo
primo/a	El, La	cousin	Sustantivo
problema (Irregular in terms of gender rule—Greek origin.)	El	problem	Sustantivo
profesor/a	El, La	teacher/professor	Sustantivo
Promover (o—ue)		to promote	Verbo Irregular
pronto		soon	Expresión
proyecto	El	project	Sustantivo

psicología	La	psychology	Sustantivo
público	El	people	Sustantivo
público/a		public	Adjetivo
puerta	La	door	Sustantivo
quedar		to be located	Verbo Regular
querer (e—ie)		to want/wish/love	Verbo Irregular
quince		15	Adjetivo
quisiera (querer)		I would like (very polite request)	Expresión
radio	El, La	radio	Sustantivo
rancho	El	ranch	Sustantivo
razón	La	reason	Sustantivo
real		real/royal	Adjetivo
recepcionista	El, La	receptionist	Sustantivo
recibir		to receive	Verbo Regular
recomendar (e—ie)		to recommend	Verbo Irregular
recto		straight	Adjetivo, Adverbio
reducir (c—zc)		to reduce	Verbo Regular
refrigerador	El	refrigerator	Sustantivo
regresar		to return	Verbo Regular
relación	La	relationship	Sustantivo
repetir (e—i)		to repeat	Verbo Irregular: E-I
reservación	La	reservation	Sustantivo
residencia	La	dormitory	Sustantivo
residencia estudiantil	La	residence hall	Sustantivo
responsable		responsible	Adjetivo
restaurante	El	restaurant	Sustantivo
rico/a		rich	Adjetivo
rojo/a		red	Adjetivo
romántico/a		romantic	Adjetivo
romper (se)		to break	Verbo Regular
rosa	La	rose	Sustantivo
rosado/a		pink	Adjetivo
rubio/a		blonde	Adjetivo
ruta	La	route	Sustantivo
sábado (s)	El, Los	(on) Saturday/s	Sustantivo
saber (otros irregulares -yo)		to know	Verbo Irregular
sacar		to take	Verbo Regular

sacar (buenas/malas) notas		to get (good/bad) grades	Verbo Regular
sala	La	living room	Sustantivo
secador	El	drier	Sustantivo
secreto	El	secret	Sustantivo
secreto/a		secret	Adjetivo
seguir (e—i)		to follow/continue	Verbo Irregular
según		according to	Adverbio, Preposición
segundo/a	El, La	second	Adjetivo, Sustantivo
seis		6	Adjetivo
semestre	El	semester	Sustantivo
Señor (Sr.)	El	Sir, Mr.	Sustantivo
Señora (Sra.)	La	Mrs. Madam, lady	Sustantivo
Señorita (Srta.)	La	Ms. Miss, young lady	Sustantivo
sensación	La	sensation	Sustantivo
sentir (e—ie)		to feel, regret, to be sorry	Verbo Irregular
septiembre		September	Sustantivo
ser (muy irregular)		to be	Verbo Irregular
ser soltero/a		to be single	Expresión, Verbo Irregular
servir (e—i)		to serve	Verbo Irregular
sesenta		60	Adjetivo
setenta		70	Adjetivo
si		if	Preposición
sí		yes	Adverbio
siete		7	Adjetivo
silencio	El	silence	Sustantivo
silla	La	seat	Sustantivo
simpático/a		nice	Adjetivo
sin		without	Preposición
sobre		about	Preposición
sobrino/a	El, La	nephew/niece	Sustantivo
sociología	La	sociology	Sustantivo
sofá	El	sofa	Sustantivo
son las… >2:00		it is… >2:00 clock time	Expresión
sótano	El	basement	Sustantivo
su		his, her, your	Adjetivo
su		their/your	Adjetivo
suegra	La	mother-in-law	Sustantivo

suegro	El	father-in-law	Sustantivo
sugerir (e—ie)		to suggest	Verbo Irregular
supermercado	El	supermarket	Sustantivo
teatro	El	theatre	Sustantivo
teléfono	El	phone	Sustantivo
teléfono	El	telephone	Sustantivo
televisión	La	TV	Sustantivo
televisor	La	tv (actual electronic)	Sustantivo
temer		to fear	Verbo Regular
tener (go + e—ie)		to have	Verbo Irregular
tener calor (go + e—ie)		to be hot	Expresión, Verbo Irregular
tener celos (go + e—ie)		to be jealous	Expresión, Verbo Irregular
tener éxito (go + e—ie)		to be successful	Expresión, Verbo Irregular
tener frío (go + e—ie)		to be cold	Expresión, Verbo Irregular
tener ganas de... (go + e—ie)		to feel like...(doing something)	Expresión, Verbo Irregular
tener hambre (go + e—ie)		to be hungry	Expresión, Verbo Irregular
tener miedo (de) (go + e—ie)		to be afraid (de)	Expresión, Verbo Irregular
tener paciencia (go + e—ie)		to be patient	Expresión, Verbo Irregular
tener prisa (go + e—ie)		to be in a hurry	Expresión, Verbo Irregular
tener razón (go + e—ie)		to be right	Expresión, Verbo Irregular
tener sed (go + e—ie)		to be thirsty	Expresión, Verbo Irregular
tener sueño (go + e—ie)		to be tired / sleepy	Expresión, Verbo Irregular
tener...años (go + e—ie)		to...years old	Expresión, Verbo Irregular
tercer/a		third	Adjetivo
tercero	El	third	Sustantivo
terminar		to finish	Verbo Regular
terrible		terrible	Adjetivo
tienda	La	store	Sustantivo
tío/a	El, La	uncle/aunt	Sustantivo

tomar apuntes		to take notes	Verbo Regular
tome asiento		sit down	Expresión
tonto/a		silly; dumb	Adjetivo
trabajador/a		hard-working	Adjetivo
trabajar		to work	Verbo Regular
tráfico	El	traffic	Sustantivo
trece		13	Adjetivo
treinta		30	Adjetivo
treinta y cinco		35	Adjetivo
treinta y cuatro		34	Adjetivo
treinta y dos		32	Adjetivo
treinta y nueve		39	Adjetivo
treinta y ocho		38	Adjetivo
treinta y seis		36	Adjetivo
treinta y siete		37	Adjetivo
treinta y tres		33	Adjetivo
treinta y uno		31	Adjetivo
tres		3	Adjetivo
trescientos		300	Adjetivo
tu		your	Adjetivo
tú		you (friendly, familiar)	Pronombre
unido/a		united	Adjetivo
uno		1	Adjetivo
urgente		urgent	Adjetivo
usar		to use	Verbo Regular
Usted (Ud.)		you (formal)	Pronombre
Ustedes (Uds.)		you all (formal & both formal and informal in latin america)	Pronombre
usual		usual	Adjetivo
vacaciones (pl.)	Las	vacation	Sustantivo
veinte		20	Adjetivo
veinte y cinco / veinticinco		25	Adjetivo
veinte y cuatro / veinticuatro		24	Adjetivo
veinte y dos / veintidós		22	Adjetivo
veinte y nueve / veintinueve		29	Adjetivo
veinte y ocho / veintiocho		28	Adjetivo
veinte y seis / veintiséis		26	Adjetivo

veinte y siete / veintisiete		27	Adjetivo
veinte y tres / veintitrés		23	Adjetivo
veinte y uno / veintiuno		21	Adjetivo
ventana	La	window	Sustantivo
verano	El	summer	Sustantivo
verbo	El	verb	Sustantivo
verde		green	Adjetivo
veterinario/a	El, La	veterinarian	Sustantivo
vibración	La	vibration	Sustantivo
viejo/a		old	Adjetivo
virgen	La	virgin	Sustantivo
visitar		to visit	Verbo Regular
vivir		to live	Verbo Regular
vocabulario	El	vocabulary	Sustantivo
volar (o—ue)		to fly	Verbo Irregular
volver (o—ue)		to return	Verbo Irregular
vosotros/as		you all (Spain only)	Pronombre
voz	La	voice	Sustantivo
vuestro/a		your	Adjetivo
yerno	El	son-in-law	Sustantivo
yo		I	Pronombre
yo también		me, too (I also)	Expresión

Glosario Inglés

Inglés	M/F	Español	Clasificación
(on) Monday/s	El, Los	lunes	Sustantivo
(on) Saturday/s	El, Los	sábado (s)	Sustantivo
(on) Sunday/s	El, Los	domingo(s)	Sustantivo
(on) the weekend	El	fin de semana	Sustantivo
(on) the weekends	Los	fines de semana	Sustantivo
(on) Thursday/s	El, Los	jueves	Sustantivo
(on) Tuesday/s	El, Los	martes	Sustantivo
(on) Wednesday/s	El, Los	miércoles	Sustantivo
(very) well thank you		(muy) bien, gracias.	Expresión
0		cero	Adjetivo
1		uno	Adjetivo
10		diez	Adjetivo
100		cien	Adjetivo
100 > 101…199		ciento >101…199	Adjetivo
11		once	Adjetivo
12		doce	Adjetivo
13		trece	Adjetivo
14		catorce	Adjetivo
15		quince	Adjetivo
16		diez y seis / dieciséis	Adjetivo
17		diez y siete /diecisiete	Adjetivo
18		diez y ocho / dieciocho	Adjetivo
19		diez y nueve / diecinueve	Adjetivo
2		dos	Adjetivo
20		veinte	Adjetivo
200		doscientos	Adjetivo
21		veinte y uno / veintiuno	Adjetivo
22		veinte y dos / veintidós	Adjetivo
23		veinte y tres / veintitrés	Adjetivo
24		veinte y cuatro / veinticuatro	Adjetivo
25		veinte y cinco /veinticinco	Adjetivo

26		veinte y seis / veintiséis	Adjetivo
27		veinte y siete / veintisiete	Adjetivo
28		veinte y ocho / veintiocho	Adjetivo
29		veinte y nueve / veintinueve	Adjetivo
3		tres	Adjetivo
30		treinta	Adjetivo
300		trescientos	Adjetivo
31		treinta y uno	Adjetivo
32		treinta y dos	Adjetivo
33		treinta y tres	Adjetivo
34		treinta y cuatro	Adjetivo
35		treinta y cinco	Adjetivo
36		treinta y seis	Adjetivo
37		treinta y siete	Adjetivo
38		treinta y ocho	Adjetivo
39		treinta y nueve	Adjetivo
4		cuatro	Adjetivo
40		cuarenta	Adjetivo
5		cinco	Adjetivo
50		cincuenta	Adjetivo
6		seis	Adjetivo
60		sesenta	Adjetivo
7		siete	Adjetivo
70		setenta	Adjetivo
8		ocho	Adjetivo
80		ochenta	Adjetivo
9		nueve	Adjetivo
90		noventa	Adjetivo
about		acerca de	Preposición
about		sobre	Preposición
above/on top		encima	Adverbio
accident	El	accidente	Sustantivo
according to		según	Adverbio, Preposición
accountant	El, La	contador/a	Sustantivo
across from; facing		enfrente de	Preposición
actor	El	actor	Sustantivo
actress	La	actriz	Sustantivo
adjective	El	adjetivo	Sustantivo
African		africana	Adjetivo
African		africano	Adjetivo
African man	El	africano	Sustantivo

African woman	La	africana	Sustantivo
after		después de	Preposición
among; between		entre	Preposición
angel	El	ángel	Sustantivo
anthropology	La	antropología	Sustantivo
apartment	El	apartamento	Sustantivo
April	El	abril	Sustantivo
architect	El, La	arquitecto/a	Sustantivo
art	El, Las	arte*	Sustantivo
artistic		artístico/a	Adjetivo
at ... >2:00 clock time		a las >2:00	Expresión
at 1:00 or times related to one		a la	Expresión
attic	El	ático	Sustantivo
August		agosto	Sustantivo
autumn/fall	El	otoño	Sustantivo
bad		malo/a	Adjetivo
balance	El	balance	Sustantivo
banana	La	banana	Sustantivo
bank	El	banco	Sustantivo
basement	El	sótano	Sustantivo
bathroom	El	baño	Sustantivo
beautiful		bello/a	Adjetivo
beautiful		hermoso/a	Adjetivo
because		porque	Conjunción
bed	La	cama	Sustantivo
bedroom	El	dormitorio	Sustantivo
before (time/space)		antes de	Preposición
behind		detrás de	Preposición
big; large		grande	Adjetivo
biology	La	biología	Sustantivo
birthday	El, Los	cumpleaños	Sustantivo
black		negro/a	Adjetivo
blonde		rubio/a	Adjetivo
blue		azul	Adjetivo
book	El	libro	Sustantivo
bookstore	La	librería	Sustantivo
bored		aburrido/a	Adjetivo
boyfriend	El	novio	Sustantivo
brother	El	hermano	Sustantivo
brother-in-law	El	cuñado	Sustantivo
brown		café	Adjetivo
brown		marrón	Adjetivo

brunette		moreno/a	Adjetivo
building	El	edificio	Sustantivo
business administration	La	administración de empresas	Sustantivo
but		mas	Preposición
cabin	La	cabina	Sustantivo
cafeteria	La	cafetería	Sustantivo
calculator	La	calculadora	Sustantivo
car	El	auto	Sustantivo
car	El	carro	Sustantivo
car	El	coche	Sustantivo
cat	El, La	gato/a	Sustantivo
chair	El	asiento	Sustantivo
channel	El	canal	Sustantivo
Chinese		chino/a	Adjetivo
Chinese language	El	chino	Sustantivo
Chinese man	El	chino	Sustantivo
Chinese woman	La	china	Sustantivo
church	La	iglesia	Sustantivo
colleague	El, La	colega (used for male or female)	Sustantivo
collection	La	colección	Sustantivo
come in		pase	Expresión
computer science	La	informática	Sustantivo
concert	El	concierto	Sustantivo
congratulations		enhorabuena	Expresión
course	El	curso	Sustantivo
court	La	corte	Sustantivo
cousin	El, La	primo/a	Sustantivo
culture	La	cultura	Sustantivo
curious		curioso/a	Adjetivo
daughter	La	hija	Sustantivo
daughter-in-law	La	nuera	Sustantivo
December		diciembre	Sustantivo
delicate		delicado/a	Adjetivo
dentist	El, La	dentista (used for male or female)	Sustantivo
detail	El	detalle	Sustantivo
dining room	El	comedor	Sustantivo
distance	La	distancia	Sustantivo
doctor	El, La	doctor/a	Sustantivo
doctor	El, La	médico/a	Sustantivo
doctor's office	El	consultorio	Sustantivo

dog	El, La	perro/a	Sustantivo
door	La	puerta	Sustantivo
dormitory	La	residencia	Sustantivo
drier	El	secador	Sustantivo
education	La	educación	Sustantivo
education	La	pedagogía	Sustantivo
engineer	El, La	ingeniero/a	Sustantivo
English		inglés	Adjetivo
English		inglesa	Adjetivo
English language	El	inglés	Sustantivo
English man	El	inglés	Sustantivo
English woman	La	inglesa	Sustantivo
enormous		enorme	Adjetivo
essential		esencial	Adjetivo
excellent		excelente	Adjetivo
except		fuera de	Preposición
exchange in terms of currency		cambiar	Verbo Regular
excuse me, when you need to physically move		con permiso	Expresión
excuse me; when you cough or sneeze		perdón	Expresión
expensive		caro/a	Adjetivo
express		expreso/a	Adjetivo
extreme		extremo/a	Adjetivo, Sustantivo
family	La	familia	Sustantivo
famous		famoso/a	Adjetivo
fantastic		fantástico/a	Adjetivo
far from		lejos de	Adverbio
fat		gordo/a	Adjetivo
father	El	padre	Sustantivo
father	El	papá	Sustantivo
father-in-law	El	suegro	Sustantivo
February		febrero	Sustantivo
fire department	El	cuerpo de bomberos	Sustantivo
first		primero/a	Adjetivo
floor	El	piso	Sustantivo
for; in order to		para	Preposición
for; through; by; because of		por	Preposición
fortunate/lucky		afortunado/a	Adjetivo
French		francés	Adjetivo
French		francesa	Adjetivo

French language	El	francés	Sustantivo
French man	El	francés	Sustantivo
French woman	La	francesa	Sustantivo
from		desde	Preposición
from where?		¿de dónde?	Preposición
funny; comical		cómico/a	Adjetivo
garage	El	garaje	Sustantivo
general		general	Adjetivo, Sustantivo
geography	La	geografía	Sustantivo
German		alemán	Adjetivo
German		alemana	Adjetivo
German language	El	alemán	Sustantivo
German man	El	alemán	Sustantivo
German woman	La	alemana	Sustantivo
girlfriend	La	girlfirend	Sustantivo
god-father	El	padrino	Sustantivo
god-mother	La	madrina	Sustantivo
god-parents	Los	padrinos	Sustantivo
good		bueno/a	Adjetivo
good afternoon		buenas tardes	Expresión
good bye		adiós	Expresión
good evening		buenas noches	Expresión
good morning		buenos días	Expresión
goodbye		chao	Expresión
grandfather/grandmother	El, La	abuelo/a	Sustantivo
grandson/granddaughter	El, La	nieto/a	Sustantivo
gray		gris	Adjetivo
green		verde	Adjetivo
guide	El, La	guía	Sustantivo
gymnasium	El	gimnasio	Sustantivo
hairdresser	La	peluquería	Sustantivo
handsome		guapo/a	Adjetivo
hard-working		trabajador/a	Adjetivo
he		Él or él	Pronombre
his, her, your		su	Adjetivo
history	La	historia	Sustantivo
home	El	hogar	Sustantivo
hospital	El	hospital	Sustantivo
hotel	El	hotel	Sustantivo
house	La	casa	Sustantivo
How are you? (formal)		¿Cómo está Usted (Ud.)?	Expresión

How are you? (informal)		¿Cómo estás tú?	Expresión
How great!		¡Qué chévere!	Expresión
How is it going? (informal)		¿Qué tal?	Expresión
how many?		¿cuántos?	Pronombre
how much?		¿cuánto?	Pronombre
how? How!		¿cómo? ¡cómo!	Adverbio
husband	El	esposo	Sustantivo
I		yo	Pronombre
I agree		estoy de acuerdo	Expresión
I am sorry		lo siento	Expresión
I would like (very polite request)		quisiera (querer)	Expresión
if		si	Preposición
illusion	La	ilusión	Sustantivo
important		importante	Adjetivo
impossible		imposible	Adjetivo
in		en	Preposición
in front		delante de	Preposición
in the afternoon		de la tarde	Expresión
in the early morning		de la madrugada	Expresión
in the evening		de la noche	Expresión
in the morning		de la mañana	Expresión
individual		individual	Adjetivo
inexpensive, cheap		barato/a	Adjetivo
infinite		infinito/a	Adjetivo
inside of		dentro de	Preposición
intelligent		inteligente	Adjetivo
interactive		interactivo/a	Adjetivo
interesting		interesante	Adjetivo
invention	La	invención	Sustantivo
island	La	isla	Sustantivo
it is… >2:00 clock time		son las… >2:00	Expresión
it is… 1:00 (time related to 1:00 o'clock)		es la… (1:00)	Expresión
it's bad weather		hace mal tiempo	Expresión
it's cold		hace frío	Expresión
it's good weather		hace buen tiempo	Expresión
it's sunny		hace sol	Expresión
it's windy		hace viento	Expresión
January		enero	Sustantivo
July		julio	Sustantivo
June		junio	Sustantivo

kitchen	La	cocina	Sustantivo
laboratory	El	laboratorio	Sustantivo
lamp	La	lámpara	Sustantivo
language	El	idioma	Sustantivo
lawyer	El, La	abogado/a	Sustantivo
lazy		perezoso/a	Adjetivo
letter	La	letra	Sustantivo
library	La	biblioteca	Sustantivo
like, as		como	Preposición
likewise, it's mutual		igualmente	Adverbio
lion	El	león	Sustantivo
literature	La	literatura	Sustantivo
living room	La	sala	Sustantivo
machine	La	máquina	Sustantivo
main plaza/center of town	La	plaza mayor	Sustantivo
map	El	mapa	Sustantivo
March		marzo	Sustantivo
material	El	material	Sustantivo
math	Las	matemáticas	Sustantivo
May		mayo	Sustantivo
me, too (I also)		yo también	Expresión
medicine	La	medicina	Sustantivo
melody	La	melodía	Sustantivo
memory	La	memoria	Sustantivo
Mexican		mexicano/a	Adjetivo
Mexican man	El	mexicano	Sustantivo
Mexican woman	La	mexicana	Sustantivo
Mexico		México	Sustantivo
microwave	El	microondas	Sustantivo
mirror	El	espejo	Sustantivo
miserable		miserable	Adjetivo
moment	El	momento	Sustantivo
more		más	Adjetivo
mother	La	madre (mamá)	Sustantivo
mother-in-law	La	suegra	Sustantivo
movie theatre	El	cine	Sustantivo
Mrs. Madam, lady	La	Señora (Sra.)	Sustantivo
Ms. Miss, young lady	La	Señorita (Srta.)	Sustantivo
music	La	música	Sustantivo
my		mi (mis)	Adjetivo
my last name is …(Ramos)		mi apellido es … (Ramos)	Expresión

my name is… (José)		me llamo …(José)	Expresión
nation	La	nación	Sustantivo
near		cerca de	Preposición
necessity	La	necesidad	Sustantivo
nephew/niece	El, La	sobrino/a	Sustantivo
new		nuevo/a	Adjetivo
next to		al lado de	Preposición
nice		simpático/a	Adjetivo
nose	La	nariz	Sustantivo
not much		no mucho	Expresión
not very well		no muy bien	Expresión
note	La	nota	Sustantivo
notebook	El	cuaderno	Sustantivo
November		noviembre	Sustantivo
numbers	Los	números	Sustantivo
nurse	El, La	enfermero/a	Sustantivo
objective	El	objetivo	Sustantivo
ocean	El	océano	Sustantivo
October		octubre	Sustantivo
of / from		de	Preposición
office	La	oficina	Sustantivo
old		viejo/a	Adjetivo
older		mayor	Adjetivo
on top of		encima de	Preposición
opinion	La	opinión	Sustantivo
option	La	opción	Sustantivo
orange		anaranjado/a	Adjetivo
orange		naranja	Adjetivo
order	La	orden	Sustantivo
original		original	Adjetivo
our		nuestro/a	Adjetivo
outside		afuera de	Adverbio
outside of		(a)fuera de	Preposición
oven	El	horno	Sustantivo
paper	El	papel	Sustantivo
parents	Los	padres	Sustantivo
park	El	parque	Sustantivo
patient		paciente	Adjetivo
patient	El, La	paciente	Sustantivo
pen	El	bolígrafo	Sustantivo
pen	La	pluma	Sustantivo
pencil	El	lápiz	Sustantivo

people	El	público	Sustantivo
personal		personal	Adjetivo
pharmacist	El, La	farmacéutico/a	Sustantivo
phone	El	teléfono	Sustantivo
photo	La	foto	Sustantivo
pine	El	pino	Sustantivo
pink		rosado/a	Adjetivo
place in the community	El	lugar en la comunidad	Sustantivo
plant	La	planta	Sustantivo
please		por favor	Expresión
pleased to meet you		encantado/a	Adjetivo
pleased to meet you		mucho gusto	Expresión
police department	La	policía	Sustantivo
policeman	El	policía	Sustantivo
policewoman	La	mujer policía	Sustantivo
political science	Las	ciencias políticas	Sustantivo
politics	La	política	Sustantivo
poor		pobre	Adjetivo
posible		posible	Adjetivo
possessive	El	posesivo	Sustantivo
possibility	La	posibilidad	Sustantivo
president	El, La	presidente	Sustantivo
pretty		bonito/a	Adjetivo
pretty		guapo/a	Adjetivo
problem	El	problema (Irregular in terms of gender rule—Greek origin.)	Sustantivo
project	El	proyecto	Sustantivo
psychology	La	psicología	Sustantivo
public		público/a	Adjetivo
purple		morado/a	Adjetivo
radio	El, La	radio	Sustantivo
ranch	El	rancho	Sustantivo
real/royal		real	Adjetivo
reason	La	razón	Sustantivo
receptionist	El, La	recepcionista	Sustantivo
red		rojo/a	Adjetivo
refrigerator	El	refrigerador	Sustantivo
relationship	La	relación	Sustantivo
relatives	Los	parientes	Sustantivo
reservation	La	reservación	Sustantivo
residence hall	La	residencia estudiantil	Sustantivo
responsible		responsable	Adjetivo

restaurant	El	restaurante	Sustantivo
rich		rico/a	Adjetivo
romantic		romántico/a	Adjetivo
rose	La	rosa	Sustantivo
route	La	ruta	Sustantivo
school year	El	año escolar	Sustantivo
science	La	ciencia	Sustantivo
seat	La	silla	Sustantivo
second	El, La	segundo/a	Adjetivo, Sustantivo
secret	El	secreto	Sustantivo
secret		secreto/a	Adjetivo
see you later		hasta luego	Expresión
see you tomorrow		hasta mañana	Expresión
semester	El	semestre	Sustantivo
sensation	La	sensación	Sustantivo
September		septiembre	Sustantivo
she		ella	Pronombre
shopping center/mall	El	centro comercial	Sustantivo
short		bajo/a	Adjetivo
silence	El	silencio	Sustantivo
silly; dumb		tonto/a	Adjetivo
sink	El	lavabo	Sustantivo
Sir, Mr.	El	Señor (Sr.)	Sustantivo
sister	La	hermana	Sustantivo
sister-in-law	La	cuñado	Sustantivo
sit down		tome asiento	Expresión
small		pequeño/a	Adjetivo
so, so		así, así	Expresión
sociology	La	sociología	Sustantivo
sofa	El	sofá	Sustantivo
son	El	hijo	Sustantivo
son-in-law	El	yerno	Sustantivo
soon		pronto	Expresión
Spanish		español/a	Adjetivo
Spanish language	El	español	Sustantivo
Spanish man	El	español	Sustantivo
Spanish woman	La	española	Sustantivo
special		especial	Adjetivo
spring	La	primavera	Sustantivo
stadium	El	estadio	Sustantivo
step-child	El, La	hijastro/a	Sustantivo

step-father	El	padrastro	Sustantivo
step-mother	La	madrastra	Sustantivo
step-sibling	El, La	hermanastro/a	Sustantivo
store	La	tienda	Sustantivo
stove	La	estufa	Sustantivo
straight		derecho	Adjetivo, Adverbio
straight		recto	Adjetivo, Adverbio
strong		fuerte	Adjetivo
structure	La	estructura	Sustantivo
student	El, La	estudiante	Sustantivo
summer	El	verano	Sustantivo
supermarket	El	supermercado	Sustantivo
table	La	mesa	Sustantivo
tall		alto/a	Adjetivo
teacher	El, La	maestro/a	Sustantivo
teacher/professor	El, La	profesor/a	Sustantivo
telephone	El	teléfono	Sustantivo
terrible		terrible	Adjetivo
thank you (very much)		(muchas) gracias	Expresión
The pleasure is mine.		El gusto es mío.	Expresión
theatre	El	teatro	Sustantivo
their/your		su	Adjetivo
they (all men or neuter)		ellos	Pronombre
they (all women)		ellas	Pronombre
thin		delgado/a	Adjetivo
third		tercer/a	Adjetivo
third	El	tercero	Sustantivo
This is my friend, Ana.		Esta es mi amiga, Ana.	Expresión
title of respect (usually with elders)		Don/Doña	Sustantivo
to		a	Preposición
to analyze		analizar	Verbo Regular
to answer		contestar	Verbo Regular
to arrive		llegar	Verbo Regular
to ask (a question)		preguntar	Verbo Regular
to ask for		pedir (e—i)	Verbo Irregular
to attend		asistir	Verbo Regular
to be		estar	Verbo Irregular
to be		ser (muy irregular)	Verbo Irregular
to be able/can		poder (o—ue)	Verbo Irregular

to be afraid (de)		tener miedo (de) (go + e—ie)	Expresión, Verbo Irregular
to be cold		tener frío (go + e—ie)	Expresión, Verbo Irregular
to be divorced		estar divorciado/a de	Expresión, Verbo Irregular
to be hot		tener calor (go + e—ie)	Expresión, Verbo Irregular
to be hungry		tener hambre (go + e—ie)	Expresión, Verbo Irregular
to be in a hurry		tener prisa (go + e—ie)	Expresión, Verbo Irregular
to be jealous		tener celos (go + e—ie)	Expresión, Verbo Irregular
to be located		quedar	Verbo Regular
to be married		estar casado/a	Expresión, Verbo Irregular
to be patient		tener paciencia (go + e—ie)	Expresión, Verbo Irregular
to be pleasing (like)		gustar	Verbo Regular (Requires IOP)
to be right		tener razón (go + e—ie)	Expresión, Verbo Irregular
to be single		ser soltero/a	Expresión, Verbo Irregular
to be successful		tener éxito (go + e—ie)	Expresión, Verbo Irregular
to be thirsty		tener sed (go + e—ie)	Expresión, Verbo Irregular
to be tired / sleepy		tener sueño (go + e—ie)	Expresión, Verbo Irregular
to believe		creer	Verbo Regular
to borrow; to loan; to lend		prestar	Verbo Regular
to break		romper (se)	Verbo Regular
to build		construir (i—y)	Verbo Regular
to cancel		cancelar	Verbo Regular
to care / to take care of		cuidar	Verbo Regular
to change		cambiar	Verbo Regular
to charge (a bill)		cobrar	Verbo Regular
to clean		limpiar	Verbo Regular
to combine		combinar	Verbo Regular
to cost		costar (o—ue)	Verbo Irregular
to cut		cortar	Verbo Regular
to die		morir (o—ue)	Verbo Irregular
to divide		dividir	Verbo Regular

to do, make		hacer (go)	Verbo Irregular: Go verb
to drive		conducir (c—zc)	Verbo Regular
to eat		comer	Verbo Regular
to fail		fracasar	Verbo Regular
to fear		temer	Verbo Regular
to feel like...(doing something)		tener ganas de... (go + e—ie)	Expresión, Verbo Irregular
to feel, regret, to be sorry		sentir (e—ie)	Verbo Irregular
to finish		terminar	Verbo Regular
to fly		volar (o—ue)	Verbo Irregular
to follow/continue		seguir (e—i)	Verbo
to forget		olvidar(se)	Verbo Regular
to function		funcionar	Verbo Regular
to get (good/bad) grades		sacar (buenas/malas) notas	Verbo Regular
to get, obtain		conseguir (e—i)	Verbo Irregular
to go		ir	Verbo Irregular
to have		tener (go + e—ie)	Verbo Irregular
to have to/must		deber (followed by an infinitive)	Verbo Regular
to help		ayudar	Verbo Regular
to hope, wish, wait for		esperar	Verbo Regular
to know		saber (otros irregulares -yo)	Verbo Irregular
to know/to be familiar		conocer (c—zc)	Verbo Regular
to learn		aprender	Verbo Regular
to lie		mentir (e—ie)	Verbo Irregular
to live		vivir	Verbo Regular
to look for		buscar	Verbo Regular
to maintain		mantener (irreg yo)	Verbo Irregular
to meet/encounter		encontrar (o—ue)	Verbo Irregular
to miss, lack		faltar	Verbo Similar a Gustar
to need		necesitar	Verbo Regular
to open		abrir	Verbo Regular
to owe		deber	Verbo Regular
to pass/to pass by		pasar (pasar por)	Verbo Regular
to pay		pagar	Verbo Regular
to play a sport or game		jugar (u—ue)	Verbo Irregular
to prefer		preferir (e—ie)	Verbo Irregular
to promote		promover (o—ue)	Verbo Irregular
to put		poner (go)	Verbo Irregular
to put in bed		acostar (o—ue)	Verbo Irregular
to read		leer	Verbo Regular
to receive		recibir	Verbo Regular

to recommend		recomendar (e—ie)	Verbo Irregular
to reduce		reducir (c—zc)	Verbo Regular
to remember		acordar (o—ue)	Verbo Irregular
to rent		alquilar	Verbo Regular
to repeat		repetir (e—i)	Verbo Irregular
to return		regresar	Verbo Regular
to return		volver (o—ue)	Verbo Irregular
to return/give back		devolver (o—ue)	Verbo Irregular
to run		correr	Verbo Regular
to say good-bye		despedir (e—i)	Verbo Irregular
to say/tell		decir (e—i)	Verbo Irregular
to serve		servir (e—i)	Verbo Irregular
to sleep		dormir (o—ue)	Verbo Irregular
to study		estudiar	Verbo Regular
to suggest		sugerir (e—ie)	Verbo Irregular
to take		sacar	Verbo Regular
to take notes		tomar apuntes	Verbo Regular
to talk, speak		hablar	Verbo Regular
to teach		enseñar	Verbo Regular
to the left		a la izquierda	Adverbio
to the left		a la izquierda	Adverbio
to the right		a la derecha	Adverbio
to the right		a la derecha	Adverbio
to turn		girar	Verbo Regular
to turn off		apagar	Verbo Regular
to turn/flip		doblar	Verbo Regular
to understand		comprender	Verbo Regular
to use		usar	Verbo Regular
to visit		visitar	Verbo Regular
to wake up		despertar (e—ie)	Verbo Irregular
to want/wish		desear	Verbo Regular
to want/wish/love		querer (e—ie)	Verbo Irregula
to work		trabajar	Verbo Regular
to write		escribir	Verbo Regular
to...years old		tener...años (go + e—ie)	Expresión, Verbo Irregular
to; at		a	Preposición
toward		hacia	Preposición
traffic	El	tráfico	Sustantivo
trash	La	basura	Sustantivo
TV	La	televisión	Sustantivo
tv (actual electronic)	La	televisor	Sustantivo

ugly		feo/a	Adjetivo
uncle/aunt	El, La	tío/a	Sustantivo
under		debajo	Preposición
under; underneath		debajo de	Preposición
united		unido/a	Adjetivo
United States	Los	Estados Unidos	Sustantivo
United States citizen	El, La	estadounidense	Adjetivo, Sustantivo
unpleasant		antipático/a	Adjetivo
until		hasta	Adverbio
urgent		urgente	Adjetivo
usual		usual	Adjetivo
vacation	Las	vacaciones (pl.)	Sustantivo
verb	El	verbo	Sustantivo
very well		muy bien	Adjetivo, Adverbio
veterinarian	El, La	veterinario/a	Sustantivo
vibration	La	vibración	Sustantivo
virgin	La	virgen	Sustantivo
vocabulary	El	vocabulario	Sustantivo
voice	La	voz	Sustantivo
washing machine	La	lavadora	Sustantivo
we		nosotros/as	Pronombre
weak		débil	Adjetivo
wedding	La	boda	Sustantivo
well		bien	Adjetivo, Adverbio
What is your name?		¿Cómo se llama Ud.?	Expresión
What is your name?		¿Cómo te llamas tú?	Expresión
What time is it?		¿Qué hora es?	Expresión
what?		¿qué?	Pronombre
what? What!		¿cómo? ¡cómo!	Adverbio
What's new?		¿Qué hay de nuevo?	Expresión
when?		¿cuándo?	Pronombre
where?		¿adónde?	Adverbio
where?		¿dónde?	Adverbio
which ones?		¿cuáles?	Pronombre
which?		¿cuál?	Pronombre
white		blanco/a	Adjetivo
who?		¿quién?	Pronombre
who? (pl.)		¿quiénes?	Pronombre
why?		¿por qué?	Pronombre
wife	La	esposa	Sustantivo

window	La	ventana	Sustantivo
winter	El	invierno	Sustantivo
without		sin	Preposición
yellow		amarillo/a	Adjetivo
yes		sí	Adverbio
you (formal)		Usted (Ud.)	Pronombre
you (friendly, familiar)		tú	Pronombre
you all (formal & both formal and informal in latin america)		Ustedes (Uds.)	Pronombre
you all (Spain only)		vosotros/as	Pronombre
young		joven	Adjetivo
younger		menor	Adjetivo
your		tu	Adjetivo
your		vuestro/a	Adjetivo
you're welcome		de nada	Expresión

Objetivos por unidad

UNIDAD 1:

1   Learn the vowels in Spanish.

2   Learn the alphabet and all the sounds in Spanish (including some regional differences).

3   Learn how to form consonant and vowel groups and how to pronounce them.

4   Learn about similarities and differences between Spanish and English sounds and cognates (words that look and mean the same as words you already know).

UNIDAD 2:

1.   Learn the beginning concepts and rules for dividing words into syllables to determine the stress of a word. Learn about enunciation and intonation to achieve authentic pronunciation.

2.   Learn how to write basic sentences and ask/answer a variety of simple questions.

3.   Learn how to greet others in formal and informal situations and say goodbye politely.

4.   Learn to introduce yourself and others and provide basic personal information in a polite way

5.   Learn numbers for providing information.

6.   Learn what subjects, pronouns, and adjectives are while recognizing if they are singular or plural, feminine or masculine.

7.   Learn what SER and TENER mean, when to use the verbs and their conjugations.

8.   Learn how to express likes and dislikes.

UNIDAD 3:

1. Learn how to identify the gender and number of Spanish words to achieve agreement.

2. Learn about definite articles and their usage rules.

3. Review how to divide words into syllables and the rules associated with each word's stressed syllable to achieve authentic pronunciation.

4. Gain the ability to read, write, listen and speak about vocabulary related to school and professions while indicating your preferences about your studies.

5. Understand the structures associated with telling time and the date.

6. Recognition of some irregular verbs and how to conjugate them.

7. Learn the question words (interrogatives) in Spanish.

8. Learn to express how you are and where you are.

9. Understand some grammatical structures in Spanish to form sentences and questions correctly.

UNIDAD 4:

1. Codify the sounds in Spanish alphabet.

2. Listen to the different Spanish accents.

3. Understand the Spanish intonation.

4. Learn about family and adjective vocabulary to be able to describe your family and home.

5. Identify objects in the home and discuss what you want in your home.

6. Expand your ability to speak about what you do presently.

7. Review grammar structures for more consistent usage in speech and writing.

8. Understand the concept of indirect objects and indirect object pronouns.

9. Differentiate clarifying, emphasizing and redundancy reduction with the indirect object pronouns.

10. Understand the concept of direct objects and direct object pronouns

11. Create sentences with both direct and indirect objects pronouns.

12. Express activities related to daily routines and personal care.

13. Speak and write Spanish avoiding redundancy.

UNIDAD 5:

1. Learn and use various manners to show possession

2. Learn and apply the concepts for Spanish phonics that lead to spelling changes.

3. Learn the differences between "conocer vs saber".

4. Review Spanish language characteristics.

5. Fluency through linking words.

6. Learn the rules for Spanish punctuation and capitalization.

7. Review some of the more challenging grammar concepts to date.

8. Progress in reading comprehension and gain exposure to another mood in Spanish.

Índice de Contenido:

Seseo	1.1, 1.2
Ser o Estar	5.7
Singular (number)	3.3, 3.8
Sounds in Spanish	3, 3.3, 4.1
Stem of the verb	4.6
Stress in the sentences	4.3
Stressed syllable	3, 2.1, 3.3, 4.2, 5.4
Structure gustar and similar verbs	2.8, 4.7
Subject	2.6, 4.7,
Subject pronouns (vocab)	2.6
Subjects, specialties (vocab)	3.5
Syllable division	2.1, 3.2, 3.3, 5.4
Tener (to have)	2.7, 3.9, 4.5, 4.6
Tener que (Grammatical structure)	3.9, 4.7
Tenses	3.6
Titles (vocab)	2.7, 4.6

Tone	4.3, 5.4
Unique verbs SER, ESTAR	2.7, 3.4, 3.5, 3.6, 3.8, 4.6, 5.7
Unique verbs Tener, Ir	4.6
Usted, ustedes (formal form) (culture)	2.4, 2.7, 4.5
Verbs	3.6
Verbs, most common (vocab)	3.6
Verbals/verboides	3.8, 4.7
Vosotros/as form (culture)	2.6
Vowels in Spanish	1, 5.4
Weather	3.5
Weather (vocab)	3.5
What or Which	3.7
What, idiomatic (vocab)	3.7
ZC verbs (Irregular verbs by phonetic)	4.6, 5.2

Temas Culturales	Unidad
Ceceo	2
Culture & language	4.1
Addressing people	2.4
Definite articles with a proper name	3.2,
Español = castellano	5.3
Greetings	2.2, 2.3
Hispano	4.2
Hispanohablante	4.2
Latino	4.2
Cuba, Celia Cruz	2.7, 5.3
Madrid, Spain	5.8
Name & last name	2.7, 5.6
Nickname	5.6,
Panama	4.10
Redundancy, avoid	4.9, 4.13
Religion	5.6
Seasons by Hemispheres	3.5
Spanish sayings	5.1, 5.6
Usted, ustedes (formal form)	2.4, 4.5
Vosotros/as form	2.6
Cognates	4
Colors	4.4
Days of the week	3.3
Equivalents (Spanish-English)	4
Expressions in Spanish	2.1
Family	4.4

TEMAS DE VOCABULARIO	Unidad, objetivo
Adjectives	2.7, 3.7, 4.4, 5.3
Alphabet	1.1
Areas of knowledge	3.5
Boot verbs	4.6
Cognates	1.4
Colors	4.4
Date	3.5
Days of the week	3.3
Definite and indefinite articles	3.1
Diacritic Stress	3.3
Direct Object Pronouns	4.10
Family	4.4
Formal/informal Greetings	2.4
Go verbs	3.6
goodbyes	2.4
Indirect Object Pronouns	2.8
Interrogative pronouns	3.7
Irregular Verbs	3.6, 4.6
Meeting someone	2.4
Months	3.3
Nationalities	2.7
Numbers	2.5
Objects in home	4.5
Places	3.3, 3.7, 5.3
Possessive adjectives	5.1
Possessives	2.7

Field of knowledge (classes, majors)	3.5		Preposition DE	5.1
Greetings, goodbyes, & replies	2.3		Professions	2.7,3.9
House	4.5		Punctuation	5.6
Idiomatic expressions with What	3.7		Reflexive pronouns	4.12
Interrogative pronouns	3.7		Regular verbs	3.6
Meeting someone	2.3		Replies	2.4
Month of the year	3.3		Rooms of the home	4.5
Most common verbs (vocab)	3.6		School supplies	3.6
Nationalities	2.7		Seasons	3.3
Numbers	2.5		Subject pronoun	2.6
Object of the house	4.5		Time	3.5
Personal pronouns	2.6		Titles	2.7
Places	3.3, 3.8, 5.3		Verb: decir	3.6
Possessives	2.7		Verb: ESTAR	3.7
Professions	2.7, 3.9		Verb: GUSTAR	2.8
Replies (vocab)	2.3		Verb: GUSTAR and similar verbs	3.9
Rooms of the house	4.5		Verbs irregular by phonetics	5.2
School supplies	3.6		Verbs that require a direct pronoun	4.10
Season of the year	3.3		Verbs that require an indirect pronoun	4.8
Subject pronouns	2.6		Verbs with reflexive pronoun	4.12
Subjects, specialties	3.5		Verbs: SABER vs CONOCER	5.3
Titles	2.7,4.6		Verbs: SER y TENER	2.7
Weather	3.5		Weather expressions	3.5

Made in the USA
Coppell, TX
06 October 2021